METAPHOR IN
ILLNESS WRITING

Contemporary Cultural Studies in Illness, Health and Medicine

Series editor: Gavin Miller

Recent books in the series

Metaphor in Illness Writing: Fight and Battle Reused
Anita Wohlmann

METAPHOR IN ILLNESS WRITING

Fight and Battle Reused

Anita Wohlmann

EDINBURGH
University Press

Edinburgh University Press is one of the leading university presses in the UK. We publish academic books and journals in our selected subject areas across the humanities and social sciences, combining cutting-edge scholarship with high editorial and production values to produce academic works of lasting importance. For more information visit our website: edinburghuniversitypress.com

© Anita Wohlmann 2022, 2024

Edinburgh University Press Ltd
The Tun – Holyrood Road
12(2f) Jackson's Entry
Edinburgh EH8 8PJ

First published in hardback by Edinburgh University Press 2022

Typeset in 10.5/13 Sabon by
Cheshire Typesetting Ltd, Cuddington, Cheshire
and printed and bound by CPI Group (UK) Ltd,
Croydon, CR0 4YY

A CIP record for this book is available from the British Library

ISBN 978 1 3995 0086 9 (hardback)
ISBN 978 1 3995 0087 6 (paperback)
ISBN 978 1 3995 0088 3 (webready PDF)
ISBN 978 1 3995 0089 0 (epub)

The right of Anita Wohlmann to be identified as the author of this work has been asserted in accordance with the Copyright, Designs and Patents Act 1988, and the Copyright and Related Rights Regulations 2003 (SI No. 2498).

Contents

Acknowledgements   vi
Series Editor's Preface   viii

Introduction   1
1. Metaphor Use: Strategies and Methods   26
2. Susan Sontag: Using Metaphor 'to see more, to hear more, to feel more'   58
3. Audre Lorde: Stretching, Risks and Difference   80
4. Anatole Broyard: A Style for Being Ill; or, Metaphor 'Light'   105
5. David Foster Wallace's Troubled Little Soldier: Narrative and Irony   132
6. From Theory to Practice: A Method for Using Metaphor   158
Conclusion   188

Bibliography   194
Index   213

Acknowledgements

My interest in metaphors started with literary representations of the female body by nineteenth-century North American women writers. Located at the Obama Institute of Transnational American Studies at Johannes Gutenberg University Mainz, Germany, and in collaboration with the research programme 'Life Sciences – Life Writing', the project developed under the energetic and inspiring guidance of Mita Banerjee and Alfred Hornung into a research project supported by the German Research Foundation (grant no. WO 2139/2-1). I will always be profoundly grateful for the support I have received from colleagues in Mainz, including among many others my PhD supervisor Oliver Scheiding.

When I was invited to join the research project 'Uses of Literature: The Social Dimensions of Literature' at the University of Southern Denmark in 2017 (grant no. DNRF127), a new phase began in every point of view. I found a generous, warm-hearted and intellectually stimulating home, and my research project on metaphors took a decisive turn: the varied uses of literature that we studied under the guidance of Niels Bohr Professor Rita Felski profoundly influenced my approach to metaphors. I am eternally grateful to Rita Felski, Anne-Marie Mai and Peter Simonsen for their trust and kindness, their continuously productive feedback, and their support and guidance every step of the way.

Each chapter specifies the individuals to whom I owe particular thanks. In addition, my profound gratitude goes to everyone who read excerpts of the book, commented on articles I wrote alongside, listened to early and more developed thoughts, inspired me with new ideas, challenged my often too simplistic arguments – and to everyone who was there to cheer me up when writing was tedious and, too often, felt overwhelming: Alan Bleakley, Alastair Morrison, Anders Juhl Langscheidel Rasmussen, Arthur Frank, Bryan Yazell, Christina Gerlach, Christine Marks, Cindie Aaen Maagard, Daniel Teufel, Danielle Spencer, Elin Abrahamsson, Ella Fegitz, Emily Hogg, Johanne

Gormsen Schmidt, Klaus Petersen, Maura Spiegel, Marie-Elizabeth Lei Holm, Miriam Halstein, Moritz Schramm, Patrick Fessenbecker, Pernille Hasselsteen, Sophy Kohler and Susanne Michl. (My apologies to everyone who should be part of this list and isn't.)

At Edinburgh University Press, I want to thank Michelle Houston, Susannah Butler and Fiona Conn as well as series editor Gavin Miller and copyeditor Robert Anderson for their consistent support and the incredibly encouraging spirit along the way.

Anna Fenton-Hathaway's extraordinary skills at copyediting provided not only the most generous and warm-hearted moral boost along the way, but our collaboration is also the reason why this book is, despite its focus on theory and detailed close readings, relatively readable. Anna, I cannot thank you enough.

I am also very grateful to Horacio Salinas who kindly provided one of his stunning photographs for the cover image of this book.

Lastly, what would I do without you, friends and family, in my old and new home? You know who you are.

Series Editor's Preface

*Contemporary Cultural Studies in Illness,
Health and Medicine
Series Editor: Gavin Miller*

Over the last fifty years or so, texts and other cultural productions on illness, health and medicine have flourished across a variety of genres and media. This book series fosters critical readings of such cultural productions, with an openness to variety in genre, medium and cultural capital. The series expects scholarly rigour and theoretical acumen, but no single theoretical or methodological standpoint is stipulated. Readers will encounter innovative and sustained critical readings that respond to the cutting – or bleeding – edge of contemporary cultures of illness, health and medicine.

Introduction

Metaphors are never inherently harmful, stigmatising or prescriptive; nor are they per se healing, inviting or generative. Such verdicts reveal the binaries through which metaphors are often conceptualised. *Metaphor in Illness Writing: Fight and Battle Reused* reaches past these binaries to explore the varied usability of common, conventionalised metaphors, arguing that, even when a metaphor appears problematic and limiting, it can in fact be reused and reimagined in unexpected and creative ways.

The terms 'reuse' and 'reusable' quickly evoke the environmental discourse of sustainability and with it concepts like recycling, upcycling and downcycling, second-hand economies and repair. These concepts are more timely than ever in our world; they also speak to what is at the heart of this book, namely the assumption that metaphors – though seemingly abundant – are precious resources that we can and need to work with rather than throw away. Practices of reuse are especially relevant when a metaphor has become internalised, when it seems worn-out, or when it starts to be considered a risk. Rather than considering such metaphors useless or expendable, this book proposes other options: we can extend a metaphor's longevity, we can repair it, or we can repurpose it (if need be) and thereby – in the spirit of upcycling – discover new value.

Both the varied usability of metaphor and the value of reuse is demonstrated by contemporary North American[1] writers including Susan Sontag, Audre Lorde, Anatole Broyard, David Foster Wallace and Arthur Frank – whose work I discuss alongside that of Siri Hustvedt, Joan Didion, Eve Ensler and Sarah Manguso. In their writing on illness, all work with the multiple entailments of an extremely common metaphor: *illness is a fight* or *battle*. All of these writers echo the criticism that this metaphor has provoked: it justifies brutality and extreme measures in the treatment of illness; its martial associations can be intimidating; it considers the body (and its illness) an enemy, thus supporting a problematic body–mind duality; and it suggests only one desirable outcome (victory) and associates losing the fight or capitulating with failure and humiliation.

And yet, despite all its problematic implications, these patient-writers continue to use the metaphor. In remaining attached to notions of battle, fight and warfare, these accomplished writers are not alone. The militaristic metaphor is one of the most frequently used metaphors for cancer and other illnesses (Semino et al., 'Online Use'; Hommerberg et al.). Patients and health professionals alike make references to fight and battle unconsciously by way of ubiquitous and clichéd, internalised expressions. Yet the metaphor is also used deliberately, as it seems to express what illness, to many, actually feels like.

Sontag, Lorde, Broyard, Wallace and Frank use the fight metaphor self-reflexively and purposefully: they ponder its benefits and harms, tinker with the notion of battle, elaborate it by drawing out more and more meanings, combine it with other metaphors and stretch the metaphor until it fits their life stories, individual circumstances and worldviews. In the process, they activate the metaphor's generative potential in ingenious, creative and empowering ways. The controversial fight metaphor, in their hands, constitutes a space for agency, resistance, self-knowledge, repair – even pleasure.

How can we understand the malleability of metaphors when metaphors are so often (and often for good reasons) considered prescriptive, normative and even stigmatising? By which specific strategies and practices do the writer-patients I mention exploit that malleability to accommodate active *re*use, maybe even creative *mis*use? Are such practices transferable from literary writing to other contexts? And if so, how can that process be enabled and conceptualised?

Metaphor in Illness Writing offers some answers to these questions by promoting a more capacious understanding of metaphors and their role in illness writing – as well as in health care more generally. Rather than locking metaphors into either/or categories and assuming default qualities, the case studies I examine in the following chapters decouple metaphor from too-rigidly defined functions. My analysis focuses on aesthetic choices that can activate and amplify metaphor's varied usability (the first premise of this book). In examining practices of usability, I foreground metaphor analysis and offer close readings of manifest practices of remaking, restoration and repair. As will become clear, practices of reusing metaphor are not restricted to the ingenuity of internationally recognised literary writers. Patients and health professionals, too, continually rethink and reuse metaphors in creative, defiant and playful ways. Such imaginative uses are the result of distinct strategies, from which we can learn (the second premise of this book) to expand our own uses of metaphors.

In analysing the varied usability of metaphor in literary writing and health care more generally, this book advances existing approaches to metaphor and contributes to the work being done in the areas of Medical Humanities[2] and Narrative Medicine,[3] where cross-fertilisations between literary studies and health care practice are studied.

WRITING ABOUT ILLNESS: NARRATIVE AND METAPHOR

Illness narratives have been an ample resource in Medical Humanities, Narrative Medicine and literary studies. Alternatively labelled 'illness narrative' or '(auto)pathography', the genre has been dated back to the 1950s, when it emerged out of or alongside the contexts of patient advocacy activism, civil rights movements, a changing doctor–patient relationship and the general boom of life writing and self-help literature (e.g. Hawkins). Psychiatrist and anthropologist Arthur Kleinman has demonstrated the importance of subjective narratives of illness as opposed to (or complementary with) biomedical definitions of diseases. In didactically oriented illness narratives, writers want to share their knowledge with other patients in order to encourage and empower (e.g. Hawkins). Other writers construct illness narratives as socio-cultural critique, to call for protest against prevailing policies, norms and values in health care and beyond (e.g. Lorde, *Cancer Journals*).

Typologies of illness narratives such as journey, rebirth, restitution, chaos and triumph have been identified across the genre (e.g. Hawkins; Frank, *Wounded*). Although sometimes problematically oversimplified (for a critique, see Woods, 'Beyond'), these conceptual frames are used to make sense of an experience in the face of meaninglessness and disruption. Indeed, it has been argued that writing about life-altering disease is not only a means of ordering experience but also of symbolic repair (Brody; Frank, *Wounded*). That is, the ill experience a form of healing through storytelling because 'Narrative form alters experience, giving it a definite shape, organising events into a beginning, a middle and an end, and adding drama – heightening feelings and seeing the individuals involved as characters in a therapeutic plot' (Hawkins 15).

While largely analysed in terms of autobiographical writing, scholars have also examined the genre's entanglement with other narrative forms such as conversion or redemption narratives or adventure stories (Couser, *Recovering*; Hawkins; Hunter). With their recognisably literary plots and frames, illness narratives raise challenging questions for literary criticism, where approaches informed by critique and suspicion are dominant: 'For scholars trained in such habits of reading', Jurecic claims, 'the idea of trusting a narrative to provide access to the experience of another person indicates a naïve understanding of how such texts function' (*Illness* 3). How is one to critically challenge these texts while still affirming the claims they make to their own truth and lived experience?

In foregrounding the *narrative* dimensions of illness writing, researchers have echoed the predominant focus on narrative in the field of Medical Humanities more generally. Since the 'narrative turn' in the latter part of the twentieth century, narrative has been considered not only a literary form but also a social discourse, a speech act and a cognitive schema (Tammi). As an essential 'part of the fabric of our lived experience' (Eakin 2), narrative has also been studied as a cognitive instrument which we use to construct reality and through which we understand ourselves – our identities, experiences and lives – in time (e.g. Bruner; Eakin; Mink; Ricœur, *Time* and 'Narrative'). Moreover, researchers have demonstrated how medical information and caregiving are structured and enriched by stories (e.g. Greenhalgh and Hurwitz; Hunter). The umbrella term 'narrative' brings together scholars and researchers from multiple disciplinary backgrounds and has become a productive and unifying reference point in Medical Humanities and Narrative(-based) Medicine.

This predominance has also attracted criticism. Narrative, it has been argued, has mattered both too much and for the wrong reasons, namely when a normative, overly broad, overly enthusiastic yet limited understanding of narrative is employed (e.g. Garden; Tammi; Woods, 'Limits' and 'Beyond'). Typical assumptions about narrative consider its hallmarks to be 'sequence, succession, causality, or closure' (Tammi 22). But whether or not these features adequately define narrative – and to what extent they can provide access to our own stories, let alone those of others (Butler) – remains in question. Do human beings really live by the diachronic continuity that narrative seems to impose?, critics ask (e.g. Strawson). (Chronic) pain, disability, dementia or trauma and their representations seem to resist narratibility and narrativisation (Conway; Garden; Kirmayer; Marks, 'Metaphors'). Angela Woods identifies an additional blind spot in granting primary status to narrative: narrative coherence can be harmful when it forces inchoate experiences into a false or constraining order, or when it promotes decidedly Western conceptualisations of the self as an autonomous agent ('Limits' 73–4).

Partly in response to such critiques, the 'Critical Medical Humanities' have taken up a more self-reflexive and sceptical stance towards some of the premises and tenets of the field (e.g. Viney et al.). While some scholars have tried to bypass 'narrative' by using other terms – such as 'illness writing' (Schmidt) – or have ventured into adjacent genres – such as the illness essay (Jurecic, 'Illness Essay'), others have retained the term and have clarified their postclassical (and thus much broader) understanding of what narrative encompasses, including paintings, dance, music or comics (e.g. Spencer). As Stella Bolaki wonders in *Illness as Many Narratives*, would 'moving beyond narrative ... be necessary or desired if we were to define narrativity more broadly and multiply existing narratives' (6)? Bolaki ultimately concludes that 'there is room to challenge *and* expand narrative's conception and role within the medical humanities field' (6). In fact, there is intriguing research in narrative theory that confounds the traditional alignment of narrative with qualities such as order, coherence and linearity; this line of research has generated notions of the *disnarrated*, the *unnarratable* and *non-narration* (Abbott; Prince; Warhol). And, of course, narrative techniques such as stream-of-consciousness, gaps, silences, leaps and fragments challenge simplistic conceptualisations of narrative. In other words, narrative is not necessarily a natural, all-encompassing and always available structure that automatically implies a subjugation of chaos and complexity into neat, culturally legitimised forms.

Controversy around narrative's limitations has produced intriguing new perspectives on what may lie beyond narrative. Of the field of Medical Humanities, Woods asks: 'What place is there for formlessness, for meaninglessness, for silence?' ('Beyond' 125). She suggests that there is both fascinating material and applicable concepts the Medical Humanities might borrow from visual media such as photography and drawing, as well as from music and haiku poetry (124). Phenomenology and philosophy more generally, also offers an alternative to the teleology of narrative by foregrounding the present moment (e.g. Carel, *Illness*). Catherine Belling makes a plea for the 'lyric mode', which does not rely on plot and temporal succession but on moments of reflection and contemplation, where the time is 'always "now"' and 'the mind is to itself' (2). And Sara Wasson proposes a focus on the episodic, which foregrounds open-endedness and fragmentary states rather than closure or telos. She suggests 'dwelling with the scene as *a moment in itself*, not only implying future decline, not only about a temporal trajectory, but about something instant, present, embodied and *now*' (6; original emphasis). As Belling notes, metaphor, too, foregrounds the present moment by yanking us 'outside the current of plot' through tiny shocks of surprise and flashes of immediate, seemingly inevitable insight (5; also see Wood, *How* 202, 209). Such jolts to consciousness are particularly prevalent in new, vivid metaphors, which are often associated with atemporality and sensory experiences rather than causality and linearity (see Chapter 4).

Metaphor is, of course, not a cure-all to the limits of narrative, nor is it a shiny new thing in Medical Humanities research. Susan Sontag's essays on illness metaphors are ground zero for critical inquiries into metaphors and presumably the most cited sources in the field on this topic. More recently, Alan Bleakley's comprehensive survey *Thinking with Metaphors in Medicine* offers a book-length account of metaphor in health care.[4] Numerous other studies have discussed the role of metaphor in health care as a central element in, for example, psychotherapy (Agstner; Kirmayer); doctor–patient and science communication (e.g. Casarett et al.; Kendall-Taylor and Haydon); and in the expression of illness experiences more generally (Conway; Woolf). From the perspective of literary studies, Christine Marks has found metaphor to be a contributing factor to the healing process some people find in writing their illness narratives: metaphors, she argues, are agents of transformation but also help create connection ('Metaphor' 14, 18). Medical anthropologist Gay Becker sees metaphors as fulfilling a similar function as narrative, namely as a tool for people trying to mend a severe disruption in their lives and both locate new meanings and re-establish a sense of continuity ('Metaphors' 404). In moments of existential loss (such as strokes or infertility), Becker's interviewees used metaphor as a cultural resource 'to create linkages between past and future' but also 'to create bridges back to normalising ideologies' (*Disrupted* 189).[5]

Other scholars have been less sanguine about the role of metaphor. Their critiques echo, in some ways, those brought against narrative. Elaine Scarry, Lisa Diedrich and Kathlyn Conway, for example, question the capacity of language, whether literal or figurative, to share the experience and meanings of serious pain and suffering. Conway asserts that many writers struggle intensely to express something that is, in fact, 'unmanageable and beyond language' (95). 'They try direct language. They try metaphor. They quote other famous writers' (95). Despite these efforts, 'Words fail in the face of suffering. Language intrudes itself between the sufferer and the listener, creating a distance from the felt experience' (97).[6] This scepticism about language is an important reminder that metaphor is not, of course, a solution to problems of narrative and to what is inexpressible in illness. Moreover, especially in view of metaphor's darker side – its potential to prescribe and stigmatise – we should neither over- nor underestimate its power. And yet, as Marks argues, however insufficient metaphors may be in giving 'direct expression to pain', they 'open up new ways, new dimensions, and new landscapes in which we may never actually come into direct contact with the referent, but may feel its presence with a new force' ('Metaphors' 305). In *The Empathy Exams*, Leslie Jamison reaffirms the creative and transcendent qualities of metaphorical language when she maintains that 'Metaphors translate emotion into surprising and sublime language' (123). Jamison adds that metaphors 'also help us deflect and diffuse the glare of revelation' (123), which can be understood as metaphor's dulling effect which may obscure and conceal, or, in a more positive light, as an escape from situations in which direct, literal words seem unbearable.[7] These multiple dimensions of metaphor – connecting, generative, sensory, reflective and protecting – provide an important complementary space to the promises and limits of narrative.

Rather than pitting one against the other, though, what would happen if we thought about metaphor and narrative *together*? After all, to think about life or illness in terms of a journey is both a common metaphor and an often-used narrative frame. Even the literary theorist Paul Ricœur, who wrote about metaphor and narrative separately – first metaphor in 1975, followed by three volumes on narrative between 1983 and 1985 – admits that 'these works were conceived together' (*Time* ix). In his attempt to understand interpretation and meaning, metaphor and narrative were, to him, the obvious points of entry (Dowling 109): both produce 'semantic innovation' either through 'impertinent attribution' (metaphor) or the 'work of synthesis' (narrative); moreover, from both metaphor and narrative, 'a new thing springs up in language' based on 'a productive imagination' that reconfigures or redescribes a 'preunderstood order of action' (narrative) or 'sensory, emotional, aesthetic and axiological values' (metaphors) (*Time* ix–xi). A number of researchers after Ricœur have explored how we can understand the intersections of metaphor and narrative, suggesting that metaphors do not only propel narratives of their own – variously labelled 'metaphor scenarios', 'metaphorical stories' or 'paranarratives'; they are also often embedded in narratives and thus interact with the narrative that surrounds them (for a more elaborate discussion, see Chapter 1).

The intertwined nature of metaphor and narrative has also been examined in the context of health care, most prominently by Michael Hanne and colleagues in the special issue of *Genre* titled 'Binocular Vision: Narrative and Metaphor in Medicine'. Even earlier, Anne Hunsaker Hawkins points out how 'Over and over again, the same metaphorical paradigms are repeated in pathographies: the paradigm of regeneration, the idea of illness as battle, the athletic ideal, the journey to a distant country, and the mythos of healthy-mindedness' (27). But even if illness narratives do not rely on such common paradigms, she finds that a central metaphor typically 'functions as an organizational principle' in the attempt to produce an illness narrative (26). This conceptual function of metaphors also informs Arthur Frank's work on illness narrative typologies: suggesting that the writers of illness narratives are 'shipwrecked' and 'wounded' storytellers, he proposes narrativisation of these experiences as a life-saving rescue or reparative and healing intervention (53–5). Rita Charon, maybe inadvertently, exemplifies the importance of thinking with narrative and metaphor together, too. In relaying an encounter with a patient, she emphasises 'how medicine and *stories* need one another' ('Novelization' 33; my emphasis). Her account of that case is, however, filled to the brim with metaphors – the body as a home, as a garden, as a metal pipe, as a communication device. These metaphors help her explore the range and depth of meanings and experiences that her patient struggles to voice. The interpretation of the patient's story is thus closely bound up with the work that metaphors do.

I believe these examples illustrate clearly that metaphor analysis and narrative analysis *together* are more productive than either one is individually; their combination can also yield more complex understandings of what happens at the boundaries of both metaphor and narrative. Despite their mutual entanglements, however, researching metaphor and narrative together is not without its challenges, as I discuss in Chapter 1. Moreover, there is good reason to focus on metaphor proper: for one, the label is often applied too broadly and treated synonymously with figurative language; for another, since this book is concerned with the reusability of metaphor, discrete definitions of metaphor and of metaphor analysis are crucial.

DEFINING METAPHOR

Metaphor is typically understood as a type of figurative language: we depart from the literal meaning of words and invoke a figurative, non-standard, surplus meaning. Aristotle defined metaphor as 'the application of a word that belongs to another thing' (105). And for George Lakoff and Mark Johnson, 'the essence of metaphor is understanding and experiencing one kind of thing in terms of another' (*Metaphors* [1980] 5). Definitions of metaphor tend to be very broad and encompass 'an array of forms, in all of which one thing is regarded as something that it is not' (Cohen, *Thinking* 6).⁸ Within such loose definitions, metaphor becomes an umbrella term for figurative language in general, one that also covers symbols, similes, analogies, allegories, metonymies, synecdoches and idiomatic expressions.

In health care and Medical Humanities research, such a broad understanding of metaphor is common. For example, a simile such as stem cells are 'like tomato seeds' or an idiomatic expression such as 'he or she did not lay a hand on me' are both called metaphors (Casarett et al. 258; Verghese, 'Linguistic Prescription'). One might dismiss such terminological distinctions as negligible or beside the point, but I am not interested in terminology for terminology's sake. (In fact, in this book, I myself sometimes disregard the differences between metaphors and similes.) The point I wish to make is this: metaphor is a highly elusive, complex and controversial phenomenon. For example, in metaphor scholarship, it has been debated whether a simile is even making a figurative claim – whether it actually invites us to speculate about an implied, non-literal meaning (Ricœur, *Rule* 220). Is there really a so-called mapping or transfer that takes place from which an additional meaning unfolds? Doesn't a simile merely perform a comparison, suggesting, literally, that x shares similarities with y? This line of questioning does not pertain only to simile, either: the assumption that figurativeness is the defining feature of metaphor has also been contested by Donald Davidson, who famously claimed that metaphors 'mean what the words, in their most literal interpretation, mean, and nothing more' (32).⁹ In other words, the notion of figurativeness, which warrants a broad definition of metaphors, might simply be too broad to be helpful for a better understanding of the inner workings of metaphor. Since this book is concerned with the varied usability of metaphors and examines strategies of rethinking them from the inside, it is important to spell out the inner functioning of metaphor *proper*.

A no less important reason for defining metaphor narrowly is that the distinction can actually make a difference to internal perception, mutual understanding and effective communication. Consider the case of metaphor and symbol: while both bring together two distinct ideas or concepts, a metaphor makes a statement about similarities or resemblances, whereas a symbol suggests that one thing stands for the other. Flowers at the bedside, for example, are commonly understood as a symbol of concern and sympathy, love and care; they can also be used as a metaphor that expresses an idiosyncratic, highly subjective experience of illness. Sylvia Plath exemplifies this point dexterously in the poem 'Tulips' in which the speaker, a woman in a hospital, compares the red tulips she received to a 'dozen red lead sinkers round my neck' and to 'an awful baby', thus expressing the speaker's despondent, maybe even psychotic state (161). While my example is taken from the world of poetry, it is easy to imagine actual contexts in which such diverse meanings and implications may impact mutual understanding. Knowing when to treat metaphor *as* metaphor and by which frameworks to analyse it seem highly relevant.[10]

Definitions of metaphor draw on different terminologies.[11] Due to their transparency, the terms 'source' and 'target', which are common in cognitive metaphor theory, will be used here. Lakoff and Johnson write that 'In a *metaphor*, there are two domains: the target domain, which is constituted by the immediate subject matter, and the source domain, in which important metaphorical reasoning takes place and that provides the source concepts used in that reasoning' (*Metaphors* [2003] 265; original emphasis). For example, if one compares illness to a fight or journey, the target domain (illness) is described through the features we associate with the source domain (fight or journey). In each metaphor, a mapping or transfer takes place, in which the features of one domain, typically the source, are carried over to the other, the target. The nature of the relationship between source and target has been conceptualised in multiple ways including comparison (e.g. Fogelin; Quintilian), substitution and resemblance (e.g. Jakobson), interaction (e.g. Black; Richards), tension (e.g. Ricœur), or blending (e.g. Fauconnier and Turner).

In taking my terminology from Lakoff and Johnson, I acknowledge their study's trailblazing function in the field of metaphor research.[12] *Metaphors We Live By* has assumed almost a cult status in metaphor research, as well as in other contexts, and it is *the* reference point for arguments about the relevance and ubiquity of metaphors beyond the poetic realm. This prominence has perhaps obscured a fuller account of the field: long before *Metaphors We Live By* challenged the notion that metaphors are mere ornamental or stylistic devices, literary critics such as I. A. Richards, Max Black and Paul Ricœur ('Metaphor' 52-3) had made the same claim. Still, Lakoff and Johnson managed to propel waves of research on the significance of metaphors by arguing that metaphors are not only a matter of everyday language but also impact how we think and act. That is, not only is there no way we can*not* use metaphors, it is through metaphors that we understand the world. In doing so, our way of thinking – our 'ordinary conceptual system' – is metaphorical (Lakoff and Johnson, *Metaphors* [1980] 3). As a consequence, *Metaphors We Live By* has animated a multidisciplinary interest in the functions and effects of metaphors, in areas from science communication, literature studies, cultural studies, linguistics and language philosophy to psychotherapy, anthropology and the cognitive sciences – including, more recently, neurology.

But research into the cognitive side of metaphors also poses challenges.[13] Not only do its methods and study designs often favour quantitative approaches, some of the tenets in cognitive metaphor theory have also come under criticism. Scholars in disability studies, for example, have taken offense with the many references to an allegedly natural, universal human body assumed in *Metaphors We Live By*. Amy Vidali, for example, demonstrates the underlying ableism in Lakoff and Johnson's approach,[14] which she traces across both *Metaphors We Live By* and their more recent study on metaphors, *Philosophy in the Flesh: The Embodied Mind and Its Challenge to Western Thought*. When Lakoff and Johnson continually claim that spatial metaphors such as 'up is good' and 'down is bad' 'arise from the fact that we have bodies of the sort we have' (*Metaphors* [1980] 15–17), they posit a norm that considers other forms of embodiment deviant. Vidali illustrates the repercussions of such norms in the able-bodied metaphor 'knowing is seeing', which for Lakoff and Johnson is based on a prototypical and natural understanding of the human body and which also implies that blindness equals 'misunderstanding and disorder' (Vidali 34). Vidali shows how a disability approach to metaphor allows us to challenge the assumptions on which some of our metaphors rest.

Another problem with cognitive-inflected approaches to metaphor has been voiced by Marjorie Garber, who accuses cognitive scientists of treating metaphor as a means to an end. To better understand how the brain works, she writes, cognitive scientists 'read *through* metaphor' (235). According to Garber, this approach 'erases the history of literary scholarship and analysis, discounts the role of interpretation and reading, and above all, denies or resists the creative, transgressive and excitingly unstable power of language. Reducing literature to concepts, even to conceptual metaphors, is a mode of appropriation that makes the literary disappear' (252).

Neither Vidali's nor Garber's critique does full justice to the diversity in cognitive metaphor research (see, for example, the research on cultural aspects of metaphors in Chapter 6), but their assessments do help contour what literary studies can offer. As Garber suggests, fluidity of language and instability of meaning are central tenets for literary scholarship, and they are powerful creative resources for writers, too. These features of metaphor are foundational to Ricœur's *The Rule of Metaphor* – in French, *La Métaphore vive* ('The metaphor lives/is alive') – which explores, among many other features, two central ideas about metaphor that anchor my own research: tension and comparison.

To Ricœur, the interpretation of a metaphor is in constant tension between 'is' and 'is not' (*Rule* 293).[15] This simultaneity creates, on the one hand, absurdity, inconsistency and 'semantic impertinence'; on the other, it enables a 'stereoscopic vision' through which an appearance of solidity and depth becomes possible ('Metaphor' 50, 56). Such double vision and oscillatory movement is crucial to what metaphor can achieve: rather than assimilating one thing into another, there is a 'tensive apprehension' from which 'a new vision of reality springs forth', a 'revelation of a new dimension of reality and truth' (68). It is this revelatory, creative and innovative aspect that makes metaphor – and poetic language more generally – '"living", "alive", "intense"' (*Rule* 296). The relevance of metaphor lies, for Ricœur, both in its necessity – we do not have enough words to apprehend or convey our endlessly rich reality – and in the pleasure and delight we experience when metaphors 'breathe force and energy into discourse' (73).

But there is also another side to metaphor: metaphor invites make-believe. We are encouraged to see one thing 'as if' it were another, and this 'seeing as' is powerful because it redescribes reality in such a way that we are tempted to assume that metaphor makes a statement on the ontological level – suggesting a 'being as' (5). While there is a risk that this illusory, suggestive quality of metaphor could involve disguise or abuse (298),[16] Ricœur argues that once the '"tensional' character of language' is recognised, it spills over into a '"tensional" character of truth' (301). That is, through metaphor, we may perceive an experience or idea *more* distinctly, with heightened insight and greater access to a sensory or perceived truthfulness even though we also know this apprehension to be founded on a mistake or misallocation – a literal untruth. To suggest that illness needs to be fought exudes such clarity and plausibility to so many because illness *is* experienced *as* a fight. Yet if we identify this statement as a metaphor, we need to consider in what ways illness is also *not* a fight and how it only *seems as if* it were.

Ricœur calls standardised and internalised metaphors 'dead' metaphors; they have lost the tensional ambiguity and vitality that fresh metaphors hold (296). What Ricœur does not sufficiently acknowledge, however, is that the life–death binary needlessly constrains metaphors. To stay within Ricœur's meta-metaphorical terminology: a metaphor that is allegedly 'dead' has not only enormous staying power; it can also be reanimated, for example when the tensional dynamic of language is restored. In *The Rule of Metaphor*, Ricœur speaks indeed of the potential to reanimate and rejuvenate worn-out, dead metaphors, and he even attests to these revived metaphors a 'baffling fecundity' (346) when 'the positive operation of de-lexicalizing ... amounts to a new production of metaphor and, therefore, of metaphorical meaning'. 'Writers', Ricœur goes on to suggest curtly, 'obtain this effect by various concerted and controlled procedures – substituting a synonym that suggests an image, adding a more recent metaphor, etc.' (344–5). Unfortunately, Ricœur does not elaborate on these examples of creative reuse.

Elsewhere, Ricœur observes that it is the sentence and discourse in which a metaphor is embedded that determines a metaphor's semantic impertinence, not the level of the word (2, 5). Moving beyond an approach that takes the word as the most important unit of reference (1), we see that metaphor interacts with countless other strategies of textual meaning-making, including irony or negation – rhetorical forms that, like metaphor, oscillate between a truth and the opposite. When paired with strategies such as these, a 'dead' metaphor's tensional ambiguity – as my examples in the following chapters demonstrate – can be revived.

My second anchor in defining metaphor is the notion of comparison. Comparison theory of metaphor dates back to Quintilian, Cicero and Aristotle.[17] Following Aristotle, 'to use metaphor well is to discern similarities' (115) and thus 'to see – to contemplate, to have the right eye for' what is comparable in two things (Ricœur, *Rule* 231). The comparison theory of metaphor has been criticised for being too limited and narrow to adequately describe what happens in a metaphor. One of the strongest arguments within this critique is that a metaphor not only suggests a comparison or similarity between two ideas, it also *brings into existence* this assumed similarity. Robert J. Fogelin has re-energised a comparativist view of metaphor more recently by suggesting that metaphors are figurative comparisons. He follows an Aristotelian view of metaphor, which considers similes and metaphors as basically the same, differing 'in only a trivial grammatical fashion' namely metaphor's ellipsis of 'like' or 'as' (27). This omission implies that metaphors tend to have more rhetorical force, that they do indirectly what similes do explicitly (29). For his part, Ricœur follows neither comparison theory nor substitution theory. Instead, his tension theory is tied to the notions of resemblance and interaction (*Rule* 204).[18] While he does speak of comparing when he explains the relationship between tenor and vehicle, his notion of comparison is a matter of 'co-presence': 'To compare can be to hold two things together in order to let them act together; it can also mean perceiving their resemblance' (94). For Ricœur, resemblance is constituted by 'a tension between identity and difference' (4); it is a relationship or kinship between two domains suggesting that 'X is like Y in some senses, but not in all' (252). That is, metaphors do not proclaim a similarity or sameness; they extend an invitation, namely to 'see as':

'the metaphorical vehicle is *as* the tenor – from one point of view, not from all points of view. To explicate a metaphor is to enumerate all the appropriate senses in which the vehicle is 'seen as' the tenor' (252); an interpretation of a metaphor necessarily also implies the senses in which 'X is *not* Y' (253). In other words, metaphor does not mirror a resemblance between two ideas but *establishes*, or invites us to establish, that resemblance. Importantly, as Ricœur himself allows, this invitation can fail or succeed (253).

When I use the term 'comparison' here and in the following chapters, I do so with Ricœur's notion of tension in mind. In fact, I would argue that a similar notion of tension also exists in comparison theory. Like metaphor, comparison has been cast in binary (and even mutually exclusive) terms, with opposed functions and effects imputed to it. Critics, especially postcolonial scholars, have associated comparison with colonisation, homogenisation and Eurocentrism (e.g. Radhakrishnan; Friedman). From this critical angle, comparison is an instrument of domination that conveys hierarchies and value-judgements and is therefore limiting and reductive. It is 'an outreaching and overbearing mode of thinking that blurs borders and connects things that may not belong together (or should not be seen next to each other)' (Epple and Erhart 12). Proponents of comparison, however, stress that comparing is a fundamental scientific practice that enables new knowledge and theory-building. As a heuristic strategy, comparison can broaden our perspective and decentre ourselves. If seen as an experiment in thinking, comparison helps us relativise and maybe even escape our limited perspectives rather than solidifying them (Felski, 'Comparison' 754).[19] A more neutral way of assessing comparison's affordances is to understand it as a 'form of relational thinking' about the ties between two objects (Felski 754). Seen as a practice, comparing is not only context-dependent and always contingent but can also be put to multiple, unpredictable uses (Epple and Erhart 18). Relating the uses of metaphors to practices of comparison opens the door to other productive concepts such as juxtaposition and collage (Friedman, 'Why' 759), 'light comparison' (Gordon 333) and the 'beside' (Sedgwick 8). When brought to bear with metaphor, these additional comparative practices can be helpful to identify and understand metaphor's varied usability.

How to examine, then, this varied usability?

CLOSE READING

Each chapter in this book offers a close reading of the illness-as-fight metaphor as it is used in different contexts; each chapter also combines that close reading with metaphor analysis. In Chapter 1, I demonstrate in detail how such an approach can look like: first I identify the source and target domain and then move on to the salient features that are mapped between illness on the one side and battle, fight or war on the other. In the following chapters, I pay particular attention to additional entailments the source domain supplies and I explore how these entailments are activated by each writer. My close readings also take narrative criteria into account. As will become clear in Chapter 1, metaphor can be reimagined via narrative scenarios which may feature, for example, new characters, new settings and new timelines. Moreover, a focus on narrative features is necessary to understand how the immediate narrative context in which the metaphor is embedded impacts the meaning and interpretation of the metaphor. For example, when they criticise and unpack the illness-as-war metaphor, the writers in my case studies make different narrative choices – such as type of narration, tone or narrative frame – and these choices influence the metaphor's use and meanings. Together, the specific features of metaphor and narrative contribute to a better understanding of how a metaphor is reused and reimagined.

In addition to these close readings, each analysis also zooms out from the individual texts under discussion and offers a broader perspective of the paradoxes or problems that the reimagination, reuse and creative misuse of metaphors involve. This broader perspective brings in other texts by the same writers (such as speeches, diaries, academic writing) as well as illness writing by other authors who have tackled similar problems. Still, *Metaphor in Illness Writing* remains dedicated to close reading and therefore does not delve into historical analyses of the illness-as-fight metaphor. Such studies can be found in Alan Bleakley, who traces the metaphor back to the mid-seventeenth century, and in Lorenzo Servitje, who analyses in *Medicine Is War* how nineteenth and early twentieth-century writers like Mary Shelley, Joseph Conrad and Arthur Conan Doyle helped forge military metaphors for infectious diseases and contributed to popularise and naturalise the connection between warfare on the one side and medicine, public health and hygiene on the other (3). Similarly, Laura Otis examines nineteenth-century literature and how it negotiates new discoveries in cell biology. Otis foregrounds metaphors of invasion and discusses how the cell–self association informs concepts of identity and individuality.

Since I foreground close reading as the central methodological frame of my analysis, I want to clarify the benefits of this approach and how it makes sense for the aim of this book. Close reading is used for fine-grained textual analysis primarily in literary studies, but also in other disciplines such as anthropology. In Narrative Medicine, close reading is considered a 'signature method' because it requires (and helps practice) a close attention to detail, including nuances of language, tone, time, space, plot and other textual features (Charon, 'Close' 157). First articulated in Richards's *Practical Criticism* and William Empson's *Seven Types of Ambiguity*, a close reading is 'the detailed analysis of the complex interrelations and ambiguities (multiple meanings) of the verbal and figurative components within a work' (Abrams 181). A close reader focuses on word choice, allusions, metaphors, symbols, images, tone and point of view (Pamboukian 16). In paying meticulous attention to language and its ambiguities, ironies and paradoxes, close readers try to figure out how details in a short passage relate to the meaning of the text as a whole in order to achieve a deeper understanding of a text's layered meanings (Pamboukian 16–17).

In literary studies, close reading fell out of favour – even while continuing to be used – when it was accused of being myopic by proponents of emerging critical movements such as New Historicism (Gallop 182). In eliding historical information, archival research, biography and other contextual information, close reading was criticised for being naively ahistorical, depolitical, self-sufficient and solipsistic. Indeed, some critics mocked close reading as a last-resort pedagogical workaround for accommodating college students' limited historical or humanistic knowledge (Smith 59). Others found that it fell short as a robust, clearly defined method that could draw level with the systematic research methods in other fields (Smith 59). Close reading has also been accused of being a tool for elitism, sexism and racism, in its emphasis on aesthetic dimensions above all else, as well as for its association with a narrowly defined literary canon of presumably timeless works of literature (Gallop 181). The latter criticism was raised in response to New Criticism, a school of literary criticism heralded by Cleanth Brooks, T. S. Eliot and Monroe Beardsley, among others, whose aim was to make the study of literature more rigorous, exact and scientific (North 24).[20]

Defenders of close reading have clarified that Richards's understanding of close reading has unjustly and incorrectly been conflated with the New Critics (e.g. North 26). To Richards, close reading was a form of deeply practical criticism: he saw no great difference between the aesthetic experience of literature and everyday experiences (*Principles* 16–17). For him, the close reading of literary texts could be 'a means of ordering our minds' (*Practical* 349), and literature is so useful not because of its complicated ingenuity and literary sophistication but because it helps readers 'cultivate many of their most useful practical faculties' (North 29). This openness makes close reading a 'widely applicable skill', Jane Gallop argues, which lets readers 'discover things they would not otherwise have noticed' (183).[21] In other words, 'Literature makes us better noticers of life; we get to practice on life itself; which in turn makes us better readers of detail in literature; which in turn makes us better readers of life' (Wood, *How* 65).

Apart from the benefits of better noticing, close reading has been associated with creating new insights and pleasures. In his plea for 'Serious Noticing', James Wood argues that literary texts can 'help us see the world more closely and carefully – to see better, to look again at our surroundings, natural and manmade, to look more closely at the body, to open the pores of our senses and *feel* the world' (n. pag.). In paying attention to minute, seemingly irrelevant details, and in trying to figure out their meaning, we may feel more alive and more present in the world, for instance by gaining an unexpected insight into a person or character. When details *refuse* to grant us such insight or access – as when a simple frown elicits contradictory readings (Wood, *How* 92) – we are reminded of the limits of objective knowing and the subjective quality of our perception. The serious noticing that close reading requires renders us self-conscious – of our own biases, assumptions, ways of seeing. Each act of interpretation, we realise, is a creative act that is contingent on multiple factors. Attention to detail thus 'makes us the writer as well as the reader; we seem like co-creators of the character's existence' (*How* 92). In this sense, even as close reading may indeed be 'ordering our minds', it is also attuning us to the forces that shape this order.

This 'tutoring' function that Wood ascribes to literature (65) has been taken up by Rita Charon and her team at Columbia University.[22] In Narrative Medicine, which Charon conceptualises as a practice of paying close attention to a text and/or a patient, close reading helps create affiliation ('Attention'). The close reading of literary texts – and thus the close attention to both *what* and *how* information is shared – is configured as a 'laboratory and training ground' (Charon, 'Close' 158) through which students and practitioners can hone fundamental skills in health care, namely active listening and narrative competence. The latter is defined as 'the skills to open up the stories of their patients to nuanced understanding and appreciation' (*Narrative* vii). Following Charon,

> A medicine practiced with narrative competence will more ably recognise patients and diseases, convey knowledge and regard, join humbly with colleagues, and accompany patients and their families through the ordeals of illness. These capacities will lead to more humane, more ethical, and perhaps more effective care (110).

In suggesting that narrative competence[23] can be cultivated and that close reading is a transferable method with important social functions, Charon is not alone. Though phrased less idealistically, Joseph North demonstrates in his history of close reading that the technique has been conceived of and used not only as a method of literary criticism but also as a form of intervention invested in social change beyond textual boundaries (34–5). Adding to this recent interest in revitalising the values of close reading, Maria C. Scott shows how close reading can be a significant tool that complements psychological approaches to the relationship between empathy and fiction-reading (12).

Inspired by these approaches that bridge textual analysis and application-oriented contexts and responding to the call for more metaphor literacy and reflexivity in Medical Humanities (e.g. Bleakley 204; Holmes 272; Reisfield and Wilson; Semino et al., 'Online Use' 6), this book lays out a method[24] for engaging with metaphor that includes several steps, such as to identify, describe and evaluate the multiple effects, functions and uses of metaphors. (A more elaborate definition is provided in Chapter 6.) Arguing that close reading and careful metaphor analysis are transferable methods from literary studies, I show how they can be put into practice in everyday life and, more specifically, in health care. The close reading of metaphors invites a detailed attention to its tensions and ambiguities, which enables deeper understanding and a thickening of meanings. Given that metaphors are so foundational to human thought and action, a method that specifies how to approach metaphor is a valuable tool in general and a vital one in health care more specifically.

CHAPTER OVERVIEW: THE CASE STUDIES

The primary texts I have selected as case studies for metaphor's varied reusability were published between 1978 and 1992 by North American writers who are, for the most part, canonical in Medical Humanities and Narrative Medicine.[25] Each text features a sustained and creative grappling with the illness-as-fight metaphor. This engagement is demonstrated by the fact that the writers do not use such metaphors in passing, but instead thematise this use self-consciously and self-reflectively by identifying the meanings and effects of the fight (and other) metaphors for their illness experiences. All writers lived with or continue to live with severe somatic and mental illnesses – cancer, clinical depression and migraine among them – and they openly discuss these experiences in their writerly work. The texts are thus autobiographical, with one exception: David Foster Wallace's text

'The Planet Trillaphon as It Stands in Relation to the Bad Thing' is not openly about Wallace's own experiences with depression even though it shares similarities with Wallace's life. Juxtaposed, at times, with other illness writing – for example by Eve Ensler, Siri Hustvedt, Joan Didion and Sarah Manguso – the selected texts testify to the capaciousness of metaphor's reusability and offer a rich and complex ground to examine how this capaciousness can be activated.

Chapter 1 focuses on Arthur Frank's illness memoir *At the Will of the Body* (1991), in which Frank engages with the 'illness is war' metaphor by contesting the aptness of the comparison, by activating previously unused elements of the source domain and by altering the setting and roles of the metaphor's actors (imagining, for example, soldiers who do not only fight and destroy but also watch and guard). The chapter charts the current state of research on metaphors' functions and effects and demonstrates how metaphor is often conceptualised on the opposite ends of a single spectrum: metaphors are considered familiarising or defamiliarising, prescriptive or descriptive, harmful or healing. Rather than following this line of thinking, I propose that we consider metaphor as a flexible agent that can move between these poles. The chapter describes two approaches for metaphor analysis: the first emphasises the lyric, sensory quality of metaphor and draws on metaphor theory and the strategies of poetic metaphor innovation identified by Lakoff and Turner in *More Than Cool Reason: A Field Guide to Poetic Metaphor*; the second is a narrative approach that examines the inherent mini-narratives and narrative scenarios metaphors can unfold. This focus on narrative criteria also includes character, setting, tone, parallel stories and frame narratives. Together, these two approaches lay the groundwork for the subsequent analyses in the book. Applied to Frank's creative rethinking of the warfare metaphor, the approaches highlight the semantic flexibility and inherent unpredictability of the metaphor, revealing how the comparison of illness to fight and battle can inspire new, surprising insights even as it saturates and thickens its inherited meanings.

Chapter 2 is dedicated to Susan Sontag, whose polemical essays 'Illness as Metaphor' (1978) and 'Aids and Its Metaphors' (1989) warn against using metaphors for illness. In the latter essay, Sontag proposes that metaphors need to be 'belabored' and 'used up' (179), and this is exactly what her essays proceed to do. In laying out her argument and reasoning, Sontag engages in three strategies that illustrate how metaphors can be 'belabored': she traces in which health care contexts the source domain of war appears, she compares how the source domain is used differently for different diseases, and she examines what happens when source and target domain are switched (for example when illness is used as a metaphor in contexts unrelated to health). In reading Sontag's essays alongside her diary entries (1974–80), her son David Rieff's memoir *Swimming in a Sea of Death* (2008) and Sontag's essay 'Against Interpretation' (1964), the chapter also illustrates that, despite Sontag's categorical condemnation of metaphors, she continued to use them herself and found them to be, at times, empowering and nourishing. In expanding my scope to an analysis of Sontag's style of writing which she herself described as adversarial, I ask which other form or style might better accommodate what Deborah Nelson calls Sontag's search for a 'pedagogy of the senses' (117) and thus a type of writing that elicits metaphors' close connection to affect and sensory experience.

Chapter 3 focuses on Audre Lorde, who described her experiences with breast and liver cancer in *The Cancer Journals* (1980) and *A Burst of Light: Living with Cancer* (1988). Famously, Lorde fashions herself as an 'Amazon warrior' in *The Cancer Journals*, and, in doing so, she uses the militant metaphor as a space of resistance. That is, by elaborating and intensifying the metaphor and by foregrounding notions of strength and community, she uses the war metaphor for her own self-mythologisation, which then fuels her agenda as a social activist who fights for patients' rights and against patriarchal, heteronormative power structures and norms. Lorde's use of the militant metaphor entails ethical questions, which this chapter explores by juxtaposing Lorde's writing with Eve Ensler's illness narrative *In the Body of the World* (2013), which has been accused of homogenising the diversity of women's suffering. By contrast, Lorde's journals and her political essay 'The Master's Tools Will Never Dismantle the Master's House' (1979) foreground difference rather than sameness or similarity. For Lorde, therefore, comparison helps shape a relational ontology rather than an ontology of essence (Mignolo 112–13). The chapter applies this reasoning to the comparative gesture that metaphors make and examines Lorde's strategies of reuse of the warrior metaphor. In short, by stretching the concept of war and combining it with other metaphors, Lorde illustrates how the same metaphor can be a space for social critique and resistance *and* a resource for self-knowledge and repair – or even unexpected elation and pleasure.

Chapter 4 is dedicated to Anatole Broyard and his essay collection *Intoxicated by My Illness* (1992). Broyard's writing is an exception in this book because he primarily invents new metaphors. Yet he also, like the other writers, uses and reuses the battle metaphor by reimagining it as a sports game and a courtroom battle. Broyard's approach to metaphors is crucial to this book because he prefers metaphor over narrative.

Accordingly, *Intoxicated*, this chapter argues, is less a narrative account of his experiences as it is an illness *essay*, an attempt with a speculative quality (Jurecic, 'Illness' 2), that is replete with asides and anecdotes. Broyard proposes and models an engagement with metaphors that is an expression of an individual style, a style whose hallmarks are vanity, exaggeration, an embracing of mistakes and a preference of quantity over quality. Broyard's (partly) incongruous claims have (rightly) been criticised for being unrealistic. The chapter proposes a different reading of their outlandishness, juxtaposing his singular aesthetic with concepts such as camp, hyperbole, the genre of tall tales and Linda Gordon's notion of 'light comparison'. These concepts bring to light Broyard's affirmative, reparative strategies which emphasise what can be gained from reusing and creatively misusing metaphors when this reuse is not too rigidly bound by rationality and congruity.

Chapter 5 examines David Foster Wallace's metaphors of severe clinical depression in the semi-autobiographical short story 'The Planet Trillaphon as It Stands in Relation to the Bad Thing' (1984). In contrast to the other writers who have achieved an almost canonical status in Medical Humanities and Narrative Medicine, this text is rarely mentioned in either field. In 'The Planet Trillaphon', Wallace uses and reuses the battle metaphor by questioning, expanding and elaborating it in creative ways. In doing so, he explores its downsides, such as defeat and failure, as well as the dangers of (over)identification and sameness in any comparative gesture. The chapter analyses how Wallace, rather than mitigating or softening these darker sides, in fact uses elaboration to intensify them. In contrasting Wallace's explorations with Joan Didion's writing on migraine, this chapter, on the one hand, explores the multiple meanings of defeat. On the other hand, it examines the narrative choices Wallace makes, such as second-person narration, irony and understatement, which open up too-narrow or too-rigid assertions about defeat, for example when it appears as the only option. Wallace's ingenious use of these narrative devices in 'The Planet Trillaphon' render his text *meta-metaphorical* in so far as the narrative mirrors qualities that are typical of metaphor: contradiction, relationality and a constant tension between distance, proximity and conflation.

Chapter 6 distils the insights from the previous chapters and proposes how they can be transferred to contexts outside of literary texts. The chapter thus addresses readers who are practically oriented and reviews the metaphor guidelines and recommendations that have been proposed. Complementing the existing research, the chapter identifies five distinct steps for approaching metaphor and illustrates them with the help of metaphors used by health care professionals and patients.

These five features comprise (1) identifying an expression as a metaphor, (2) naming the salient features of a metaphor, (3) evaluating a metaphor, (4) analysing the context of a metaphor and (5) activating the generative potential of a metaphor. The chapter concludes by broadening the scope from metaphor to other forms of figurative language, namely simile and symbol, and explains why a distinction between these different forms is useful and relevant in the context of health care.

* * *

In analysing the varied usability of metaphors through a close reading of illness writing and a linking of metaphor with narrative, *Metaphor in Illness Writing* advances research in Medical Humanities in several ways: it offers a more capacious understanding of metaphors by considering the varied, unpredictable and surprising usability of metaphors; it devises an approach to metaphors grounded in both metaphor theory and narrative theory in order to demonstrate the nuanced and complex ways in which even problematic metaphors can be fruitfully engaged; and it identifies the distinct choices that prominent writers make when they actively and creatively engage with metaphors. By analysing how metaphor and narrative intersect and interact with one another, the following chapters make a contribution to research at the boundaries of metaphor theory and narrative theory. With its focus on strategies, practices and transferability, *Metaphor in Illness Writing* echoes the call for greater metaphor competency and metaphor literacy among health care workers, which is needed, researchers have argued, to enhance understanding on both sides of the care equation. The final chapter responds to that call by offering a method for analysing metaphors and for translating the insights of this book into non-literary, practice-oriented contexts.

NOTES

1. In the following chapters, I use the basic yet ambiguous modifier 'American' by which I designate primarily US-American culture and discourses, acknowledging, of course, that the term is much broader in its meanings.
2. I am using the terms 'Medical Humanities' and 'Health Humanities' interchangeably here, while appreciating the arguments made by proponents of the more inclusive term 'Health Humanities', which is considered less elitist and more application-oriented while also embracing a broader understanding of health that includes health professionals such as

Introduction 23

  paramedics, pharmacists, nurses and physiotherapists as well as complementary and alternative health care (Allsopp 71; Crawford et al.). Besides Health Humanities, scholars have suggested 'Critical Medical Humanities' as a more appropriate label for a field that takes 'seriously the challenges of critical and cultural theory, community-based arts-in-health, and the counter-cultural creative practices and strategies of activist movements' (Atkinson et al. 78).
3. The term 'Narrative Medicine' is sometimes used interchangeably with Medical Humanities or as a subfield within Medical Humanities. Rita Charon's concept of Narrative Medicine in the US emerged simultaneously with the publications on Narrative-based Medicine by Trisha Greenhalgh and Brian Hurwitz. My use of the term mostly refers to Charon's programme, mostly because of its rootedness in literary theory, analysis and methodology.
4. Another book-length study has been published: Geraldine W. van Rijn-van Tongeren's *Metaphors in Medical Texts*.
5. In Guy Becker's study *Disrupted Live*, metaphor plays a double role: Becker speaks of 'metaphors of transformation' such as death and rebirth (184) through which her interviewees framed their experiences of disruption and their return into a sense of continuity. At the same time, metaphor itself is implicated in this process of transformation because metaphor, as Becker argues, shares with transformation 'alterations to ways of seeing', 'shifts in vision' and thus a 'looking at things differently' (174). What is transformed or amended is the position of the interviewees to the dominant cultural model that frames the life course in terms of continuity. The cultural model itself, Becker maintains, cannot be changed but metaphors grant 'plasticity with which individuals work around such models when those models pose a source of conflict and cease to work for them' (404–5). For example, Becker interviewed a woman who could not get pregnant without reproductive medicine (400). When an egg by her sister was fertilised with her husband's sperm, the mother-to-be found it hard to see the foetus in her as her own baby. She learned to view the situation from a new perspective when she used a metaphor: she compared her sister's egg to fire and her womb as the fuel that keeps the fire alive and nurtures it. The metaphor served as a 'transforming bridge' (384) that helped the mother accept her particular status as a mother and restored her with a sense of continuity.
6. In *The Language of Pain* (2010), David Biro is much more optimistic about the healing and alleviating power of metaphors. He even suggests meta-metaphors, such as weapon, mirror and X-ray to describe the power of metaphors in expressing pain.
7. In the context of palliative care, Deanna Hutchings finds that metaphor's indirectness can function like a protective veil for patients. See Chapter 7 for a discussion of this dimension.
8. Robert J. Fogelin makes a similar observation when he identifies a 'tendency to use the term "metaphor" in a generic way that covers a wide

9. Davidson maintains that a metaphor 'makes us see one thing as another by making some literal statement that inspires or prompts the insight' (47). Therefore, for Davidson, metaphors belong 'exclusively to the domain of use' (33). For a more elaborate discussion of the debate between semantics and pragmatics, see Harries.
10. For an in-depth discussion of Plath's poem, see my article 'Symbol or Simile? Sylvia Plath's Poem "Tulips" and the Role of Language in Medicine'.
11. I. A. Richardson, for example, coined the terms 'tenor' and 'vehicle' (with 'ground' as the common features between tenor and vehicle). Harald Weinreich proposed the terms 'donor field' (*Bildspender*) and 'recipient field' (*Bildempfänger*). In rhetoric, the terms 'primum comparandum' and 'secundum comparatum' are common. And Max Black speaks of the subsidiary or secondary subject (vehicle) and the principal or primary subject (tenor).
12. Moreover, studies in cognitive metaphor theory, such as Zoltan Kövecses's *Metaphor*, provide a detailed and useful guide for metaphor analysis.
13. For literary scholarship, one of these challenges regards methodology: Literary approaches analyse metaphors in specific texts and focus on the originality and singularity of metaphors (Semino and Steen). As a consequence, literary criticism is confronted with several challenges, such as how to approach metaphors from a more systematic perspective, or how to distinguish between well-known, ubiquitous metaphors in everyday language and more innovative, uncommon and surprising metaphors, as for example in poetry or literary fiction (Fludernik, *Beyond*).
14. I am grateful to Stella Bolaki for making me aware of Vidali's work.
15. For Ricœur, the tension takes place on three planes: (1) between source and target domain, (2) between two interpretations, literal and figurative, and (3) between identity and difference in relation to the resemblance that is suggested (*Rule* 292).
16. This can happen, for example when the assertions of metaphor are taken literally which then requires that metaphors need to be exposed and unmasked (*Rule* 298).
17. Ricœur specifies that, for Aristotle, comparison is an expanded form of metaphor. For Cicero and Quintilian, it is the other way around: metaphor is an abridged comparison ('Metaphor' 47–8).
18. Ricœur's contribution to metaphor theory is his joining of the notion of resemblance with interaction theory. The interaction theory of metaphor was suggested by I. A. Richards and defended by Max Black. Both argued that the mapping or transfer of features does not only go one way (from source to target) but that there is an interactive, reciprocal exchange between source and target so that a new meaning emerges. Rather than basing the exchange on resemblance, interaction theorists suggests that there is merely a sort of relation (Ricœur, *Rule* 226).

(Text continues from previous page: range of tropes and also in a specific way as the name of a particular trope' (32, fn. 1).)

19. Rita Felski, for example, sees many promises in comparison, which can 'deliver a sobering jolt to consciousness and a brake on narcissism, initiating a humbling sense of the limits of one's own perspective. Without explicit or implicit comparison, it is hard to see how one could ever escape, for even a moment, the confines of one's own experience and become aware of alternate ways of conceiving or inhabiting the world' ('Comparison' 754–5).
20. In order to achieve this aim, New Critics disconnect the interpretative process from the role of the author (to not commit the 'intentional fallacy') and from a text's effect on the reader (to avoid the 'affective fallacy'). A reading inspired by New Criticism focuses thus on the text only, which is considered an autonomous entity of literary value. By contrast, Richards's vision of literary criticism was more open. While he foregrounded close attention to the text itself, he also considered vital the reader's responses to and experiences of a literary work. Rather than discriminating between good and bad poetry, Richards argued that 'It is the quality of the reading we give them that matters, not the correctness with which we classify them' (*Practical* 349).
21. Similarly, Barbara Herrnstein Smith finds practices of close reading highly flexible – in terms of the material that is closely studied as well as the discourses, theories and spirit in which it is used (58).
22. Following Charon, a 'committed and close reading gradually opens the reader to self-expression and self-examination. In Wayne Booth's terms, we come to know ourselves through 'the company we keep' (Charon, 'Close' 171).
23. Likewise, concepts such as 'cultural competence' and 'structural competency', which aim at reducing stigma and inequality in health care, are inspiring approaches. I refer to them again in Chapter 6.
24. I understand method here as a guide for analysing metaphors. Toril Moi argues that the use of the term method in literary studies can be confusing at best, inaccurate at worst, because the term does not mean the same in scientific research where a method is 'a systematic protocol, a clearly defined series of steps to be taken in a specific order in order to reach a replicable result' (192). While the method that I am proposing does suggest a protocol, the steps can be used flexibly, as I explain in the final chapter, and the method neither produces nor aims for replicable results.
25. The chosen text genres comprise, following a broad definition, 'narrative' texts, including journal entries, essays and a short story. Even though Lorde, for example, is also a poet, I did not include lyric poetry because the role of metaphor in the lyric form warrants a study of its own (see, for example, Alan Bleakley and Shane Neilson's *Poetry in the Clinic: Towards a Lyrical Medicine*, 2021).

1. Metaphor Use: Strategies and Methods

If metaphors can be used and reused for multiple purposes, how can such varied engagements be analysed? To answer this question, this chapter first distinguishes between metaphors' functions and their uses and fleshes out and nuances some of the binary assumptions about metaphors that I describe in the introduction. Metaphors' functions tend to be cast in mutually exclusive roles: they familiarise or defamiliarise, they are prescriptive or descriptive, they limit or open up. Accordingly, the effects of metaphors are presented in binaries, too: they are considered risky, even dangerous, on the one hand, or empowering and therapeutic on the other. While one might question whether or not it is beneficial to reproduce such binary classifications – I should also add that other scholars such as Alan Bleakley prefer lists over binaries (see Chapter 6) – the categories allow me to point to a gap in the existing research which only few studies have tackled so far, namely the observation that *how* people actually *use* metaphors criss-crosses such neat categorisations and evaluations.

Taking Arthur Frank's memoir *At the Will of the Body* (1991) as an exemplar of innovative metaphor use, this chapter examines several of these frames. In metaphor theory, metaphor analysis focuses on the implied conceptual mappings of a metaphor and offers vocabulary for describing writers' creative strategies in rethinking those mappings. Narrative analysis emphasises the narrative context in which metaphors tend to be embedded, exploring how parallel stories but also narrative criteria such as character, setting and tone can challenge existing mappings of metaphor or inspire new ones. One of Frank's chapters in particular – 'The Struggle Is Not a Fight' – sustains the battle metaphor for illness over the course of several pages, while ingeniously interweaving it with other, parallel narratives. Both Frank's careful questioning of the metaphor's mappings as well as his use of additional narratives lead to a gradual thickening and saturation of the metaphor. The argument here is that a combined analysis, including approaches from both metaphor theory and narrative theory, *together* illuminate the full range of metaphorical engagement better than they do separately.

FUNCTIONS OF METAPHORS

One major function of metaphor is to name, clarify and crystallise: metaphors help fill gaps in language. This is particularly relevant for illness because, compared to the experiences of love, battle and jealousy (3–4), we lack a rich language for it, as Virginia Woolf argued in her 1925 essay 'On Being Ill'. And yet medical textbooks are filled with metaphors which help designate the anatomy of the human body (Bleakley 10). The McGill Pain Questionnaire, too, proposes metaphorical expressions, such as stabbing or burning, to help patients describe their ailments (Melzack 281). Metaphors thus step in to help express what cannot be said literally when there is a gap in the lexicon (Black 439). In science studies, too, the use of metaphors has been tied to their explanatory function: when scientists try to explain complex and abstract findings, they tend to compare them to something more concrete: DNA, for example, becomes the book of life; Paul Ehrlich famously described the cure against syphilis as a magic bullet (e.g. Kay; Kistner).[1]

This explanatory and descriptive function of metaphors may at times intersect with their prescriptive and normative function, for example when a comparison transmits unexamined cultural myths, hierarchies and values (Eubanks; Nünning 'Steps'). Relatedly, metaphors may also work as rhetorical devices, subtly making a compelling case for how to see a complex issue. After all, a metaphor such as 'the book of life' has religious connotations which can be extrapolated to suggest certain moral judgements when it comes to defining how scientific discoveries about DNA should be used. In naming and clarifying, that is to say, metaphors can also narrow down and freeze meanings, or solidify cultural or moral attitudes. And when metaphors are institutionalised or become associated with a hegemonic cultural discourse, they can be instrumentalised in power dynamics between the 'definers' on the one hand and the 'defined' on the other.

At the same time, metaphors serve a generative function when they are considered to be not only a 'product – a perspective or frame, a way of looking at things' but also 'a process by which new perspectives on the world come into existence' (Schön 137). When used as modes of inquiry and discovery (Doty 81–2), they may generate new ideas, inspire innovation and entail a vividness to the way we see and perceive the world. In this sense, metaphors are tentative and exploratory rather than prescriptive. Like an encounter or event in which our imagination becomes suddenly activated in an unforeseen way, they invite us to see something in a different way, opening up our thinking.

Binaries like prescriptive/descriptive and narrowing down/opening up appear across the scholarship on metaphor, as the above discussion illustrates. Perhaps the most prominent binary in the health humanities discourse around metaphor is that of familiarisation/defamiliarisation. When metaphors are considered familiarising, they are said to establish a link between the properties of the known entity, which are mapped onto the unknown. As Oliver Sacks puts it, metaphors 'make the strange familiar' when they help the caregiver or patient understand, via 'imaginative collaboration', a foreign experience, thus helping 'to bring into the thinkable the previously unthinkable' (8). Familiarisation is also the desired outcome in science communication (e.g. Bono; Martin, *Woman*). The flip side of such familiarisation is that metaphors may domesticate and even essentialise that which is strange and alien (e.g. Radhakrishnan). For example, in a study by David Casarett et al., a doctor tried to explain 'bone marrow' to a patient and compared the bone marrow to an elephant, elaborating by saying: 'It has a long memory. It remembers everything it has ever seen before' (258). While Casarett et al. found that such metaphors are usually welcomed by patients (and contribute positively to patients' ratings of their doctors' communicative skills), the same metaphor can also have the inverse effect, that is, it can *de*familiarise and thus make strange what we thought we knew. Imagine a patient who knows very well what bone marrow is; he or she might interpret the elephant comparison as condescending or even infantilising. In the humanities, defamiliarisation is a welcome function of artworks: poetry or poetic language should jolt us out of the habitual by imparting 'the sensation of things as they are perceived and not as they are known' (Shklovsky 12). Metaphors, in this sense, are 'peculiarly crystallized works of art' (Cohen, 'Cultivation' 7). Like a stunning painting, they can yank us out of the ordinary and familiar.

The functions of metaphors can also sway between being empowering and disempowering. In a mixed-methods study on online writing about experiences with cancer, Elena Semino and her colleagues identified that the same battle or war metaphor can be used to give praise, courage and motivation, while it also appears in contexts in which a person's sense of agency is decreased and his or her negative feelings are reinforced ('Online Use' 3–5). These findings lead Semino et al. to suggest that health professionals need to develop skills to identify the semantic nuances of illness metaphors and evaluate their diverging functions ('Online Use' 6).

While the functions of metaphors have often been compared to resources and tools[2] – Chambers suggests, for example, that metaphors, for him, are 'equipment for living' as well as 'equipment for sickness' (Chambers 12–13) – their utility as tools has also been challenged. Chambers himself cautions that once a metaphor no longer proves useful, he says, people will drop it and use a different one (13). According to Ted Cohen, subjecting metaphors to the logic of intended functionality underplays their inherent ambiguity and indeterminacy. He doubts that a metaphor's function can be controlled by 'effective procedures for dealing with metaphors', arguing that

> there can be no routine method for (1) detecting metaphors when they appear, just as there are no foolproof rules for determining when someone is joking, or (2) unpacking the metaphor once it is known to be one, just as there is no standard method for explaining a joke. ('Cultivation' 11)

Like literary texts and artworks, the way in which people use metaphor is 'not always strategic or purposeful, manipulative or grasping' (Felski, *Uses* 7–8): metaphors can operate in unintentional, unplanned and surprising ways. In other words, how we use a metaphor may build on but is not restricted to the functions of naming and clarification – nor even to the function of prompting new thinking.

In *What's the Use?*, Sara Ahmed offers a helpful distinction between function and use. To Ahmed, 'Use does *not* necessarily correspond to an intended function. This *not* is an opening' (24). In decoupling use from function, Ahmed argues that use comes first, and *then* things become functional (24). If an object has an intended function, there are many other possible uses that circumvent the assumption of how it can or should be used. Function is thus based on assumptions, whereas use is about practice.

METAPHOR IN PRACTICE: CREATIVE USES

Creative metaphor practices have been documented in diverse research contexts.[3] I will foreground here examples from research in health care, in which patients or relatives have used a metaphor, then reused it and adapted it until it fits their needs or yielded a new idea. Such varied uses are described in the contexts of therapeutic encounters, online writing about illness, and conversations between medical practitioners and the relatives of patients.

In psychotherapy and art therapy, the importance of metaphors and images has a long history,[4] and it is therefore not surprising that some of the most fascinating and productive uses of metaphors come from this area. Psychiatrist Laurence J. Kirmayer, for example, describes the varied usability of metaphors in the context of his medical practice, where he has found that metaphors are crucial tools for working through his patients' psychological problems. To Kirmayer,

> Metaphors are tools for working with experience. A metaphor expresses something that the body knows how to do, a way of working with or transforming a concept. Tools are pluripotential. Their shape suggests a use to the hand but they can be used in many ways not originally intended (although this sometimes involves misuse, as when the handle of a screwdriver is used to hammer nails). Metaphor provides ways of acting on our representations, or making presentations to others, that transform the conventional representation, unpack new meanings, open up the situation. The logic of a metaphor can only be appreciated when we see how it is applied, and there are always new uses to which a metaphoric tool can be put. So metaphors cannot be reduced to any finite diagram or set of images. Metaphoric connotation is inexhaustible because, like a tool, a metaphor can always be used to fashion something new. The more we know of the world, the further we can extend our metaphors and the more skillfully we can use them to reshape experience. (Kirmayer 335)

Kirmayer demonstrates this inexhaustibility with examples from colleagues' therapeutic practice as well as his own. For example, in an article from 1993, he discusses several vignettes in which psychotherapists identified their patients' metaphors and then continued to develop them. In the cases he describes, the therapists invited their patients to further explore their own metaphors, to elaborate on the details and, occasionally, to accept new elements proposed by the therapists themselves – for example when one suggests a rope to a patient who feels like she is helplessly drowning (177). In a case where a patient described himself as 'a black stone' and suggests he is 'a black-hearted bastard', the therapist invites the patient to reconsider the original image – the stone – by noting that, apart from the negative connotations that the patient activates (hard, cold and unfeeling), he may also acknowledge additional, more positive qualities, such as a stone's strength, density and immutability (177–8). Similarly, psychotherapist Irene Agstner has written about how she helps her cancer patients to reimagine their own metaphors. Agstner, whose work is informed by gestalt therapy and role play activities, emphasises visualisation strategies to help her patients further develop their own metaphors. Agstner argues that such exercises require extensive descriptions; by verbalising the potential actions or situations within the metaphor, patients are encouraged to see how new opportunities are in fact graspable (72).[5]

A research project on Swedish bloggers with advanced cancer illustrates further metaphor uses (Gustafsson et al. 2020).[6] In contrast to Kirmayer's and Agstner's examples, the bloggers do not write in a therapeutic context; and yet their writing seems to have therapeutic effects. Anna Gustafsson and her colleagues suggest that these bloggers 'cope by metaphors', thus riffing on Lakoff and Johnson's famous title *Metaphors We Live By*. The bloggers seem to develop, on their own, sophisticated verbal approaches to common metaphors such as illness as battle, illness as journey and illness as imprisonment. In engaging the battle metaphor but combining it with personification, for example, they manage to externalise the cancer, which Gustafsson and her colleagues interpret as a form of beneficial compartmentalisation. Other bloggers studied by Gustafsson and colleagues change the target domain of the battle metaphor: instead of fighting against a personified cancer enemy, they 'fight against negative thoughts and emotions' (270), a shift that can be seen as an indication of 'acceptance and positive reinterpretation and growth' (270). Overall, this study demonstrates how staying within a metaphor, exploring it and developing it further, can be a meaningful part of coping with advanced illness.[7]

Medical anthropologist Cheryl Mattingly also examines the varied usability of common metaphors in health care.[8] Instead of its coping function, however, Mattingly sees in metaphor use a potential site of agency and resistance. In a 2011 article, Mattingly describes a case in which the intended function of a metaphor was upended by its deliberate misuse. While one might consider this example a failure, namely a failure by the health care professional to use an appropriate metaphor, Mattingly is not interested in putting blame on anyone. Rather, she foregrounds the creative ways with which the receiver of the metaphor reacted to its problematic implications and brings out that reaction's political implications. The case Mattingly observes concerns the infamous vegetable metaphor that often appears in relation to reduced or absent cognitive function. The comparison to a vegetable is used by a nurse to convince the parents of a baby with severe spina bifida to sign a do-not-resuscitate form (DNR). The child is dependent on machines and unable to breathe or eat on her own, she has had almost thirty surgeries, and her heart has stopped several times. But she has survived and is alive. The doctors and nurses have come to the conclusion that each new measure to prolong the baby's life will also prolong her agonies.

In a conversation with the parents in which a nurse from the team seeks to explain the necessity of the DNR decision, she refers to the child's cognitive functions (which are close to but not entirely extinct) by describing the baby as a vegetable. The parents, however, refuse to sign the DNR. In their retort to the nurse's vegetable metaphor, the mother replies:

> we're going to be her [the child's] garden ... Everybody, her brothers and her sister, is going to water her with no problems. We tell her she's going home with us. We going [sic] to be her garden and they're going to be the sprinklers. And she will grow. (Mattingly, 'Machine-Body' 377)

For Mattingly, the case illustrates how, within an established power hierarchy expressed via an infamous metaphor, the parents managed to find a way of resisting that hierarchy by using a strategy termed 'poaching' (376). That is, by 'shifting the semantic selection and highlighting other qualities of vegetables', the mother undermines and reappropriates the metaphor's intended meaning (376). The example illustrates, of course, that metaphor creativity can entail problematic outcomes given that the dilemma is unresolved and the patient's possible suffering continues. Undoubtedly, metaphor creativity is not a commendable endeavour per se, and researchers have cautioned against the problems of overzealous metaphor uses.[9]

What makes Mattingly's work so foundational for the issue of reusability is that she does not only apply the methods of metaphor analysis but also articulates them when she explains why the nurse's metaphor 'failed' and via which strategies the mother reused it. Mattingly identifies which features were implicitly mapped by the nurse (vegetables lack a brain; both are brain dead) and which features were activated by the mother, for whom vegetables 'live in gardens. They are cultivated. They are watered. They are not only alive, they even grow if they are cared for' (377). Mattingly ends her analysis with an important call: instead of putting blame on practitioners, she suggests, 'one should ask, What culturally, within the practice of biomedicine, makes this analogy make sense? What is it about the metaphors of biomedicine that encourages this particular line of persuasion?' (379). In other words, Mattingly calls for a better understanding of why metaphors like the body-as-plant or the ubiquitous body-as-machine comparisons work so well in medical contexts. Metaphor analysis – attending to which features are typically foregrounded in a metaphor and which features are ignored – is key to this endeavour.

Mattingly's explicit application of metaphor analysis offers a compelling account of how metaphors are used, reused and imaginatively misused – whether intentionally or not. As a method in its own right, metaphor analysis, then, promises to be a particularly productive methodology for analysing the varied and capacious ways in which metaphors can be used.

METAPHOR ANALYSIS I: ARTHUR FRANK'S USES OF THE BATTLE METAPHOR

In this book I examine contemporary anglophone illness writing by professional writers. This selection of texts has several advantages. In contrast to the transcripts from conversations, these texts are finely crafted expressions of the writers themselves. Moreover, in contrast to the bloggers' writing in Gustafsson's study, the texts I analyse engage with a metaphor over a longer stretch of time, during which the writers explore and grapple with a metaphor's various meanings.[10] In doing so, the writers embed their uses of metaphor within longer personal narratives, and, as experienced and professional writers, they employ literary strategies and play with form, genre and narrative conventions. Ultimately, their writing process can be expected to be more self-reflexive than that of other patients – and, if that is true, this self-reflexivity may inform their use of metaphor.

Frank's *At the Will of the Body* is a case in point for this hypothesis. Indeed, Frank dedicates his entire chapter 'The Struggle Is Not a Fight' to the illness-as-battle metaphor. Frank is, at first, critical of the metaphor and does not consider it apt, even though, as he acknowledges, there is some truth to it.

> People with other diseases are just plain sick; those with cancer 'fight' it. During my heart trouble no one suggested I fight my heart, but one of the first things I was told about cancer was, 'You have to fight.' ... But I do not believe illness should be lived as a fight. (83)

Despite his scepticism and criticism of the metaphor, Frank continues to grapple with it during his writing. He identifies its problems, he reimagines some of its features and, eventually, juxtaposes it with a related yet distinct metaphor.

Metaphor analysis, as Mattingly has shown, can help reveal more specifically what is at stake in a given metaphor. Following the terminology suggested in Cognitive Metaphor Theory, the battle metaphor consists of the source domain 'battle' and the target domain 'illness'. This implies that characteristics of battle, fight and war are mapped onto the target domain 'illness'. This mapping can be articulated in the following way. Both battle and illness:

- require actors with heroic characteristics, such as courage, strength and determination
- can entail liminal experiences between life and death
- can place people under siege[11]
- require good defence strategies
- put people under the command of someone/something else
- focus on the fight against an enemy, who is imagined as a wrongful or alien invader
- can cause wounds and scars
- can result in victory or defeat
- rely on the understanding that surrender is not an option because it suggests defeat and cowardice.

These are some of common mappings or salient features of the battle metaphor. It is important to note, however, that these characteristics are idealisations. They may even be founded on clichés or myths. As Anders Engberg-Pedersen observes on the rhetorical strategies used in COVID-19 discourses, warfare imagery triggers powerful associations. However, '[i]n the US and in Europe, much of this mental imagery dates back to WWII, which in the wider imagination has become synonymous with the "ideal war" – victorious, reasonably swift, with clear distinctions between good and evil, and, in the end, spectacularly decisive' (Engberg-Pederson). The reality of warfare is, however, quite different – especially in more recent history when the war on terror has replaced earlier forms of combat. Today, we are dealing with wars that seem 'distant, pointless, non-spectacular', entailing 'weary allies and elusive enemies' as well as feelings of 'first boredom and finally indifference in a population tired of war without end' (Engberg-Pederson). If the war or battle metaphor is used, it is crucial then to keep this shift of meaning in mind and to imagine other options which the war rhetoric obfuscates, such as the possibility for worldwide solidarity given 'our shared vulnerability and destructibility' (Meretoja).

Besides these common mappings, there are additional elements in the source domain of battle and war that are typically *not* or only rarely transferred or carried over. In a battle or war, for example,

- soldiers receive a salary for their work and
- soldiers are extensively trained so that they can handle the lethal weapons and machinery that supports their fight.[12]

This list of bullet points is somewhat tedious, of course, and runs counter to the intuitive way we tend to apprehend metaphors (Furniss and Bath 151). Metaphors, especially new ones, are rarely processed so fussily; they *happen* to us, lighting something up in a split second. To break down a metaphor into source, target and mappings destroys a metaphor's immediacy and magic. These steps are nonetheless an important part of metaphor analysis, helping us to identify and clarify the basic assumptions that underlie a metaphor. Moreover, distinguishing between source and target and identifying the salient features illuminates which aspects remain hidden or out of focus, as well as which elements are implicitly used and which remain 'unutilized' (Kövecses, *Metaphor* 91–4). Unidentified mappings can be a crucial factor in misunderstandings. They can also be a source of creativity.

Frank activates such unidentified mappings in his sustained engagement with the battle metaphor. While he objects to its common meanings, he does not reject it altogether. In fact, he turns to describing how he and his wife developed their own reading of the metaphor. The following is a lengthy passage from his memoir, but it is worth quoting in full because it illustrates how he continuously works through the metaphor across his writing:

> The fight metaphor does capture something of what living with illness is like. Cathie and I talked about cancer as a life during wartime. We did not mean that we were waging a war against the enemy, cancer. Rather we were searching for words to describe lives that had been overrun. We thought of ourselves as civilians whose home had become a battlefield. Demands and crises followed one after the other so fast that we felt buffeted. As soon as we worked through the emotions of one crisis we were 'hit' by another, ranging from a new side effect of chemotherapy to a feared infection of my line ...
>
> But our talk never suggested that we were fighting cancer. We never thought of 'the cancer' as a thing to be fought. That would have personified it, and it is this personification I object to. Cancer is not some entity separate from yourself. As I lay in my hospital room awaiting surgery, I had to find some way to understand these tumors inside me. Were they something alien, smuggled in from outside and not really part of me? Or were they as much a part of me as my brain and muscles?
> ...
> I could never split my body into two warring camps: the bad guy tumors opposed to the naturally healthy me. There was only one me, one body, tumors and all. Accepting that I was still one body brought me a great sense of relief.
> ...
> Though I did not personify my tumors, it seemed useful to visualize them. This process had nothing to do with fighting cancer. I simply allowed images of the tumors to appear, with as little conscious direction as possible, and visualized them disappearing. Actually I visualized my white blood cells more often than my tumors. In normal times white cells 'kill' the cancer cells the body constantly produces. I imagined the white cells, but an image of

them attacking the tumors never came to me. They were simply there, on guard, standing silhouetted on mountain cliffs. My imagination gave the white cells the form of ancient Greek soldiers, perhaps because my white cell count reminded me of the number of Greeks at the battle of Marathon, a word that has particular connotations for me as a runner.

I had learned many times that running a marathon is a struggle but it cannot be a fight. You cannot fight for twenty-six miles; it's too far. At least for a middle-aged recreational runner the trick in marathon running is to coddle the body. If you treat yourself as gently as possible, your body's energy will unfold over the distance. In the far reaches you may realize sources of energy you never knew the body had. The body knows how to run; you have to learn to let it.

During cancer I tried to let my body do what it wanted with the tumors. The white cells, my Greek guards, were there, watching. The tumors had no identity, no faces, hardly even shapes. Flaccid and without purpose, they were vulnerable. They had no basis for survival. It wasn't necessary to 'attack' them; they simply disappeared. The tumors were superfluous. My life was ready to move on and had no time for them. (*At the Will* 83–6)

Over eight pages, Frank resourcefully explores the source domain of the battle metaphor for cancer, identifying commonly unused features and activating new mappings.[13] How can we understand more systematically the ways in which he is engaging with the metaphor?

METAPHOR ANALYSIS II: POETIC STRATEGIES

In *More than Cool Reason: A Field Guide to Poetic Metaphor*,[14] George Lakoff and Mark Turner identify four modes of poetic reworking: questioning, elaborating, extending and combining (71). These four modes complement the analysis of a metaphor's mappings and help us chart how Frank pushes the conventional battle metaphor into unconventional, maybe even poetic, uses (53).

Frank starts his chapter with *questioning* the aptness of the comparison. To question a metaphor, Lakoff and Turner maintain, implies an 'explicit commentary' on its limitations and boundaries (*At the Will* 71); this commentary is visible when a writer carefully and overtly scrutinises the appropriateness and validity of a given comparison. For Frank, the battle metaphor seems inappropriate because it applies only to a limited range of illnesses: heart attacks, he notes, are not considered enemies to be fought. Moreover, the comparison of a tumour to an alien invader that needs to be driven out does not convince Frank. However, instead of dropping the metaphor entirely, Frank continues to think with it.

For example, he *elaborates* the battle metaphor. Following Lakoff and Turner, elaborating a metaphor means filling an existing slot[15] or constituent elements in unusual ways; it is an 'imaginative filling in of special cases' (71). Frank uses the existing element of the fighter and reimagines it in an innovative way: soldiers do not only fight and destroy, they also protect and guard. In Frank's case, this means that instead of activating the notion of white blood cells as killers who attack the enemy-cells on the body-battlefield, Frank imagines them as ancient Greek guards standing on watch atop a cliff, emanating a sense of calm and steadiness rather than frenetic aggression.

Frank also *extends* the meaning of the warfare metaphor. Extension implies that a new slot is created in a source domain and that elements that are usually not mapped are now activated. Frank creates a new slot when he references civilians. His home, he argues, has become a battlefield during his illness, and he comes to experience his life as a life in wartime. The regular comparison, namely the body as battlefield, is rejected because Frank has trouble imagining his body split into two warring camps. Instead, the new slot he activates is the perspective of civilians and how they experience and are impacted by a war. Drugs and side effects are compared to bombs that destroy homes and mark lives with a sense of being overrun, powerless and controlled by external forces.

Finally, Frank *combines* the warfare metaphor with another metaphor when he evokes the notion of a marathon race. Following Lakoff and Turner, composing or combining is 'the simultaneous use of two or more such metaphors in the same passage, or even in the same sentence' (70). In leaping from the Battle of Marathon to a running race, Frank combines the illness-as-battle metaphor with illness-as-race. In doing so, he shifts the perspective from a life-and-death matter to a sports event. This combination allows Frank to propose an attitudinal shift that foregrounds gentleness rather than belligerence and coddling rather than steely rigour. Combination thus produces 'a richer and more complex set of connections' (Lakoff and Turner 71).

In addition to these four central modes, Lakoff and Turner mention a fifth poetic strategy of *personification*. Via personification, 'we understand other things as people' and, in doing so, we can draw on 'our knowledge about ourselves to maximal effect' (72). While Frank maintains that he did not personify his tumours but simply visualised them, the white cells he also visualises do appear as human-like actors, taking 'the form of ancient Greek soldiers' (85). In this part of the passage, personification allows Frank to project his own attitudes about illness (which he defines as 'peaceful' and accepting) onto his illness.

Frank makes metaphor use the focus of his chapter. Other writers may employ such metaphors less consciously, however, or pay little overt attention to them. When Lakoff and Turner speak about modes, strategies and engagement, then, who do they assume is doing this work? Their wording ('poetic creativity') suggests that it is the poets themselves who wield modes of metaphorical thought in order to 'invoke' something in their readers (71). Yet in general, Lakoff and Turner locate these modes in the reader; it is readers who do the work, even though the manner of that work is 'indicated or at least suggested' by the text (67). In my opinion, trying to locate the origin of these modes or strategies is a slippery slope. I agree with Lakoff and Turner that the poet or writer may not be the sole origin, especially because this would suggest an intentionality that may not always be present. Clearly, the reader plays an active and creative role, as she may see a reuse of a metaphor unbeknown to the writer.[16] For reasons of simplicity, I have decided to follow Lakoff and Turner's phrasing and designate the writers as the grammatical subjects of these strategies; however, this choice does not imply that the writers are the sole origin of a metaphor's creativity.

METAPHOR, NARRATIVE, ALLEGORY AND PARABLE

Metaphor analysis, as I have illustrated, is useful for articulating the varied usability of a metaphor. It has its limits, however. What metaphor analysis does not account for is the temporal unfolding and narrative embeddedness of metaphors – factors that are instrumental in how metaphors are used, reused and creatively misused across time. Frank's engagement with the battle metaphor is sustained over an entire chapter, and even beyond, as I will show. By the end of 'The Struggle Is Not a Fight', he has come to think of his illness as a wrestling match – a contest, in other words, 'between two persons, each trying to throw the other by grasping his body or limbs' ('wrestle, n.'). To wrestle also means 'To strive or labour (esp. to obtain the mastery, superiority, or advantage) *with* or *against* difficulties, circumstances, forces, personal feelings, etc.' and 'To twist or writhe about; to wriggle, move sinuously; to work backwards and forwards' ('wrestle, v.'). The connotations of 'wrestle' are clearly very different from fight and battle, suggesting pliability, intimacy and reciprocity. The focus is not on violence but on hard work, not on steely and straightforward determination but on going back and forth, wriggling and moving sinuously.

Frank's metaphor shift from battle to wrestle is not only a shift of focus or emphasis, as it also comes with a framed narrative: the biblical story of Jacob's wrestling with the angel. This story is introduced in the chapter before Frank discusses the fight metaphor. It is 'a story I lived with as part of my personal mythology of illness. This is what it is to be ill: to wrestle through the long night, injured, and if you prevail until the sun rises, to receive a blessing. Through Jacob's story, illness became an adventure' (81). Here we see that Frank's engagement with the battle metaphor is not only deeply interwoven with his personal story of illness, but also with a biblical story, which is in itself highly figurative. When at the end of the metaphor chapter Frank returns to Jacob and concludes, 'The wrestling is a struggle but not a fight' (89), we also need to account for how Frank's use and reuse of the battle metaphor is shaped by the power of this narrative frame.

To take this idea even further, we should note that Frank's continued interest in the fight metaphor also exceeds the boundaries of his memoir. For example, in the afterword of *The Wounded Storyteller*, Frank discusses metaphors of battle in the context of Plains Indians in North America, such as the Crow, for whom a victorious fight is not simply defined as conquest, killing and survival but also as a form of recognition (207).[17] The practice of 'counting coups' involves for example that an enemy's weapon is taken, which demonstrates superiority in warfare (207). Harming the enemy is secondary. Elsewhere, in a review article on four illness narratives, Frank chooses the title 'Metaphors of Pain' and discusses the pain-as-weapon metaphor, which he finds in three of the texts he reviews (185), discussing what the metaphor accomplishes in each text. These examples, taken from across Frank's academic and writing career, confirm Frank's interest in the metaphor's capacity and potential as well as his continued engagement with it over time. For this reason, metaphor analysis also invites narrative analysis, allowing us to examine how a metaphor unfolds, changes and thickens with time.

One obvious way of attending to the narrative dimensions of Frank's wrestling metaphor is a closer look at allegory and parable.[18] A parable is 'a very short narrative about human beings presented so as to stress the tacit analogy, or parallel, with a general thesis or lesson that the narrator is trying to bring home to his audience' (Abrams 7). Steen defines parables as an 'anecdote that is meant to be understood as a … metaphor for a moral or spiritual aspect of life, in particular good behavior' (418). Parables, like allegories, thus have a literal, primary level of meaning as well as a figurative dimension, and these two dimensions are upheld throughout the narrative. Readers are invited to ask themselves how the literal story may link up with a specific context or moral. Knowing that a parable like the Good Samaritan or George Orwell's allegorical novel *Animal Farm* is not only about the literal events described in the texts, readers engage actively in a process of comparing. In this sense, allegories and parables are similar to metaphors, but with an added narrative and temporal dimension. For Cohen, metaphor encompasses allegories, parables and analogies. In all of these forms, Cohen argues, 'one thing is regarded as something that it is not' (*Thinking* 9). In other words, these forms are

> grounded in the idea that A can be understood (or 'seen') as B, and in virtually every interesting case this will be not because A and B share some property but because B has some property that A can be thought of as having, or imagined to have, when in fact the property is not literally a property of A. (*Thinking* 10; original emphasis)

I would not go so far as Cohen and subsume parable, analogy and allegory under the cloak of metaphor. Moreover, I do not think that Frank's sustained engagement with the battle metaphor in his chapter is a parable or allegory. For one, there is no figurative meaning for us to intuit or extrapolate. Frank does the work of extrapolation very literally and before our eyes when he dissects the figurative implications of the metaphor; he does not suggest that this process of dissection is to be understood figuratively. For another, one might wonder if Frank is even telling a story in the chapter 'The Struggle Is Not a Fight'. Isn't he actually pondering a problem, enriching it with personal anecdotes, hypotheses and ideas – criteria that put the chapter closer to an essay?

With his concept of 'extended metaphor', Paul Werth comes the closest to capturing what Frank is doing. Werth usefully distinguishes between two ways in which metaphors can be extended: either because they carry an inherent temporal dimension (e.g. the metaphor 'life is a path' suggests travel that takes place over time); or because they recur throughout an extended text – a poem, play or novel, say – and each reappearance (possibly) takes on new meaning (80, 83). This latter type of extended metaphor can run like an undercurrent through a text, allowing 'extremely subtle conceptual effects to be achieved' (89).[19] In attending to these effects, Werth is arguing for a discursive approach to metaphor, one that focuses not only on the sentence level but also on the context in which the metaphor is explored. However, Werth is not discussing how we can understand the relation between the undercurrent and the main text.

I am interested in further exploring the interaction between metaphor and narrative. As shown in Mattingly's example of the parents of the hospitalised infant, an extended metaphor may counter, question or reject a story that a health care team tries to convey. But besides resistance and contestation, in what other ways do metaphor and narrative interact with one another? And how can we bring narrative analysis to bear productively on more exploratory extensions of metaphors, like Frank's?[20]

THE MICRO LEVEL: NARRATIVE ANALYSIS OF AN EXTENDED METAPHOR

Narrative concepts or terminology are not, in fact, completely foreign to metaphor analysis. For example, Mark Johnson uses the concept of 'experiential gestalts' to explain the narrative summoned in a flash of insight that metaphors sometimes produce. Experiential gestalts are 'structured meaningful wholes within experience' which consist of 'sub-patterns' (Johnson 30–1). Using the gestalt for 'war', Johnson explains that its subpatterns involve:

> PARTICIPANTS (people/nations as adversaries), PARTS (two positions, planning strategy, attack, defense, counterattack, surrender, etc.), STAGES (one adversary attacks, both sides maneuver, one side retreats, etc.), LINEAR SEQUENCE (retreat after attack, counterattack after attack, etc.), CAUSATION (attack results in defeat, etc.), PURPOSE (victory). (31; emphasis in original)

These subpatterns resemble the criteria that inform narrative analysis, such as character, events, story and plot typologies (e.g. Nünning and Nünning 106–9; original emphasis). Blending Theory or Conceptual Integration Theory – an approach to metaphor developed by Gilles Fauconnier and Mark Turner in 1994[21] – also demonstrates an openness to narrative categories. Proponents of blending theory advocate replacing the two-domain structure of source and target with a four-space model, consisting of two input spaces as well as a generic and a blended space (Kövecses, *Metaphor* 267ff.). The advantage of the Blending model is that it explains how *new* meanings, which are neither part of the source nor the target, can emerge in a metaphor (see Fludernik, 'Narrative' 353). Because the blend 'contains more than the sum of the parts of the input spaces' (Busse 179), this model can help explain metaphor creativity (Kövecses, *Metaphor* 285). The classic example for demonstrating the advantages of blending is the metaphor 'My surgeon is a butcher', which suggests incompetence, even though this feature is inherent to neither surgeons nor butchers (Kövecses, *Metaphor* 313ff.). Following the four-space model, the items activated in the metaphor are identified as 'roles' or 'agents' with particular 'identities' who perform actions with specific goals ('healing', 'severing flesh') in particular settings ('operating room', 'abattoir') that include props ('scalpel', 'cleaver') (Grady et al. 105). This approach to metaphor, too, seems to align well with narrative concepts such as characterisation, setting and the causal relations of events (or plot).

Both experiential gestalts and the insights of blending theory are helpful in examining Frank's extension of the fight metaphor from a narrative perspective. Unlike straight metaphor analysis, a narrative-inflected approach invites us to pay attention to the way he deals with character, space and time, course of action and beginning and ending – both within the metaphor and in the immediate context in which the metaphor is embedded.

The *agents* or *characters* Frank imagines to be carrying out the fight or struggle are described with a set of distinct characteristics: he imagines watchful, defensive guards who do not blindly or furiously attack but rather wait and see.[22] In leaping from the *present* to the *past*, the world of ancient Greece, Frank builds a historical bridge through which he connects his personal, idiosyncratic struggle with mythical struggles in human history. In the context of the ancient Greek legend of the Battle of Marathon, Frank does not side with the Persian attackers, but with the defensive Athenians. Standing on a mountain cliff as silhouettes (a quite dramatic *setting* or *space*), the white cells/soldiers are given a status of anonymity (they only have contours) and an elevated position (they have a good overview or vantage and, figuratively, stand above things). They appear as mysterious creatures and guardian angels, exuding a peaceful, serene *atmosphere*. Yet for all of its poise and calm, Frank's invocation of this famed battle also contains an interesting ellipsis or gap: Pheidippides, the runner who, according to legend, was sent to Athens to share the good news about the victory of the Greek troops over the Persians at Marathon, died from exhaustion after he delivered the news.[23] Did he run too fast? Did he overexert himself? Would there have been another way to accomplish his goal? And is his death a heroic ending or a sign of failure?[24]

These questions are answered, indirectly, when Frank changes the setting and time in the next paragraph. Leaving ancient Greece, we are now at an imagined sports event in the present, a place of sweat and tears, music and cheering, recreation and excitement. The marathon runner he envisions is characterised by gentleness and kindness. Drawing on his own experiences as a runner, Frank speaks of coddling, generosity and support towards the body in order to prevent overextension and enable a more fortunate ending than that of Pheidippides. Moreover, a marathon typically has a fixed route, a predetermined *course of action* with a clear *beginning and ending* at exactly 26.219 miles – a set course (of events) that appeals to anyone seeking a clearly defined and (ideally) speedy 'race' from illness to health. Moreover, in

Frank's version, the body becomes an active subject or actor, also grammatically speaking: 'The body knows' (86); it is experienced, superior and imbued with surprising amounts of energy.

My analysis of the fight metaphor's narrative features suggests that its source domain contains a rich repertoire of story seeds or kernels that can be activated and elaborated. I am drawing on concepts proposed by researchers such as Benjamin Biebuyck and Gunther Martens who have argued that metaphors 'carry in them the germs of a vast number of narrative extensions that only need to be actualised' ('Literary' 64). Metaphors thus harbour 'micronarratives' that can be unfolded at length and in depth (64). Ansgar Nünning takes up the notion of mininarrations (a term suggested by Philip Eubanks) and argues that metaphors 'are narratives that mask themselves as a single word' ('Steps' 231). Metaphors are thus not only shortened comparisons, they are also condensed or reduced simple stories. Andreas Musolff speaks of 'metaphor scenarios' (23), and Monika Fludernik argues that metaphors generate 'virtual scenarios' ('Narrative' 363) or 'virtual storylines' that 'tease the interpreter's mind with narrative elaborations' and 'make it possible to imagine alternative or subordinate stories' ('Cage' 125).[25] In Frank's example, stories about marathon battles and marathon races have been tapped. However, their narrative unfolding remains, to some extent, latent. After all, Frank does not realise them as fully fleshed-out stories. In contrast to Frank's more elaborate retelling of Jacob's story, the marathon micronarratives or kernels are not (re)told as stories per se. Instead, their narrative potential lingers – in between the lines of the text, in the readers' minds, and in the writers' imagination.

While these virtual stories or micronarratives can also be identified via the methods of metaphor analysis, the inclusion of narrative criteria has several advantages: it helps us pose new questions; it adds a different analytical vocabulary, and, as a result, it offers a more comprehensive frame for analysing how a writer is engaging with a metaphor over the course of his own and other parallel stories. A narrative analysis shows that Frank extends the fight metaphor by invoking at least two distinct virtual scenarios: (1) the ancient Greek Battle of Marathon and (2) his autobiographical experiences as a marathon runner. In activating the temporality and narrativity that this metaphor carries, Frank manages to saturate the battle metaphor with his own experiences, knowledge and attitudes.

Aside from the narrative analysis of the battle metaphor and its unfolding, there is another narrative dimension to consider: Frank's two virtual scenarios exist alongside the parable of Jacob's wrestle with the angel, and they are enfolded in Frank's own struggles. For one, quite literally, Frank struggles with his illness; for another, more indirectly, he grapples with the martial language of illness. How do these different levels of narrativity, which occur on a more global or structural level, interact with one another?

THE MACRO LEVEL: LINKING METAPHOR AND NARRATIVE

Narratologist Monika Fludernik claimed in 2009 that structural approaches to the intersection of metaphor and narrator had been 'curiously under-researched' and that it is 'high time' to analyse metaphor from a narrative perspective ('Cage' 109, 110). Narratologists' reluctance to approach metaphors more comprehensively is explained by Fludernik in the following way: metaphors 'upset the neat model in which every category has its place on a distinct level of narratological typology' (123). This confusion about whom a metaphor can be assigned to – character, narrator, author – and thus where it can be placed within a narratological paradigm is also evident in the divergent ways that narratological textbooks categorise metaphor: some list it under 'content', similar to the function of a motif (e.g. Martinez and Scheffel), whereas others see it as a matter of style (e.g. Lahn and Meister). Since 2009, Fludernik herself has contributed a great deal to close this gap. Her anthology of 2011, *Beyond Cognitive Metaphor Theory: Perspectives on Literary Metaphor,* is an excellent collection of articles exploring the intersections of metaphor and narrative. And yet, approaches from cognitive sciences seem insufficient to fully explain the creative ways in which writers use metaphors in literary texts, as Biebuyck and Martin have also argued ('Literary' 63). As recently as 2017, in a survey article titled 'Metaphor and Story-telling', L. David Ritchie claims that 'Systematic attention to story metaphors, including stories activated by shorter metaphors and by visual metaphors, has only begun' (347). Ritchie's work has been central in drawing scholarly attention to the narrative potential of metaphors; Michael Hanne has explored the role of metaphor and narrative more generally and across a range of subject areas, including medicine, education, law and politics.[26] In the following, I will highlight the work of three researchers whose work on the specific forms of interaction between metaphor and narrative seem particularly relevant to my question: How does a metaphor's narrative extension or micronarrative interact with other narrative dimensions in a text?

Focusing on the role of metaphors on the macro-structural level of a story, Fludernik ('Cage') demonstrates that metaphors are interwoven with a story's forms of narration and theme. For example, in a study on cage metaphors, she discusses a novella by Henry James, 'In the Cage' (1898), in which the cage metaphor is used on several levels of the story: the story's setting (the character is literally caged in a post office), on the level of narrative perspective (internal focalisation), the theme of the story (the moral confines of societal norms and structures) as well as in the title of the story itself ('Cage' 122). The 'global' metaphor of the cage thus does not only have a stylistic function but also acquires a structural role as it resonates on several levels of the text (123). In the case of James, Fludernik argues, all manifestations of the metaphor together amplify the general impression of imprisonment in the story. In other words, metaphors are not 'merely ornaments or rare rhetorical flourishes; they crucially model the narrative discourse and are inextricably knotted together with the semiotics of the text' (Fludernik, 'Narrative' 362). Beside the effect of intensification, Fludernik also identifies other modes of interaction. In her analysis of Chaucer's 'The Knight's Tale', she finds that extended similes can also 'introduce alternative, purely virtual fictional worlds that parallel, counterpoint or complement the main narrative' ('Cage' 124). Fludernik does not expand on this idea, but nonetheless suggests usefully that a study of metaphor at the structural level adds an important level of ambiguity to any comprehensive interpretation of the text (123).

Tamar Yacobi complements Fludernik's suggestions by elaborating how the entanglement of metaphor with different narrative agents adds to the ambiguity of metaphor in fictional texts. To Yacobi, a metaphor can be embedded in a complex network of 'speaker, addressee, echoer, object, implied author and reader; this network activates, and its understanding must coordinate, the discourse as a whole' (121). While Fludernik sees a narratological difficulty in attributing metaphors to a character, narrator, or implied author, Yacobi argues that this vagueness substantiates the importance of metaphor in an analysis of narrative. Readers are prompted to question the reliability of those in the text that use a metaphor (121): Are their intentions biased or kind? What motivations drive them? Such questions become particularly relevant when a character in a story has a limited perspective but the reader is given advance knowledge through the narration or the narrator's perspective. In that case, a metaphor may point directly to a story's thematic irony (131).[27] Yacobi concludes that a narrative perspective on metaphor can help 'enrich the functionality of the figure, along such lines as (self-)characterisation, rhetoric, irony, plot dynamics, semantic density, emotional and ideological impact' (132). Yacobi's analysis is particularly intriguing not only because she focuses on literary fiction but also because she demonstrates how the functionality of a metaphor is enriched by multiple factors in a given text. Apart from irony, therefore, the analysis of metaphor – as I demonstrate in the following chapters – can also include attention to other rhetorical and narrative strategies, such as hyperbole, paradox, negation, perspective, structure and form.

Biebuyck and Martens further expand this discussion. They understand metaphors as events which are, importantly, not events *in* a narrative but ones that happen *to* a text ('Metaphor and Narrative' 118). In this sense, metaphors have a 'performative quality' and momentarily suspend the course of narration by colliding two ideas or concepts that the reader needs to understand (118). For Biebuyck and Martens, metaphor is therefore neither a matter of a writer's or character's style nor 'a narrative tool in the hands of the narrator' (118). The narrative function of metaphors is 'autopoetic' and thus composerless; yet it is not entirely autonomous or self-sufficient either, because it attaches itself like a 'symbiont' to the main narrative (Biebuyck, 'Figurativeness'). In order to better describe the interactions between metaphor and narrative, Biebuyck and Martens distinguish between the primary or 'epinarrative' of the literary text and the 'paranarative', which is a second-order narrative that emerges from 'configurative clusters' of metaphors in a text ('Metaphor and Narrative' 120). The paranarrative – a term that Biebuyck and Martens take from Luz Aurora Pimentel – 'grafts itself onto the originary narrative and turns this into its object' (120).[28] However, rather than suggesting a stable relationship of resistance or intensification, Biebuyck and Martens propose a dynamic interconnection that is characterised by reciprocity and *potential* meanings ('Literary' 63). That is, as Frank's example illustrates, the relationship between the metaphor's virtual scenario and the narrative in which it is embedded can oscillate between numerous modes: cautious scepticism, partial endorsement, playful tinkering, individual customisation and many more.[29]

Biebuyck and Martens's conceptualisations are so intriguing because of the processual and dynamic quality they ascribe to the relationship between metaphor and narrative. Elsewhere, they elaborate on this point by suggesting that the 'paranarrative manifestly traverses the intentionality and temporal linearity of the primary order. This urges us to interpret it as a counter-telling, joyously released from the illusion of narrative sequentiality' ('Figurativeness'). 'Counter' here does not necessarily mean a form of resistance to the main narrative's themes, but a resistance to the narrative's temporal or causal order. In other words, metaphors and their paranarratives jolt us out of the epinarrative's linear or sequential order into an alternative, associative and experiential world of our imagination.

The usefulness of the approaches developed by Fludernik, Yacobi, and Biebuyck and Marten lies in the fact that they are applied to literary texts and take into consideration the dimensions of narration and thus the mediated or discursive nature of stories. While the texts that I foreground are, for the most part, autobiographical in nature and therefore do not distinguish between character, narrator and author, their discursive features nonetheless prompt important questions: for example, how is the battle metaphor that Frank engages at such length related to the larger theme of his memoir? And how do dimensions of narration – such as voice, mood, reliability, diction, address and order – impact the use and reuse of a metaphor?

Frank's grappling with the fight metaphor is clearly bound up with the theme of his chapter. Broadly speaking, we might say, he *fights against* the common expectation of *fighting against* illness. Frank tells a story of resistance in which he challenges the common language about illness and tries to overcome it. Yet, it seems to me that the goals of fighting, resisting and overcoming an oppressive 'enemy' – the elements that tend to drive a story of resistance – only partially reflect what is happening in the chapter. After all, and quite differently from Sontag's fight against illness metaphors, the chapter is not a full-frontal assault on the idea of fighting illness. Although Frank repeatedly uses negative statements such as 'Illness is not a fight' (89), his writing indicates that he is more interested in negotiating the issue than in overpowering or destroying the assertion. Note, for instance, how he carefully traces and assesses the (in)adequacy of the metaphor in multiple contexts: he lists many shortcomings, but he also acknowledges that the idea of battle does ring true (83) and confesses his own involvement in the metaphor that urged him, in a weak moment, to consider blaming himself for the illness when he tackled the question 'why me?' and brooded over potential mistakes in the past that might have caused the illness (86). Even when he dismisses the idea that his white blood cells attack and kill the tumours, he remains within the metaphor's domain and imagines them as ancient Greek soldiers (85). This engagement with the fight metaphor, I want to suggest, models on the stylistic level what Frank is working through on the thematic level, namely what it means to *wrestle* with an idea – or with an illness: he embraces it, he tries to put it in a headlock and, in the process, he becomes closely entangled with it when he tries to overbalance it and throw it to the ground.

Negation serves as a productive heuristic strategy in Frank's writing. In continually denying that fighting is the appropriate or adequate term for his experiences – 'There was no fight, only the possibility of change' (85); 'We cannot fight cancer or tumors' (88); 'Illness is not a fight against an other, but it is a long struggle' (89) – Frank simultaneously dismisses and keeps present the comparison. While negation is an expression of semantic opposition, a negative expression like 'not' also ties the true statement inextricably to the false statement, insisting on the relationship between the two (Horn and Wansing). As Daniel T. Fischlin argues, 'Negation produces a circularity of discourse in which one moves continuously between the poles of truth and falsehood, affirmation and denial' (153). In Frank's writing, negating the truth value of the fight metaphor yields surprising discoveries, namely that there is value in not fighting (88).

Here it is important to circle back to the parable of Jacob and the angel. For an entire night and all alone, Jacob struggles in a life-and-death fight with an unknown, powerful figure – an angel? God? a demon? his guilty conscience? – until, at dawn, he asks for and receives his opponent's blessing. Jacob has become a symbol for a believer who holds on to his faith despite the wrestling and struggle it may involve. Following Frank's interpretation of the story, Jacob 'does not overcome his opponent; instead he finds divinity in him' (89). Moreover, Frank's negation of the fight metaphor does not only imply opposition, rejection and overcoming, it also entails an acknowledgement of the merits of fighting. In this sense, Frank's wrestling with the fight metaphor enables him to acknowledge a paradox that lies at the foundation of his illness experience:

> The opportunity [of diseases] is to recognize that although illness just happens, we can organize its experience to make our lives meaningful. We can have both a faith that allows us to accept whatever just happens and at the same time a will to bring about the change we desire. Thus I find no contradiction between leaving illness to the body's will and seeking medical help. We are most faithful when active, just as we struggle best when we do not fight. (90)

In the parable of Jacob, Frank finds inspiration to mediate between foundational contradictions of human life. Moreover, Jacob's biblical story thickens Frank's own wrestling and tinkering with the ambiguities of the fight metaphor.[30]

NARRATIVE VERSUS METAPHOR? A PRELIMINARY SUMMARY

Frank's example suggests that it can be very productive to complement metaphor analysis with an analysis of a metaphor's narrative dimensions. While these dimensions entail a thickening of the fight metaphor in 'The Struggle Is Not a Fight', they need not automatically do so. In fact, narrativising a metaphor can also thin out a metaphor and curtail its otherwise multiple, ambiguous meanings. Fludernik's research foregrounds metaphor's potential to produce alternative and subordinate stories, but she also acknowledges that a metaphor sometimes 'comes in an already elaborated form, and therefore cuts off further, less pertinent, narrative excursions: in a narrative context the metaphor is already constrained in its semiotic impact' ('Cage' 125).[31] That is, rather than jolting us out of the habitual by suggesting new, unexpected perceptions, the metaphor's mappings are already laid out. Approaching problematic metaphors from a narrative perspective thus absolves neither metaphor nor narrative from their powerful effects.

If narrative does not necessarily thicken a metaphor, what is gained if we add a narrative perspective? Conversely, what might be lost if we approach metaphor too rigidly through the lens of narrative? What is the power of metaphor that a purely narrative approach may fail to address? These questions have been discussed by scholars who try to demarcate the boundaries between narrative and poetry, prose and lyric. Roman Jakobson famously aligned metaphor to poetry on one side and metonymy to prose on the other. For him the two figures constitute two opposite 'gravitational poles' (1076), with metaphor relying on similarity and metonymy defined by contiguity and proximity (1078). Therefore, Jakobson concludes, 'for poetry, metaphor – and for prose, metonymy, is the line of least resistance' (1078). Such a neat polarity does not reflect the mutual entanglement of metaphor and narrative, and yet Jakobson's 'gravitational poles' contour how metaphor (from the perspective of the lyric mode) is indeed different from narrative.[32] For Brian McHale, the lyric mode is not about what *happened* (as in narrative) but about what *is* (12–13).[33] Lyricality thus 'expresses a state of mind or process of perception, thought, and feeling' (Abrams 146). Drawing on Virginia Woolf and Julia Kristeva, Susan Stanford Friedman defines the lyric as a mode that 'foregrounds a *simultaneity*, a cluster of feelings or ideas' ('Lyric Subversion' 164), whereas narrative 'is inherently authoritarian' and may represent a form of tyranny via sequence and emplotment (163).[34] In aligning the lyric mode with being 'outside time' and thus with the 'timelessness' of the 'preverbal, sensual, boundaryless, rhythmic space' of femininity, Friedman ascribes to the lyric mode a subversive power against the dominance of narrative (179).[35] To Mark Doty, lyric time implies that one is 'lost in the present' and swept up in a moment of 'self-forgetful concentration' (22):

> In this lyric time, we cease to be aware of forward movement; lyric is concerned neither with the impingement of the past nor with anticipation of events to come. It represents instead a slipping out of story and into something still more fluid, less linear: the interior landscape of reverie. This sense of time originates in childhood, before the conception of causality and the solidifying of our temporal sense into an orderly sort of progression.
>
> Such a state of mind is 'lyric' not because it is musical (though the representation of these states of mind usually is) but because we are seized by a moment that suddenly seems edgeless, unbounded. The parts of a narrative are contiguous, each connecting to the previous instant and the next, but the lyric moment is isolate. Though it most often seems to begin in concentration, in wholly giving oneself over to experiencing an object, such a state leads toward an unpointed awareness, a free-floating sense of self detached from context, agency, and lines of action. (22–3)

The specific temporality of the lyric mode resembles the features that scholars ascribe to metaphor. Donald Davidson, for example, considers metaphor 'the dreamwork of language' (31).[36] Like in a dream, time and logic seem suspended when we are hooked by a metaphor. Barbara Maria Stafford, writing on analogy, describes how it 'temporarily allows the beholder to feel near, even interpenetrated by, what is distant, unfamiliar, different. Denial and accommodation, retreat and advance, absence and presence ... mark the *capriccio* dynamics of analogy's jumps from antithesis to synthesis and then back again' (2; original emphasis). The same rambling and indirect oscillation between *is true, is not true* and *shall be true* has been attributed to metaphor, too (Kurz 23). In addition to this dreamlike, flickering forms of timelessness, metaphor is also associated with another, more sudden and immediate temporal unfolding. James Wood describes metaphor as a leap (*How* 208), an explosion (204), a flash (205) and 'a tiny shock of surprise, followed by a feeling of inevitability' (209); Cohen compares metaphors to the sudden recognition we know from jokes, which cannot be explained but are typically understood instantaneously – or not ('Cultivation' 11); and Fludernik has argued, in relation to Blending Theory, that metaphor is characterised by a 'spontaneous' merging of input spaces that produce 'ad hoc solutions or scenarios' (*Beyond* 4).

Of course, as Friedman and others have argued, this allegedly particular experience of temporality cannot be exclusively reserved to metaphor or the lyric mode. Similar experiences have been described for the reading of prose texts, too (see, for example, Felski on enchantment in *Uses of Literature*). What is the use, then, of emphasising differences between metaphor and narrative when those differences are neither clear-cut nor permanent? As my discussion of Frank's chapter illustrates, an attention to metaphor and narrative – separately and together – offers a productive framework that yields insights on how a metaphor can be interwoven with an experience of illness, a style of writing and a text's theme. A metaphor's usability unfolds on multiple levels, and we need a palette of different approaches to better understand this variability.

* * *

In this discussion of Frank's engagement with the fight metaphor, I have proposed a number of approaches. I use a simplified version of metaphor analysis to identify source and target domains and the mappings that are typically activated. Lakoff and Turner's four modes of metaphor creativity help identify how Frank questions, elaborates, extends and combines the fight metaphor in order to activate new mappings and tease out new meanings. A narrative analysis on the micro-level of the fight metaphor illustrates that narrative criteria such as actors, plot, time and space can be helpful tools to chart the micronarratives or virtual scenarios that emerge when a metaphor is elaborated and expanded. And lastly, a narrative analysis of the immediate context in which a metaphor is embedded reveals how the same metaphor that is tackled on the thematic level also interacts with the structural and discursive dimensions of the text. As I concluded earlier, Frank not only proposes wrestling as an alternative to fighting, he also models what it means to wrestle with a metaphor via his writing. In doing so, he uses negation as a rhetorical strategy that reproduces, at the level of style, the flickering between true and false that we know from the way a metaphor titillates our senses and animates our perception. By staying with the metaphor and exploring it from within, Frank draws out more and more meanings, pondering the metaphor's benefits and harms, its cultural embeddedness and its normative rank within biomedical culture. Fight and battle are still the underlying concepts, but as they are expanded and reimagined in the writerly process, they rise through new layers of ideas and insights and become more and more saturated.

Frank's example illustrates that there is not *one* approach to metaphor but multiple lenses we can use to attend to a writer's varied engagements with metaphors. The next chapters will focus on one writer each – Susan Sontag, Audre Lorde, Anatole Broyard and David Foster Wallace. All of them share with Frank a critique of metaphors and a creative reimagination of the fight metaphor, which changes its functions and yields new effects and meanings in the texts I will analyse. In thinking both about these authors' use and reuse of that metaphor and about the narrative context in which this reuse takes place, the next chapters demonstrate how theme, form, structure or narration respond, in some way or another, to the metaphor that is being negotiated.

NOTES

1. Metaphors can even have a diagnostic function, for example when the inability to use and understand metaphors points to a neurological disease (e.g. Jakobson; also see Hanne 'Diagnosis'). Cohen (*Thinking*) links the 'talent for metaphor' with empathy and identification and thus the ability to imagine oneself as someone else.
2. A number of meta-metaphors have been suggested to describe how metaphors work and need to be addressed. Michael Erard thinks of metaphors as rooms: 'the windows and doors frame a view toward the reality outside. Put the windows high, people see only the trees. Put them low, they see the grass. Put the window on the south side, they'll see the sun.' For Mark Doty metaphors are 'a form of self-portraiture', 'a kind of perceptual signature, a record of an individual way of seeing' (79–80). And Cohen understands metaphors as artworks in their own right ('Cultivation' 7).
3. In communication studies, political sciences and cultural studies, for example, researchers have described situations in which metaphors were used as generative resources for problem-solving and policymaking (e.g. Schön). Others have examined how metaphors are used, reused and transformed – for example by politicians, policymakers or scientists – to change a discourse and align it to their own agenda (Musolff; Ritchie 'Gateshead') and to express 'their social relationships and their shared perception' of a situation (Ritchie and Schell 99). Lynne Cameron, for example, describes how the participants in her study transformed conventionalised metaphors and used metaphors' indeterminacy to reduce alterity and generate reconciliation. In the process, Cameron found that a vehicle term, such as building bridges (213), could be 'developed, re-deployed or dropped' (203) and that varying degrees of metaphoricity (literal, metonymic and metaphorical) were used in the process (216). L. David Ritchie and Char Schell found that in using, modifying, combining and transforming a stock metaphor (in their case, the practice of academic research is compared to life in an ivory tower), a focus group of scientists engaged in a collaborative act, in which the metaphor was introduced, 'let drop, picked up and reintroduced … then developed … and combined …' (100). Together, the participants produced a 'metaphorical narrative' (100).
4. C. G. Jung's work with mental images comes to mind, of course, as well as strategies of verbalisation and visualisation used in art, dance and movement therapy. Elisabeth Kübler-Ross's work on symbolic images, too, is an important reference in this context. More recent work on the role of metaphor in psychotherapy has been published by Dennis Tay and Loue Sana.

5. Visualisation and verbalisation are techniques that Frank and Lorde also mention explicitly.
6. The authors of the study analyse the bloggers' strategies against the background of psychological theories on coping and by using linguistic metaphor analysis.
7. The bloggers' engagement with the metaphors are interpreted as and aligned with a taxonomy of strategies for coping (Gustafsson et al. 268). In this sense, one might argue, the metaphor strategies are instrumentalised within a particular paradigm of psychological reasoning. Rather than being insightful as strategies in themselves, they are considered indicators of a coping function.
8. Also see my discussion of this case in Wohlmann, 'Analyzing Metaphors'.
9. In foregrounding playfulness and creativity, psychiatrist Laurence J. Kirmayer stresses, for example, that 'metaphor is capable of wild and limitless invention' (339). Such creativity can, however, also be a play with fire. Therefore, Kirmayer warns against overzealous interpretations, which can quickly become oppressive, obstructing the patient to find her own way with a problematic metaphor (340). Similarly, Britt Trogen offers a more critical view of metaphor creativity. Trogen observed how her fellow medical students became very innovative when, during an objective structured clinical examination (OSCE), they described to a 'standardized patient' how a vaccine works. In view of the multiple vaccine metaphors that range from 'personal trainer' to a 'fingerprint of the germ' (1411), Trogen criticises that such creativity in language is left to the whims of physicians and claims that metaphors should be tested for how well they function to express an intended meaning (1411–12). Evidence-based trials have indeed been conducted to understand, for example, metaphors' role and impact in health care settings (Casarett et al. 2010; Semino et al., 'Online Use'). To my knowledge, there are only a few studies so far that have tested the effectiveness of explanatory metaphors to communicate scientific findings and recommendations (Kendall-Taylor and Haydon 2016; Hauser and Schwarz 2015).
10. The temporal aspect is a limitation that Gustafsson and colleagues also mention, suggesting that '[a]n exploration of individuals' use of metaphors as the illness progresses might be a fruitful area for future research' (275).
11. See Per Krogh Hansen's discussion of the seventeenth-century poet John Donne, who was the first to use this metaphorical expression (218).
12. Some patients may, of course, 'train' themselves to become experts of their illnesses. But normally, the expertise with the therapeutic 'arsenal' is located with the health care team. In this sense, one might say that patients are expected to fight without preparation or training.
13. The following analysis was previously published in a more condensed form in Erin Gentry Lamb and Craig Klugman's anthology (see Wohlmann, 'Analyzing Metaphors').

14. Lakoff and Turner examine how poets engage with common metaphors and how they push such metaphors 'beyond the conventional into poetic uses' (53). In the last chapter, I present another systematic approach, namely Helen Sword's DEEPER rubric.
15. Lakoff and Turner use the notions of slot and schema in their analysis of the four modes. Using the example of 'life is a journey', they distinguish between *schema* – the basic features that we associate with journeys, such as travellers, a starting point, a path, impediments, etc. – and *slots* – which are elements in a schema that can be filled variously. The slot for the vehicle of travel can be filled, for example, with 'horse', 'car' or 'boat' (61).
16. Biebuyck ('Figurativeness'), for example, locates the narrative potential of metaphors not *in* the metaphors themselves, but in its receivers.
17. Frank also reflects on the role of metaphor and its relation to narrative by using the metaphor of the shipwreck for the interruption that illness creates and by suggesting that narrative can be a form of repair work on the wreck, restoring a sense of temporality in which past, present and future align again more smoothly (*Wounded* 53–5).
18. Allegories and parables designate entire stories that have a figurative implication. In parables (e.g. the Good Samaritan) and allegory (e.g. George Orwell's *Animal Farm*), readers suspect an implied meaning and are encouraged to look behind the surface of the literal words and story.
19. Similarly to the concept of extended metaphors, conceit is a figure of speech that is used in poetry analysis and that describes an 'ingeniously elaborate' comparison that extends over an entire poem (Abrams 42). Metaphysical poets like John Donne 'exploited all knowledge – commonplace or esoteric, practical, theological, or philosophical, true or fabulous – for the vehicles of these figures' (43). In contrast to the conventional metaphor Frank is 'exploiting', the conceits of metaphysical poets were 'novel and witty' (43). Moreover, since conceit is typically discussed in the context of poetry, narrative concerns are left aside.
20. The following analysis of Frank's metaphor draws on an earlier version, published in the chapter 'Analyzing Metaphors' in *Research Methods in Health Humanities*.
21. Following Fauconnier and Turner, the unidirectional mapping process of Conceptual Metaphor Theory is insufficient. In Blending Theory, both source and target (which are called input spaces) yield information regarding what is comparable. From the two input spaces, commonalities are abstracted in a 'generic space' and identified under headings such as agent, undergoer, a specific space, a course of action, and goals. It is in the 'blended space', then, that these commonalities are semantically brought together.
22. In a similar way, Per Krogh Hansen analyses how a patient uses the war metaphor but expands it: the soldiers are imagined as UN soldiers and thus a peace-making force. Instead of fighting aggressively, they drive back the anger and 'keep it in place' (222). For Hansen, the master metaphor

has turned into a counter-metaphor that offers resistance to the dominant cultural metaphor (223).

23. Whether or not Pheidippides (or Philippides) actually died depends on the source. Herodotus' original account does not mention a runner who was sent to inform the Athenians about the victory (Herodotus only mentions a runner who was sent to Sparta to call for help). Plutarch's later version describes a messenger by the name of Eucles, who ran, apparently in full armour, to bring the good news about the victory to the anxiously waiting Athenians (Fink 174). I am grateful to Miriam Halstein, who brought this aspect to my attention.

24. The Battle of Marathon legend is a rich story with a complex history, and there are many additional features and questions to consider. For example, Dennis Fink discusses the different styles of fighting that distinguished the Persians from the Greeks (142). Greek armies, for example, relied, among others, on hoplites and thus citizen-soldiers who had no professional training as warriors. In discussing the importance of the Battle of Marathon (188ff.), Fink also juxtaposes the typical Western view (in which the battle saved Western civilisation from the invading Persian 'barbarians') with the Persian view (in which the battle is only a minor defeat). In other words, the legend contains a number of additional features that can be activated and brought to bear with the fight metaphor.

25. The 'seed' and 'kernel' explanation for metaphor's narrative potential has been discussed critically. Biebuyck and Martens express several concerns with the 'unfolding thesis' that suggests, to them, a 'genetic epistemology' ('Literary' 64). They point out that metaphors are not stable in their position and meaning because they tend to coincide and compete with other metaphors in a text (62). Moreover, the narrative unfolding of a metaphor can be undermined when a metaphor becomes literal or turns into a metonymy (62).

26. For an overview of Hanne's work, see http://narrativemetaphornexus.weebly.com (accessed 7 November 2020).

27. Gerard Steen mentions an example of thematic irony produced by a structural metaphor: James Joyce's protagonist Leopold Bloom in *Ulysses* is, through the 'structural metaphorical correspondence' in the title, compared with Odysseus, Homer's larger-than-life hero ('Metaphor' 306). This is ironic because Bloom is actually presented as an average man.

28. The paranarrative is thus 'neither instrumental nor superior to the epinarrative. It allows the reader to gain access to alternative segments of the story world and opens up a complementary spectrum of perspectives' ('Metaphor and Narrative' 66). The paranarrative 'displays new narrative agency' and while it is 'non-linear and non-continual', it progressively develops narrative potential (66).

29. Following Biebuyck and Martens, the temporal frame is decidedly different from the ad hoc interpretation of a metaphor that is often assumed in empirical research on metaphor ('Literary' 66). It is also different from

the sequential unfolding that we know from allegories, where 'changes on the allegorical level follow meticulously the changes on the level of the manifest narration, both with respect to causality and temporality' (Biebuyck, 'Figurativeness'). Instead, the paranarrative temporality is oscillatory, resembling a conduit in which information travels back and forth (Biebuyck and Martens, 'Literary' 69).

30. I take the notion of 'thickening' from Maura Spiegel and Danielle Spencer, who draw on social worker and family therapist Michael White, the founder of 'narrative therapy'. Spiegel and Spencer suggest that thickening stories implies that one tells them 'in a new way to a responsive listener ... to discover novel significance in them so that the "thin" conclusion no longer appears fixed and essentialized' (Charon et al. 22–3). Michael White argues that stories and characterisations are harmful when they result in thin conclusions about who someone is. By externalising thin stories and conclusions, patients and therapists can 'unpack' them and deprive them of their truth status (30). Thin stories can thus be reauthored and thickened so that wider ranges of possibilities for action emerge and patients can recognise their own resources, their 'knowledges of life and practices of living' (4). The warfare metaphor, one might say with White's terminology, has become 'thin' in that it suggests rigid roles, prescribed trajectories and narrow visions. Frank's engagement with the warfare metaphor is a form of (re)thickening it that adds ambiguity and nuance.

31. A related idea has been suggested by Philip Eubanks who maintains that the relationship between metaphors and stories is defined by the licensing function of stories. Licensing stories are 'narratively structured representations of an individual's ideologically inflected construal of the world' (437). Which features of a metaphor are activated depends on the licensing story in which the metaphor is embedded; the licensing story thus limits a metaphor's ambiguity and semantic scope. For example, in the case that Mattingly describes, both the evidence-based, scientific understanding of human life as well as the parents' religious worldview function as licensing stories that endorse the vegetable metaphor's respective meanings. According to Eubanks, licensing stories tend to be 'more prominent and pervasive than mapping strategies' (424). However, a conventional metaphor can suggest quite powerful mappings, too. Indeed, as the fight metaphor illustrates, writers like Frank have to be quite creative and persistent to destabilise the existing mappings of the metaphor.

32. Of course, the lyric mode is not restricted to poetry (McHale 13). As McHale reminds us, 'Lyric can be cast in prose form ... conversely, not all poetry is *lyric* poetry' (13).

33. Also see James Phelan, who distinguishes between two modes of 'lyricality', namely '(1) somebody telling somebody else (or even himself or herself) on some occasion for some purpose that something is – a situation, an emotion, a perception, an attitude, a belief; (2) somebody telling somebody else (or even himself or herself) on some occasion about his or her

meditations on something; to put it another way, in this mode, the poem records the speaker's thoughts' (*Experiencing* 22).

34. In a similar way, James Phelan argues that the opposition between narrative as defined by sequence and the lyric as 'gestalt in stasis' or state of mind – which is Friedman's axis of distinction – does not adequately describe the differences between lyric and narrative (*Narrative* 31). Phelan, who takes a rhetorical approach to narrative, uses character and judgement to define the differences. Eventually, he considers attitude a defining criterion and maintains that the set of conventions and expectations we bring to a text are crucial in how we understand the genre we are encountering (31).

35. Friedman clarifies that the distinction between narrative and the lyric mode is not as sharp as it seems. 'Rather,' Friedman argues, 'narrative itself is potentially polyvocal and polymorphous' ('Lyric' 180). Thus, disruption and subversion can occur via narrative, too.

36. Laurence Kirmayer argues that metaphors 'allow for inventive play', which represents a counterforce to the constraints of 'hyperrationalism' that is predominant in Western thought and that labels everything irrational and non-rational as defective (323, 330).

2. Susan Sontag: Using Metaphor 'to see more, to hear more, to feel more'

There is no way around Susan Sontag (1933–2004) in a book on illness metaphors.[1] I decided to dedicate an entire chapter to Sontag's use of metaphors for two reasons. First, Sontag fits the profile of the writers I am considering in this book: she is an intellectual whose experience of severe illness inspired writing that has become canonical for the Medical Humanities; this writing not only uses metaphors but also engages them head-on. Second, Sontag's engagement with metaphors is full of contradictions and incongruities: while she dismisses the harmful uses of metaphors in her essays, she also experiences their empowering and nourishing potential in her own illness experiences and in her reflections on writing, style and interpretation.

Rather than identifying the flaws in her argument or offering neat justifications for them, this chapter takes Sontag's incongruities as a valuable point of departure. I start by identifying the specific strategies she uses to challenge the 'illness is war' commonplace, and I explore the multiple and unpredictable uses to which Sontag puts this same metaphor. As Sontag herself contends, 'metaphors cannot be distanced just by abstaining from them. They have to be exposed, criticised, belabored, used up' (*Illness* 179). While Sontag indeed does many things with and to metaphors, she never quite 'uses up' this resource. Her diverse, sustained, critical relationship with metaphor serves as the basis for what this book tries to develop: a more capacious understanding of the varied usability of metaphors and a method for a critical and mindful engagement with metaphor.

Importantly, Sontag does not limit her critique to metaphor, but also questions the value and use of autobiographical narrative and genre. In refusing to tell yet another story 'in the first person of how someone learned that she or he had cancer, wept, struggled, was comforted, suffered, took courage', Sontag chose the argumentative, polemical style of the essay (*Illness* 101). Though highly generative for her specific purpose, Sontag realised later that the essay form also foreclosed other, more tentative and exploratory approaches that would allow her to express her own uncertainties and 'integrate thought and feeling' (Jurecic, *Illness* 74). In the last section, I take Sontag's search for what Deborah Nelson calls a 'pedagogy of the senses' (117) as an inspiration to ask how metaphors are related to affect and sensory experience. Do metaphors, in a productive way, help us to see and feel more?

CONTRADICTIONS

The two most quoted metaphors in Sontag's work against illness metaphors are metaphors of her own:

> Illness is the night-side of life, a more onerous citizenship. Everyone who is born holds dual citizenship, in the kingdom of the well and in the kingdom of the sick. (*Illness* 3)

These two metaphors, as Ann Jurecic claims, are 'the twentieth century's most cited metaphors for illness' and also 'the century's most misread or misinterpreted metaphors' (*Illness* 68).[2] They are followed by another frequently quoted excerpt, namely Sontag's plea to avoid metaphors at all cost when one speaks of illness:

> My point is that illness is *not* a metaphor, and that the most truthful way of regarding illness – and the healthiest way of being ill – is one most purified of, most resistant to, metaphoric thinking. (3)

Despite this suspicion of 'metaphoric thinking' and her awareness of the harmfulness of the warfare metaphor in particular – which she criticises because it victimises and stigmatises, puts blame and guilt on patients, adds to the suffering of patients and may even kill patients (when they do not stand up for their rights) (97–100) – Sontag herself, when she was dealing with her three bouts of cancer, was deeply impacted by military metaphors, even though, as she claims in 'AIDS and Its Metaphors', she was 'unseduced' by them (98). We know from her son David Rieff's memoir that his mother fought until the bitter end, that she was inspired by triumph narratives of successful cancer battles (such as Lance Armstrong's) and that she deeply believed in the progress narrative of scientific research that is informed by the notions of conquest, victory and exceptionalism. As Kathleen Conway argues in referencing G. Thomas Couser, the protagonist of the triumph narrative 'takes action, battles heroically, and maintains an optimistic attitude' (5). Sontag subscribed to this narrative, and her two victories over cancer solidified her sense of exceptionalism (Rieff

144). The 'War on Cancer' initiative, which entered public discourse via Richard Nixon's National Cancer Act in 1971[3] and which Sontag criticised so relentlessly in her essays, was thus a significant resource for her own dealing with illness (Rieff 62, 94). These military metaphors empowered Sontag, Rieff's memoir suggests, and when Sontag briefly reflects on her own experiences in 'AIDS and Its Metaphors', there is a sense of satisfaction and pride when she reports that she was cured and managed to confound her doctors' pessimism (Sontag 100).

These incongruities in Sontag's writing and behaviour raise many questions: How could she fiercely attack illness metaphors, when, on the very same page, she employs them so conspicuously? Was this incongruity an unfortunate oversight, a flaw in her argument? Or, had the complexity of her own illness somehow distracted her when she wrote the first essay? Is this a split between her critical, distant self and her autobiographical self, which she intentionally banished from her essays but which shrewdly reinserted itself in the prologue? In *Swimming in a Sea of Death: A Son's Memoir*, Rieff explains that his mother had internalised some of the most insipid metaphors during her illness experience and had come to dismantle them only later, when she wrote her essays (see also Prosser 203 and Rieff 'Illness'). This account makes Sontag's complex relationship to metaphors the result of being '*between* postures' – between, on the one hand, the 'majestic air of paradox that gallops through her writing on photography or Camus or camp' and, on the other, 'an aching, moving irresolution' (Haslett). The concept of *betweenness* is apt, I think, but not to describe a passing stage from one certain position on metaphor to an equally certain but opposite stance. Instead, the oscillation acknowledges a coexistence of contradictory impulses, and this flickering between different postures or meanings is an important feature of an engagement with metaphors that recognises their inherent ambiguity and that allows for their semantic capaciousness to unfold.

Critical Responses to Sontag

Sontag's inconsistencies have been met by a variety of critical responses. Sociologists and cultural scholars have been particularly interested in the truth value of Sontag's claims. Barbara Clow (2001), for example, challenges the shame and punitive notions Sontag ascribes to the experience of cancer. While Sontag suggests that cancer patients are reduced 'to a state of silence or disgrace', Clow's analysis of historical sources (such as obituaries, medical literature and literature on health education) gives a more nuanced picture, which leads her to suggest that the experience of and public opinion about cancer in the early twentieth century was considered to be dreadful, indeed, but was overall less dramatic than Sontag claimed (Clow 294). In his 1978 review for *The New York Times*, literary scholar Denis Donoghue also wonders about the reliability of Sontag's evidence, noting that Sontag mostly draws on personal observations and literary fiction for her claims. He also takes issue with what he considers to be a lack of systematic organisation of her research, as well as the anger that courses through 'Illness as Metaphor'. Deborah Nelson argues that Sontag problematically inflated Wilhelm Reich's role and impact on the understanding of cancer in her analysis (102). And Ulrike Kistner points out that Sontag does not sufficiently distinguish between different types of metaphors and their impact on illness and health care. To Kistner, dead or 'substitutive metaphors' have 'zero information value' because there is no (longer a) tension between the literal and the metaphorical (18). Therefore, dead metaphors are aligned with and contribute to pre-scientific mythologisation, which abounds, as Sontag argued, when the actual, scientifically proven cause and nature of a disease is yet unknown. 'Living metaphors', however, can also function as a heuristic instrument (Kistner 28). Like scientific models, their function can be 'theory-constitutive' and thus represent a way of finding 'a new description or theory' for an experience (18). Thus, living metaphors enable rather than shut down further connections. That Sontag ignores this other function, Kistner argues, makes her critique incomplete and unconvincing.

Despite these criticisms, many scholars, especially those in Medical Humanities, have applauded Sontag's powerful exhortation, and they use her essays as the go-to reference for exploring the complexity and risks of language in health care (Oransky 468). Martha Stoddard Holmes finds Sontag's work on metaphors to be 'hugely important as a space-clearing move – a statement that elbows out the walls that constrain our thought and slaps us awake to the meanings in too-familiar words' (265). Arthur Frank reminds us that Sontag's plea was an expression of care: Sontag believed that the inability to see diseases as 'straightforward medical realities' had shortened the lives of friends with cancer ('Metaphors' 184 and see endnote 4). And Conway, whose critical analysis of the ubiquitous triumph narrative draws on Sontag's assessment of military metaphors, wonders if Sontag 'ever expected her critique of metaphor to be taken quite so literally' (79). But it is not only Sontag's repudiation of metaphors that has become a standard reference. The metaphors Sontag introduced herself – the night-side and kingdom comparisons – keep inspiring writers and critics alike (Conway 92, 95–6). Jurecic suggests that Sontag's use of these two powerful metaphors might have been a clever gambit, a way to grab her readers' attention (*Illness* 68). Similarly, Frank sees Sontag's simultaneous use and rejection of metaphors as 'a great hook for marketing' (personal email correspondence). Certainly, Sontag's incongruities have attracted a great deal of attention.

One of the advantages of such ambivalent uses is exemplified in Sarah Manguso's *Two Kinds of Decay* (2008). Manguso refuses to use metaphors when she describes some of her most atrocious experiences with a neurodegenerative disease and its treatment. For example, in the chapter 'Taste', Manguso is tempted to describe the sensation of having her blood exchanged and replaced by 'new' blood with a metaphor:

> I need to describe that feeling, make a reader stop reading for a moment and think, *Now I understand how cold it felt*. But I'm just going to say it felt like liquid, thirty degrees colder than my body, being infused slowly but directly into my heart, for four hours. (39)

In remaining with the literal description, Manguso paints the need for metaphor as superfluous, a clichéd rhetorical strategy. The literal and descriptive is sufficient, and sufficiently awful. In part, Manguso's scepticism towards metaphor is fuelled by the negative experiences she has had with metaphorical language: a neurologist, wrongly and dangerously, continued to belittle her symptoms as a 'bump in the road' (80), and in the chapter 'Causation', Manguso scrutinises, in the spirit of Sontag, the dangerous association of diseases with spiritual illnesses (21). And yet this scepticism does not prevent Manguso from using metaphors and similes in other places of her book, for example when she compares pity to 'a sea of antibodies' and 'an additional poison' (84). She even concedes the benefits of metaphoric language.[4] Paired with her scepticism about metaphors, the effect of these instances is intensified.[5]

Scholars have identified a similar intensification in Sontag's incongruent approach to metaphors. Lisa Diedrich finds that it is precisely the double nature of Sontag's argument – her use of metaphors *and* her plea for de-metaphorising language in health contexts – that 'might be useful for the person who is ill' (*Treatments* 29). According to Diedrich, in making strong, polemical claims (and undercutting them, whether intentionally or not), Sontag contributes to the transformation of how we think and speak about illness (29). Holmes considers the possibility that it might be the incongruity itself that has ensured the continued usefulness and currency of Sontag's ideas. In fact, Holmes suggests, if Sontag had actually offered a perfect argument against metaphors, she would have ended up in a dangerous 'stopping place' (265):

> A desire to retire certain metaphors is all too easily translated into a 'metaphors are bad' or 'good metaphor/bad metaphor' policy, and once we start scrutinizing 'negative images', it's all too easy to slip into a ban of all images, all representation, because of the inherent potential that our figures will do harm. And, of course, stopping metaphors is like ceasing to eat or to breathe. (Holmes 265)

Holmes's argument is very similar to mine: there is a risk in locking metaphor into binary categories when what we need is to open up our ways of thinking about and with metaphor. We may look again to Sontag, and particularly to her commentary on her essay's reception, as a model for this opening-up.

Sontag's Answer

Sontag addressed the criticism of 'Illness as Metaphor' in the subsequent essay 'AIDS and Its Metaphors', acknowledging that she had added those two famous metaphors to her preface in 'a brief, hectic flourish' that she characterises as 'a mock exorcism of the seductiveness of metaphorical thinking' (91). And, she clarifies:

> Of course, one cannot think without metaphors. But that does not mean there aren't some metaphors we might well abstain from or try to retire. As, of course, all thinking is interpretation. But that does not mean it isn't sometimes correct to be 'against' interpretation. (91)

Sontag restates the aim of her writing on metaphor: 'To regard cancer as if it were just a disease – a very serious one, but just a disease. Not a curse, not a punishment, not an embarrassment. Without "meaning"' (100). As she notes in 'AIDS and Its Metaphors', this call echoes a plea she had made in 1961 with regard to the interpretation of visual art:

> The purpose of my book was to calm the imagination, not to incite it. Not to confer meaning, which is the traditional purpose of literary endeavor, but to deprive something of meaning: to apply that quixotic, highly polemical strategy, 'against interpretation', to the real world this time. To the body. My purpose was, above all, practical ... The metaphors and myths, I was convinced, kill. (*Illness* 99)

Inevitably, her essays on illness metaphors are, of course, interpretations. Sontag, as Prosser (196) and others have argued, relies primarily on creative works as evidence for her claims, for example fiction by Thomas Mann, Henry James and Harriet Beecher Stowe as well as films by Ingmar Bergman and Akira Kurosawa. It is from these texts that she selects metaphors and interprets the meaning of a seemingly harmless metaphorical expression such as 'cancer "spreads" or "proliferates" or "diffuses"' (*Illness* 15). When she explains that 'Metaphorically, cancer is not so much a disease of time but a disease or pathology of space. Its principal metaphors refer to topography' (*Illness* 15), Sontag is the interpreter who makes metaphors intelligible and discloses to her readers their 'true meaning'. Thus, oddly, Sontag seems to act as the figure she denounced in 'Against Interpretation' who says: 'Look, don't you see that X is really – or, really means – A? That Y is really B? That Z is really C?' (5). While Sontag does not add meaning or alter the metaphors, she does reveal and expose what they 'truly' mean, reducing them to straightforward, univocal content ('Against Interpretation' 4–5).

Blaming Sontag for this inconsistency would be short-sighted. As Sontag says herself (anticipating Lakoff and Johnson's *Metaphors We Live By*), there is no way that we can speak, think or act without using metaphors. It is more productive, I think, to zero in on the specific metaphors she takes up and the strategies or tools she uses. At the end of 'AIDS and Its Metaphors', Sontag comments on the 'instrument to dissolve these [harmful] metaphors' that she wants to offer to her readers (100): rather than distancing themselves from metaphors, her readers are advised to follow Sontag's example and challenge what seem to be 'age-old' and 'seemingly inexorable' ones (179). While not all metaphors are 'equally unsavory and distorting' (179), when a metaphor does not fit or is harmful, its failings need to be exposed and criticised: 'We are not being invaded. The body is not a battlefield. The ill are neither unavoidable casualties nor the enemy. We – medicine, society – are not authorised to fight back by any means whatever' (180). Sontag models a formidable array of approaches to metaphor on the way to this conclusion, and these approaches usefully inform the method for engaging with metaphor I am developing.

SONTAG'S STRATEGIES

In 'Illness as Metaphor', Sontag identifies, collects and arranges the many source domains and comparisons that exist in relation to tuberculosis and cancer. More specifically, she (1) traces particular source domains and their metaphorical entailments, (2) compares how these source domains work differently for the understanding of different diseases and (3) refocuses her attention to consider instances where the source and target domain of the illness are switched, which allows her to trace new connections and effects.

For example, in Chapter 8 of 'Illness as Metaphor', Sontag follows the source domain 'warfare', which she considers a controlling metaphor of cancer (65). First, she identifies some of the metaphorical expressions that are associated: cancer cells are considered invasive and rogue and they colonise and assault the body, which is considered defenceless (66). She continues following the warfare language in a different area, namely that of cancer treatment, which, as her collection illustrates, draws on related military language (bombarding, killing, damaging, destroying). In the next paragraph, she presents a 'more grandiose scheme of warfare', in which, as she maintains, 'non-intelligent ("primitive", "embryonic", "atavistic") cells are multiplying, and you are being replaced by the nonyou' (68). Sontag identifies a similar implication in Wilhelm Reich's psychological theory of cancer, whose metaphorical expressions compare cancer to 'a cosmic disease' with 'alien powers' (68–9). Science-fiction scenarios in which the basic notion of warfare is expanded by notions of an 'invasion by "alien" or "mutant" cells', deadly rays and atomic radiation (69), represent a related source domain.

Next, Sontag traces another strand of the science-fiction scenario, in which the notion of cancer as a ferocious energy or as something that is magnified requires extreme measures in response. Consequently, in her reasoning, the National Cancer Act is the 'equivalent of the legislation establishing the space program' (70). Before she ends this chapter, Sontag pursues yet another dimension of the warfare imagery: she articulates the simplistic and paranoid worldview in which cancer is figured as a demonic possession associated with faith healers or a rebellion of the ecosphere.

To summarise, Sontag's strategy consists in pursuing the notion of warfare across a variety of manifestations (or entailments) and showing how thematically related target domains (cancer cells, body, treatment) are connected via the same source domain – warfare – which is an umbrella concept for a range of metaphorical expressions (from specific military action to science-fiction scenarios to political agendas). The result of this strategy of tracing and articulating is a survey of existing metaphorical entailments. It is also a testament to the richness of the metaphor and its deep entanglement in North American culture.

After establishing these entailments for a single disease, Sontag adopts a comparative approach, taking one source domain and describing how it produces different inflections when applied to different diseases. The source domain 'energy', for example, is a particularly productive concept, and, as Sontag's comparison shows, the notion of energy organises tuberculosis and cancer in different, even contrasting ways: whereas energy applied to tuberculosis implies expressions such as 'defective vitality', 'vitality misspent' and 'low energy' (63), it is the opposite for cancer, where energy is imagined as 'unexpected' and 'too much', as well as being problematically repressed and requiring release

(63). 'Economy' is another source domain Sontag considers in her comparative approach. The tuberculosis patient 'has a limited amount of energy, which must be properly spent', otherwise the 'body will start "consuming" itself' (64). The 'economic catastrophe' of cancer is of a different range: it is about 'unregulated, abnormal, incoherent growth' (64). Bringing together the source domains of energy and economy in the next paragraph, Sontag argues: 'TB is described in images that sum up the negative behavior of the nineteenth-century *homo economicus*: consumption; wasting; squandering of vitality' (64). In contrast, cancer reflects advanced capitalism's values of 'expansion, speculation, the creation of new needs' and describes 'the negative behavior of twentieth-century *homo economicus*: abnormal growth; repression of energy, that is, refusal to consume or spend' (65). In comparing tuberculosis with cancer and how they relate differently to the same source domains, Sontag teases out the semantic differences and shows how they are, nevertheless, connected. This comparative strategy has risks (see the next chapter on Audre Lorde), but, in Sontag's work, comparison allows her to create a compelling description of the many misuses of metaphors in health contexts.

Thirdly, Sontag refocuses her attention and considers examples where source and target domains have switched places. Whereas for a large part of the essay diseases are the target and she explores a number of different source domains, she also considers cases in which a disease, like cancer or the plague, becomes the source domain to describe another target, such as society or a political system. In the architect Frank Lloyd Wright's book *The Living City* (1958), for example, city life is imaged as a cancer or 'fibrous tumor', 'a place of abnormal, unnatural growth' (74–5). Both communism and the Nazi regime have been compared to cancer, Sontag notes (76).[6] These reversals of illness metaphors are explored in Sontag's final chapter of 'Illness as Metaphor', and suggest to her that illness metaphors are deeply engrained in our culture and imbued with cultural values. Since cancer and other diseases have become so fully identified with particular meanings, they can serve as source domains in order to make us see how something abstract, such as a political system, works. In other words, Sontag's strategy of refocusing the attention from source to target makes clear that our culture has projected meanings onto diseases, and that when these meanings have become accepted, the disease and its associations are projected onto the world.

What I want to stress here is how generative even Sontag's most firm interpretation is. In making metaphors her object of investigation, she exposes, criticises and belabours them. Her strategies indicate a rigorous method, and Sontag exemplifies these strategies in a specific genre, the essay, which, in Sontag's view, requires a distinct writerly stance, one in which she excelled: the cool, suspicious and 'unseduced' cultural critic (98). Within this essay form, Sontag's strategies result in a resolute judgement about metaphors that culminates in *one* meaning or function of the warfare metaphor: it stigmatises and harms, and therefore we should 'Give it back to the warmakers' (180). In other contexts, however, Sontag used the same metaphor, creating additional uses untethered from harm or stigmatisation.

'I FEEL LIKE THE VIETNAM WAR': MORE USES OF THE WARFARE METAPHOR

Such additional uses are illustrated in the Vietnam War metaphor that Sontag used in her diaries to describe how she felt, presumably during her cancer treatment (see endnote 7). The metaphor is mentioned in David Rieff's memoir: 'I feel like the Vietnam War ... My body is invasive, colonizing. They're using chemical weapons on me. I have to cheer' (35). It is unclear when Sontag actually wrote the journal note on the Vietnam War metaphor and in which larger context she situated it.[7] Due to this lack of contextual information, there is a risk of assigning too much importance to this single reference. Moreover, Sontag's journal entries are often unconnected, fragmentary and apparently contextless. As Emily Greenhouse reminds us in her 2012 review of the second publication of Sontag's diaries, Sontag tries on 'a gamut of stances' in her journals. And, of course, many diaries serve as a space for experimentation, for testing provisional arguments and playing with thoughts that seem relevant in the moment they are written down but are not yet entirely sound or thought through. These concerns do not, I think, lessen the importance of Sontag's diary entries. In fact, it is intriguing to observe how differently this metaphor can be interpreted: while some read it as a sign of Sontag's disempowerment, others see it as an act of resistance.

To Rieff, the Vietnam War reference is ambivalent: 'there is nothing victorious about her tone. Instead, all through the journals she kept during her treatment, she returns again and again to how diminished she feels' (35). He considers the comparison indicative of his mother's bitter fantasy (35) and concludes that 'my mother was painfully acquiring the cultural traits that were simultaneously the privilege and the burden of what she would later describe in her essay "Illness as Metaphor" as her new citizenship in the world of the ill' (36). Rieff also notes that his mother wondered how she could transform her illness experiences into something more liberating (35). Importantly, Rieff emphasises that, while his mother's position might be paradoxical, it was, paradoxically, also generative for her:

> Reading her diaries, I am now aware that this [the triumph narrative] was not in fact the way that my mother had experienced her surgery and subsequent treatment for breast cancer as they were taking place. But it was the way that she came to remember it and it was this 'rewriting' that informed the way she lived from that time forward … You did not give in to cancer, you fought it, and if you fought hard enough and, above all, intelligently enough, there was a chance that you could win. (91–2)

In interpreting his mother's use of the war metaphor, Rieff is suggesting different temporalities of that use.[8] In other words, at different times during her illness experience, metaphors could be either a blessing or a curse. Rieff recalls poignantly that his mother took an enormous sense of pride from having fought so hard; the fact that she twice defied her doctors' bleak diagnoses confirmed her feeling of being special and her ability to change for the better (Rieff 141). In this frame of mind, militaristic language provided her with pride and self-affirmation and helped confirm her faith in progress and science. At other times, the war metaphor also had the power to make her feel diminished, depleted and forlorn (Rieff 63).

In her reading of the Vietnam War metaphor, Deborah Nelson, too, comments on the ambivalence of Sontag's stance. She reads the metaphor against the backdrop of contemporaneous discourses on the anti-war protests and movements. In contrast to Rieff, she considers the metaphor as one that already contains Sontag's resistance and reappropriation. Thus, to Nelson, the metaphor does *not*, as Rieff argues, express Sontag's sense of diminishment. Rather, as she maintains:

> Sontag imagines herself as the Vietnam *War*, not Vietnam or by extension the Vietnamese people. If she were Vietnam, she could extend to herself the sympathy meant for the invaded, colonized, and brutalized victims of the war with whom she had long expressed solidarity. Instead, reversing all of her actual positions during the war, she is the patriot cheering US military aggression; her body initiates a war with itself as invader and colonizer, emphasizing her identification with the United States, while suppressing her identification with Vietnam as the invaded and colonized body; and 'they', her doctors, figure the US military as her deadly but potentially life-sustaining allies. Sontag figures herself primarily not as the victim but as the aggressor and as the helpless bystander who can only root for destruction. (114; original emphasis)

Nelson is aware of the fact that, in reading this metaphor through the lens of Sontag's political engagement with the anti-war movement, she risks overinterpretation. She may, as she concedes, 'put too much pressure on the journal notes of someone recovering from surgery and undergoing chemotherapy' (114). And yet Nelson's reading reminds us of the multiple contexts in which a single metaphor can be embedded – all of which necessarily impact how we interpret them.

Through their divergence, Rieff's and Nelson's readings of Sontag's metaphors highlight the temporal, provisional dimension of metaphors. Not only are metaphors historically contingent, as Sontag's critical analysis in *Illness as Metaphor* demonstrates, metaphors can also take on different meanings in much shorter time frames. And this semantic contingency applies to the person who uses metaphors as well as to the caregivers and critics who 'read' the metaphors that are used. Thus, a metaphor that is harmful and devastating in one instance can be used as a resource and agent of pride, self-affirmation and defiance in another moment or context. In other words, the meanings of metaphors can be rewritten, re-remembered and reappropriated – even by the same person.

'I AM AN ADVERSARY WRITER'

Sontag's uses of the warfare metaphor extend to her own writing *style* – in particular the military energy with which she exposes and dismantles metaphors. In her diaries, for instance, Sontag often employs a military vocabulary to describe her approach to writing. On 4 September 1975, Sontag maintains in *As Consciousness is Harnessed to Flesh*:

> I am an adversary writer, a polemical writer. I write to support what is attacked, to attack what is acclaimed. But thereby I put myself in an emotionally uncomfortable position. I don't, secretly, hope to convince, and can't help being dismayed when my minority taste (ideas) becomes majority taste (ideas): then I want to attack again. I can't help but be in an adversary relation to my own work. (397)

The perpetual cycle of attack, counter-attack and self-attack is, to Sontag, an indicator of good writing and high-quality ideas: 'The interesting writer is where there is an adversary, a problem', she says in the same entry (398). Sontag's belligerent, antagonistic position is one that she thoroughly enjoys, as she expresses in an interview in Nancy Kates's documentary film *Regarding Susan Sontag* (2014):

> For the last 100 years in our society the most interesting writers have mostly been critics of the society. The writer very often has taken some kind of adversary position. I like that adversary position. I like the position of being able to express dissenting opinions. (2:53–3:12)

By linking her intellectual work with attack and antagonism, Sontag draws on a common metaphor – argument is war – that George Lakoff and Mark Johnson discuss as one of the metaphors we 'live by'. It is a metaphor deeply interwoven in our language and ways of thinking (4). Rather than foregrounding the destructive and victimising nature of warfare metaphors, Sontag emphasises here the usefulness of the concept: it gives her pleasure and locates her in a history of other important critics and writers. Moreover, the comparison of writing to warfare is, to Sontag, a sign of quality and something that, ideally, adds value to a text. The notion of 'combat' is also prevalent in 'Illness as Metaphor', not only on the level of content but also in how Sontag approaches her topic (Donoghue 1978). Ironically, then, the metaphor 'argument is war' is a productive resource for Sontag's fight against, among others, the warfare metaphors of illness.

This ironic circumstance, I want to suggest, is not a flaw but rather a source of productive friction in Sontag's writing. Waging a war against a language saturated with war imagery is an undertaking that adds complexity and nuance to the purpose of Sontag's argument. Importantly, Sontag's style of writing impacts the results of her analysis: if one understands argument as a war, the metaphor has specific entailments. As Lakoff and Johnson elaborate, the arguer imagines an opponent; she attacks that opponent's position and defends her own; she can win or lose the argument, gain and lose ground; and she needs a plan and strategies for her line of attack (4).[9] Moreover, in a war, simplistic, binary paradigms and orthodoxies are key: the combatants are divided along a seemingly neat frontline of allies and enemies, heroes and losers, truth-tellers and liars. These specific features of argumentation imply that problematic metaphors, Sontag's opponents, are assigned only *one* meaning – military metaphors are 'unsavory and distorting' (179) – and *one* way of dealing with the problem – the retirement of such metaphors (179). In this sense, Sontag's style of writing, her antagonistic approach to metaphors, is limiting because it locks metaphors into a single semantic frame. Thus, the style of her writing *precludes* other functions or uses of metaphors on the level of content and yet it also *parades* them on the level of her style of writing. After all, as Sontag claimed about the role as the adversary writer, it is a style that signals quality and may even generate social change. Metaphor, as Sontag (perhaps unwillingly) demonstrates is thus not only a powerful instrument, it is one that can be put to multiple uses. It can entail diminishment and stigmatisation *as well as* empowerment and triumph. In other words, Sontag's writing on metaphor is so intriguing because her claims on the level of content are challenged on the level of style.

In using a belligerent, adversary style, Sontag exacerbates and aggrandises the harmfulness of metaphors, which, as I want to suggest, does not lie in a particular meaning but in the reductive way in which the warfare metaphor is tied to *one* use or function. One might argue, therefore, that Sontag is inadvertently complicit in the harmfulness of the metaphor that she denounces. This complicity is further accentuated by the genre of writing Sontag used: the essay form allows her – at least in the way that she understands it – to take an outsider position rather than acknowledge her very personal stake in the argument. Claiming that she was 'quite unseduced' by fantasies about cancer (98) and arguing that she saw the usefulness of her essay in foregrounding an idea rather than a personal story (98), she portrays herself as an objective, removed observer. She presents herself as being neither victim nor culprit in the suffering caused by metaphor, and yet she delivers judgement and draws a line regarding what is right and what is wrong. This position is problematic. Not only is her writing (inevitably) informed by her own illness experiences (and possibly her anger), Sontag also risks becoming entangled in and perpetuating the very same discourse that she criticises: something (or someone) is stigmatised through a metaphor and, subsequently, blame is put on those who uncritically use metaphors about cancer and tuberculosis.

FRUSTRATIONS: ESSAY AND NARRATIVE

Sontag herself was not unaware of these risks. She quarrelled with the alleged certainty that the adversary style prescribes and linked it to the genre in which she expressed her ideas. On May 9, 1980, she proclaimed a decision: 'I must give up writing essays because that inevitably becomes a demagogic activity. I seem to be the bearer of certainties that I *don't* possess – am not near to possessing' (*Consciousness* 519; original emphasis). The essay genre does not, of course, dictate an adversarial style, nor does it exclude the personal and autobiographical (Jurecic, 'Illness'). Yet it confined Sontag in her attempt to 'integrate thought and feeling' (Jurecic, *Illness* 74). Jurecic argues that Sontag found in narrative a better platform or frame to express such an integration. This is surprising in so far as in 'AIDS and Its Metaphors' Sontag explains her deliberate anti-narrative stance with the following reasoning:

> I didn't think it would be useful – and I wanted it to be useful – to tell yet one more story in the first person of how someone learned that she or he had cancer, wept, struggled, was comforted, suffered, took courage ... though mine was also that story. A narrative, it seemed to me, would be less useful than an idea. (*Illness* 98)

As Nelson argues, Sontag's reluctance towards autobiographical self-expression was 'part of a larger strategy to scale back the importance of feelings altogether' (120). And yet, Sontag's personal absence in her argument – the distant, suspicious essay voice – was, as Sontag realised, part of the problem: she got herself into an impasse by relying too narrowly on a single genre and its singular, argumentative focus on an 'idea' (98). But if Sontag disdained autobiographical narrative and mistrusted the essay, what was her alternative? Which form would allow her to express more uncertainties in her attempt to get closer to the human experience of suffering?

Jurecic maintains that Sontag found an answer in narrative fiction, and historical fiction more precisely (*Illness* 69).[10] In her historical novel *The Volcano Lover* (1992), for example, Sontag used 'realist narrative to create conditions for attunement with the pain of others' (77). To Jurecic, Sontag was a conflicted writer who became increasingly interested in a style of writing that would allow her to become more attuned to the reality of human experience. Indeed, in Nancy Kates's documentary film *Regarding Susan Sontag*, Sontag claims that she conceived of writing as 'a way of paying attention to the world. You're just an instrument for tuning in to as much reality as you can' (28:29–43). In Roland Barthes, Jurecic argues, Sontag found a writer whose style became an inspiration. She was fascinated with Barthes's way of 'experiencing, evaluating, reading the world; and surviving in it, drawing energy, finding consolation (but finally not), taking pleasure, expressing love' (Sontag qtd in Jurecic, *Illness* 74). Narrative (rather than ideas) and fiction (rather than non-fiction) allowed Sontag to inquire into 'the importance of emotionally powerful experience' and their capacity to shape 'moral understanding' (Jurecic, *Illness* 76). Sontag's turn to narrative fiction thus became an opportunity to explore a different voice and a different form of representation (Jurecic, *Illness* 75–6).

Jurecic ends her analysis of Sontag in a noteworthy move that ties narrative and metaphor together: Sontag's elaborations on metaphors, Jurecic argues, continues to be so powerful and inspirational because metaphors provide 'a *narrative* framework for engaging with the suffering of others' (91; original emphasis). Jurecic sees evidence in the many autobiographical narratives that Sontag's essays on metaphor inspired, including memoirs by people closest to Sontag, such as her son and her partner Annie Leibovitz,[11] who both wrote (photographic) memoirs about suffering (Jurecic, *Illness* 90–1).

Rightly and importantly, Jurecic foregrounds the narrative potential of metaphors; her analysis of the significance of narrative and storytelling is a crucial dimension of Sontag's oeuvre. However, in shifting the focus to narrative, Jurecic aligns herself, maybe too neatly, with the standard arguments in Medical Humanities, where narrative is considered so central because it allegedly addresses, better than other forms and genres, the disconnection caused by illness and where stories and storytelling are considered 'tools of understanding' (Jurecic, *Illness* 91). While these concepts are certainly correct and significant, I am hesitant to tie the power of metaphors too closely to the function of 'a narrative framework' (Jurecic, *Illness* 91). I do agree with Jurecic that metaphors have a narrative potential (see previous chapter), but I believe their power cannot be explained in narrative terms alone. Moreover, as Nelson makes clear, Sontag continued to write essays after the quoted journal entry – and she never stopped being wary of autobiographical self-expression via narrative. To Nelson, the key to Sontag's search for new ways of integrating thought and feeling lies beyond considerations of genre. Sontag was continually frustrated, in life and in writing, by the way that an excess of *feelings*, that is emotions, would dull or anaesthetise *feeling*, and thus bodily sensations (99). Sontag's primary aim, Nelson argues, was thus to develop an 'aesthetic strategy or pedagogy of the senses' (117) – a way of experiencing 'through the senses "the luminousness of things being what they are"' (Sontag qtd in Nelson 97). The last section of this chapter explores Nelson's claims about Sontag's aesthetic strategy and links that strategy to the lyric, sensory side of metaphors.

FEELING MORE THROUGH METAPHORS?

In *Tough Enough* (2017), Nelson analyses how post-war women writers and artists like Joan Didion, Diane Arbus and Susan Sontag inquired into suffering and pain, developing an aesthetic of unsentimentality or toughness to get closer to the reality of experiences without becoming dulled or swept up by feelings. Sontag, Nelson argues, pursued an aesthetic that was not informed by questions of beauty but by questions of knowledge – more specifically, a 'knowledge through the senses' (120). In her discussion of Sontag's work, Nelson reads *On Photography* and *Illness as Metaphor* through the lens of 'Against Interpretation'. Sontag's essays on metaphor are, to Nelson (and to Sontag herself),[12] new versions of the claims Sontag made in 'Against Interpretation', where Sontag criticises hermeneutic approaches to art that focus on exposing and excavating meaning, celebrate critical distance and are informed, at heart, by impious, aggressive and destructive impulses ('Against Interpretation' 6–7). In their stead, Sontag calls for an approach to works of art (and illness) that does not interpret and *add* meaning but rather attends to the reality of the artwork and thus to '*how it is what it is,* even *that it is what it is,* rather than to show *what it means*' (14; original emphasis). In the tradition of 'Against Interpretation', such an approach would allow one 'to *see* more, to *hear* more, to *feel* more' (14; original emphasis). In shifting the focus from meaning to experience, Sontag defends the importance of sensations and embodiment over interpretation and content.

In Sontag's essays on illness metaphors and photography, Nelson argues, Sontag expounds and deconstructs how feelings are, problematically, tied to morality and values. Too often, Sontag argues, metaphors and images flatten feelings into sentimentality or aggrandise them in melodramatic ways. In doing so, reality becomes distorted and actual sensations, the reality of experience, becomes dulled. Or, in Nelson's words, 'Feelings get in the way of feeling (seeing, hearing, touching), which is to say they are anesthetic or, when not properly managed, can be' (99). *Feeling,* however, and thus physical experience and sensations such as seeing or touching, are concrete and specific. As Nelson argues, Sontag was seeking ways to restore agency to the sick and found that enlisting specific and concrete senses could do so by bringing attention back from the abstract or imagined space to the actual pain of the sufferer (117). Nelson elegantly describes the tensions of Sontag's inquiry: while Sontag was interested in the ways that the capacity to feel intensely could be increased so that one can 'experience as much feeling as possible', she was also advocating self-control to prevent excess, fearing that feeling could 'run out of control, … dominate rather than enrich, … overwhelm agency rather than fuel it' (111–12). This tension, I think, also applies to metaphors. In some cases, they can augment our sensations; in other cases, they can, as Sontag's essays illustrate, evoke sensations that can spin out of control. Holmes's reflections on metaphor in her essay 'After Sontag: Reclaiming Metaphor' are particularly helpful in better understanding the tensions between perceptive intensification and dulling excess. In response to Sontag's claim that metaphors curtail agency and exacerbate suffering, Holmes counters that:

> there are many more ways[13] to use metaphors, and some of them decrease suffering rather than add to it. We can use figurative language to approach the body, as verbal pincers to get at the thing itself (or somewhere close to it) and express our own embodiment. Figurative language can even give us a better shot at proprioception, by materializing what increasingly feels immaterial and disembodied as it is reinforced by the multiple immaterialities of the contemporary world. (269–70)

Metaphors can thus be an instrument to get closer to what Nelson calls a 'knowledge through the senses … knowing what something is and how it is what it is' (120). Holmes uses the meta-metaphor of the prosthesis to describe this potential: like a prosthesis, metaphor can be a helpful device that 'extends our sense of touch, getting us closer to those things we cannot palpate ourselves or see without technology' (Holmes 270). In foregrounding the different ways in which metaphor/ prostheses are put to use, the meta-metaphor resonates powerfully with Sontag's concerns.

However, prostheses are not only enabling devices,[14] and the use of metaphor to sharpen our senses raises ethical questions, especially when this particular use is applied to illness. As Nelson rightly asks: 'At the risk of being too literal, can we imagine telling the readers whom she's most concerned with reaching – those ill with cancer – to see, hear, and feel *more*?'

Nelson finds clues in Sontag's work that suggest Sontag's support for an 'awakening of the senses [even] in times of suffering and distress' (118). The question remains: how can one prevent this awakening from becoming excess? And what amount of (self-)control does that prevention require? I wonder if metaphors – such as the war metaphor – unfolded the desired positive, affective function for Sontag when she struggled with her illnesses. Did it increase her 'knowledge through the senses'? Or did she use other metaphors that made *her* see and hear more?

One metaphor Sontag mentioned in her diary when she was sick seems particularly sensory to me: *In the valley of sorrow, spread your wings*. Rieff found this metaphor in the documents his mother left behind:

> In one of her own journals, in an entry written during the period when she was receiving chemotherapy at Memorial Sloan-Kettering for her breast cancer, my mother enjoined herself to 'be cheerful, be stoic, be tranquil.' And then she added, 'In the valley of sorrow, spread your wings.' (Rieff 178–9)

I do not want to suggest that this metaphor was particularly insightful for Sontag. As Nelson cautions, Sontag was wary of autobiographical interpretations of her work, and thus of attempts to 'access her experience, her feelings of and about disease' (120). Moreover, as Rieff acknowledges, the metaphor does not say much about how his mother felt when she was sick. It was certainly not the way she died, Rieff argues (179); but maybe it was the way she lived, Katie Roiphe suggests (2008). Rieff doubts whether or not his mother believed in the metaphor (179), and whether or not he believes in it himself (Jurecic, *Illness* 39). To Rieff, it is 'the best that can be said of old mortality' (179). Personally, I find the metaphor very powerful. And it seems particularly relevant with regard to Sontag's quest for an integration of thought and feeling. Without wanting to claim that this metaphor gives us access to Sontag's experiences, I wish to describe how it may have a prosthetic function more generally.

The metaphor powerfully extends the senses and triggers embodied impressions that have a surprisingly luminous quality. What are these sensations? And what kind of insight or knowledge do they generate? From a strictly analytical perspective, Sontag's expression combines two metaphors. The first draws on an orientational or spatial metaphor: 'Happy is up; sad is down' (Lakoff and Johnson, *Metaphors* [1980] 15). The spatial dimension is specified through the geographical information, a valley, which invokes a conventional concept: we typically refer to the top of hills or mountains to speak of states of success and joy, whereas the foot of a mountain or a valley is associated with pain, grief or sorrow. There is also a narrative potential in this first metaphor,[15] but I want to emphasise here the embodied, sensory quality of this metaphor that foregrounds a moment in the present, not a narrative trajectory.

The second metaphor compares a sorrowful person to a bird. Birds have wings and can fly. They can walk on the earth, but they can also elevate themselves from the ground and soar up towards the top of a hill and through the sky. Birds can fly away, and they can use the wind to glide. Spreading one's wings like a bird in the time of sorrow seems, however, counterintuitive: as Lakoff and Johnson explicate with regard to the spatial metaphor of 'up' and 'down', the metaphor has a physical basis: 'Drooping posture typically goes along with sadness and depression, erect posture with a positive emotional state' (*Metaphors*, 15). Thus, in sadness, we cower, crouch and duck down; we make ourselves small. Yet Sontag's metaphor suggests a contrastive posture: spreading one's wings (or arms) implies openness and expansion. It is a gesture we use when we embrace and welcome someone. It also implies tallness and breadth. When we spread our arms or wings, we *take up* more space, and we simultaneously *make* more space within ourselves (for breath, new thoughts, etc.). Lastly, many birds are associated with positive attributes: eagles with gracefulness and pride, doves with peace and hope. Sontag's metaphor resonates with the three states of mind she prescribed for herself – 'be cheerful, be stoic, be tranquil' – but it suggests many more attitudes, postures and actions. The metaphor affords an insight into the power of sensory, embodied imaginings and fantasies. Such fantasies may be counterintuitive, may contradict our actual experience and may even be ethically problematic, for example when they are used in normative and prescriptive ways. However, seen as an invitation to imagine, they suggest alternative ways of attending to sorrow, which may expand and enrich our experiences both in the kingdom of the well and in the kingdom of the sick.

SUMMARY

Susan Sontag uses one of the four modes of poetic reworking that Lakoff and Turner identified, and she excels in it: she *challenges* conventional metaphors of illness. As part of this strategy, she traces and compares various illness metaphors' source domains and demonstrates how certain targets become their own new source domains. In contrast to the other writers I discuss, Sontag does not use this strategy to reclaim or reimagine the metaphors she challenges. Her aim is to dismiss and retire problematic metaphors, such as the war metaphor. And yet Sontag, like the other authors in this book, continues to use the very same metaphor, and her work exemplifies its capacious usability. For her, it is both an embodied practice when she faces cancer and a style of writing that is, as she claims, adversary and combative. Such a continued use is possible because new meanings and uses can emerge from even the tritest metaphors. Thus, even though Sontag's essays on metaphor tend to lock them in a narrow understanding of misuse and harm, her other writing also illustrates that metaphors are at heart provisional, temporal and contextual.

Sontag's inquiry into other modes of expression that enable her to get closer to the reality of experience and sensation is a useful theoretical context to consider the sensory, affective potential of metaphors. This is a dimension that other writers, such as Audre Lorde and Anatole Broyard, explore more conspicuously. They share with Sontag an interest in integrating thinking and feeling; but, unlike Sontag, they state outright how particular metaphors have activated their senses and extended their capacities to feel and perceive.

NOTES

1. I am very grateful to the colleagues who helped me shape this chapter. Arthur Frank provided kind and productive feedback and contextualising information on Susan Sontag. With Emily Hogg, I collaborated on a project on description and interpretation, and Emily's thoughts about Sontag were an invaluable inspiration for this chapter.
2. The wide resonance of these two metaphors can be found in countless illness narratives and scholarship since Sontag published her essays in 1978 and 1989. Conway, for example, lists titles of books about illness

and disability which use the metaphors (93, note 83). Jurecic illustrates the ubiquity of the metaphors via a Google search (*Illness* 68, note 3). In the same footnote, Jurecic also quotes Rita Charon who maintains that '[i]t is the rare book in social medicine that does not cite Susan Sontag's opening sentence in *Illness as Metaphor*'.

3. Nixon himself, however, did not use military terms when he presented the National Cancer Act; the martial rhetoric was added later. For a historical contextualisation, see Nelson (101).

4. When her first central line was implanted, her doctor described the procedure in every graphic detail. 'What if', she wonders, 'I'd been told someone would be standing over me, massaging my collarbone, while I lay blindfolded? That's something I would have tolerated. And up to the point that the lidocaine began to wear off, that's almost what it felt like' (37).

5. Also see Arthur Frank's discussion of Manguso's illness narrative. Frank suggests that 'Manguso's aesthetic is also her epistemology. Each sentence is perfectly clearly descriptive; most, read by themselves, are even a bit flat. Reality is already twisted enough. Language should not make things more complicated. Maybe there's nothing to understand. Maybe remembering is all that understanding can or need be' (193). Manguso's illness narrative thus suggests, in Sontag's sense, how a metaphor-free aesthetic about illness could look like.

6. Sontag herself used a cancer metaphor in 1967 which she later regretted. In the context of the Vietnam War, she called 'the white race ... the cancer of human history', suggesting that 'it is the white race and it alone – its ideologies and inventions – which eradicates autonomous civilizations wherever it spreads ...' (Zito 1978).

7. Deborah Nelson takes the metaphor from Rieff's memoir, and Rieff does not indicate the date or context of the journal entry. To my knowledge, the quote is not part of the second volume of Sontag's diaries, which were published by Rieff and contain her journals until 1980. The subsequent, third volume is still pending.

8. Of course, the paradox Rieff is describing is coloured by his own memories and personal perception of his mother's behaviour. His mother's ambivalent position helps explain his own questionable and maybe even unethical responses to it. As personal and likely biased as they are, however, Rieff's observations remain insightful and worthy of analysis.

9. In *Metaphors We Live By*, Lakoff and Johnson suggest a thought experiment to illustrate how deeply ingrained the concept of warfare is in our culture. Rather than considering argument as war, we might replace warfare with another source domain:

> Imagine a culture where an argument is viewed as a dance, the participants are seen as performers, and the goal is to perform in a balanced and aesthetically pleasing way. In such a culture, people would view

arguments differently, experience them differently, carry them out differently, and talk about them differently. (5)

Lakoff and Johnson concede that, with dance as the source domain, we may not recognise that an argument is actually taking place (5). Still, this thought experiment elicits intriguing questions: if Sontag's style of writing had been informed by another metaphor, such as dance, would her work on metaphor have led to other conclusions? In other words, would a writing style informed by dance allow for more semantic variability? The work of Anatole Broyard and Audre Lorde suggests that this might indeed be the case.

10. In *Illness as Narrative*, Jurecic focuses on Sontag's work on suffering and pain and their representations in culture as, for example, in *On Photography* (1973) and *Regarding the Pain of Others* (2003); she also considers Sontag's essays 'Against Interpretation' (1964), her novels, and her essays on writers like Roland Barthes and Elias Canetti.
11. See Annie Leibovitz's photographic memoir *A Photographer's Life: 1990–2005* (2006).
12. Sontag comments on this link several times, for example in her diary (*Consciousness* 477; March 1978) and in 'AIDS and Its Metaphors' (99).
13. One of the ways that Holmes suggests is a shift from metaphor to simile (271). The affordances of this distinction are discussed in the final chapter.
14. Prostheses, like metaphors, can also cover up 'what can't be handled, as some prosthetic limbs function to accommodate the needs of disabled lookers rather than those of the person who wears them. Prosthesis can be enabling or deeply problematic, depending on who directs its use' (Holmes 270). In this negative dimension, the prosthesis comparison resonates with Sontag's critique that metaphors may serve some people while deeply harming others.
15. I am thinking here of the metaphor-story of illness (or life) as a journey, in which the traveller, stereotypically, goes through valleys and climbs hills.

3. Audre Lorde: Stretching, Risks and Difference

The African American writer and activist Audre Lorde (1934–92) first became known for a number of poetry collections published in the 1970s.[1] Lorde made major contributions to second-wave feminism and the civil rights movement with publications such as *Sister Outsider* (1984), a collection of speeches and essays, including the seminal essay 'The Master's Tools Will Not Dismantle the Master's House', as well as her 'biomythography' *Zami: A New Spelling of My Name* (1982). Lorde is also well known in the Medical and Health Humanities for her writing on illness, in which personal experiences are inevitably linked to her political work: *The Cancer Journals* (1980), a collection of essays, speeches and diary entries chronicles Lorde's experiences with breast cancer between 1977 and 1980; and 'A Burst of Light: Living with Cancer' (1988) is a collection of diary entries from January 1984 to August 1987 in which Lorde describes how she dealt with the recurrence of cancer in her liver. In these narratives, Lorde's dominant metaphor is, as it is for so many, that of warfare.

This prevalence has been discussed in contrasting ways: scholars have either considered the metaphor to be a tool of empowerment for Lorde, or they have read it as a trap that confines and restricts her. These opposing readings echo the mutually exclusive categories to which metaphors are often assigned: they either heal or harm; they are either aggrandising or victimising. In this chapter, I examine Lorde's writing on illness to flesh out my argument that an 'either/or' categorisation of metaphor misrecognises metaphor's varied usability. As becomes evident in *The Cancer Journals* and 'A Burst of Light: Living with Cancer', Lorde is well aware of the constraints of the warfare idea – and yet she continues to use it, consciously navigating the metaphor's constraints and activating its multiple affordances by challenging its connotations, stretching its meanings and combining it with other metaphors to produce new concepts and orientations. What these three strategies – challenging, stretching and combining – lead her to, I argue, is a more ethical form of comparison, one that foregrounds interdependence and connection without sacrificing *difference*. While Lorde's comparative innovations certainly served her anti-racist, anti-misogynist and anti-homophobic activism, I believe they also model an approach to metaphor in which comparison makes space for unexpected gains of illness. In other words, the comparative gesture inherent in metaphor becomes, in Lorde's hands, a resource for self-knowledge and repair, generating an attention to detail and beauty that sharpens Lorde's aesthetic sensibilities and produces unforeseen moments of elation and pleasure in the midst of despair.

LORDE AND THE WARFARE METAPHOR

Both *The Cancer Journals* and 'The Burst of Light' are permeated with notions of struggle, fight, weapons, battlefields and enemies. In them, Lorde repeatedly identifies as a warrior, more specifically as an Amazon warrior, and in doing so she folds a typically masculine discourse of heroic warfare and honourable wounds into an image of female strength and tenacity (*Cancer* 61). In Lorde's writing, as Tanja Reiffenrath argues, the Amazon warriors represent a transgressive act of reappropriation through which Lorde re-signifies the fraught language of illness and her personal struggle for social justice (99, 103). Following conventional understandings of the myth, the Amazon warriors are associated with female solidarity, strength and fearlessness. They are willing to go to extremes in order to excel at their skills (e.g. by cutting off their right breasts to become better archers, according to legend). Importantly, as Reiffenrath suggests, the image of Amazon warriors does not foreground a warrior model that is based on solitary heroism, but instead invokes a group of like-minded fighters whose strength is also rooted in solidarity (100). The image of Amazon warriors thus fits perfectly with a political activist like Lorde, who identified as a 'black woman warrior poet' (19) and continues to be celebrated as a feminist heroine, who advocated female solidarity across ethnic differences and a joint resistance to racist and sexist discrimination.

Amazon warriors are a topos in lesbian writing (Bolaki, *Unsettling* 222), and it is through this image that Lorde connects her identity as a black, lesbian, woman warrior poet with both ancient Greek and West African mythology (Reiffenrath 100).[2] Lorde resourcefully engages with problematic warfare imagery by drawing on mythical stories to recontextualise her contemporary personal struggle. Indeed, after a biopsy comes back positive for cancer, this engagement, and the Amazons Lorde summons through it, provide an answer to her painful question: 'Where are the models for what I'm supposed to be in this situation?' (28). Lorde's confident self-formation and self-creation via the warfare metaphor is thus, in many ways, an admirable and powerful achievement in the face of cancer.

This reading of metaphor as a tool of empowerment and reappropriation is a typical argument in the scholarship on Lorde. Researchers have applauded Lorde's strong voice and have found a playful and creative reclamation and 're-formation' of language as well as a powerful act of resistance in Lorde's use of the language of warfare (Wu 256; also see Alexander). As several critics note, Lorde's way of resisting the terror of cancer on a personal level is closely tied to her political resistance against the social structures that enable (environmental) racism, sexism and homophobia in medical care and society at large (e.g. Banner, Marks, Wu). In this sense, her multiple struggles are narratives of resistance which echo the various calls for emancipation in the 1970s and 1980s voiced by women, African Americans, gay people and patients. Therefore, the language of warfare is a unifying force that bridges multiple experiences of disruption and embeds Lorde's personal illness experience in larger, culturally recognised narratives (Marks 15ff.).

Yet focusing only on these powerful narratives of resistance does not entirely do justice to Lorde's nuanced writing. For one, Lorde vividly describes waves of feelings of self-doubt, despair and vulnerability. For another, she shifts the focus from admitting negative feelings to the matter of *difference*: when she asks, 'how did they [the Amazon warriors] handle it?' (27) and 'how long it was before the Dahomean girl Amazons could take their changed landscapes for granted?' (45), Lorde does not assert a straightforward similarity but also acknowledges the difference between herself – a middle-aged American woman – and the 'Dahomean girl Amazons' (45). In fact, all of Lorde's references to Amazon warriors are embedded in or followed by questions: 'What would happen if an army of one-breasted women descended upon Congress and demanded that the use of carcinogenic, fat-stored hormones in beef-feed be outlawed?' (14–15), she wonders. Or, 'How did the Amazons of Dahomey feel?' (34). In other words, the warfare metaphor does not only empower Lorde or fuel her defiance. It also, as she self-consciously describes, expresses her vulnerability, uncertainty and despair.

Robina Josephine Khalid takes this vulnerability as evidence for her argument that, ultimately, the warfare metaphor turns out to be a trap for Lorde rather than a tool of empowerment. Khalid claims that the warfare metaphor actually betrays Lorde and does her a disservice:

it perpetuates a binary thinking from which Lorde cannot escape, and therefore it 'reads more like a stumbling block than a source of strength' (699). Echoing Sontag's warnings against the hidden powers of metaphorical language, Khalid argues that the warfare metaphor naturalises violence and masculinist values and ultimately divides Lorde's experiences into binary categories of weakness and strength, failure and victory, a cancer body and warrior mind as well as relationships of dominance and subordination, which amplify Lorde's sense of alienation and dissociation (702–4). From this perspective, the war metaphor is un-useful at best, harmful at worst.

These contradictory assessments of Lorde's use of metaphors are typical of the binary ways in which metaphors tend to be described in the context of health care and medical practice (see Chapter 1). Such an either/or model has benefits, of course, but it is also insufficient. In Lorde's case, it suggest that the claim of empowerment de-emphasises Lorde's vulnerability and doubts, while Khalid's argument of disempowerment overlooks Lorde's agency and curiosity.

Khalid argues that because the warfare rhetoric fails to represent the heterogeneity and nuance of Lorde's subject position and experience (703), 'alternative vocabularies' such as the 'bodies as cities' (706) are needed. This suggestion is in itself problematic: rather than taking Lorde's work at face value, Khalid calls for a replacement of the metaphors that Lorde uses, implying that therein lies the solution. However, I wonder, is such a 'solution' not a form of imposing another way of thinking – one that Khalid obviously finds intriguing – onto Lorde's work and thus a way of misrecognising what Lorde actually does? Moreover, Khalid seems to underestimate Lorde's awareness of the problems of metaphorical language. In doing so, Khalid risks considering figurative language as static and straightforward. In Lorde's hands, however, language is dynamic: it can be bent and stretched to her needs. In fact, Lorde presents herself as highly conscious of the problems that metaphors entail, and she uses distinct strategies to negotiate the risks and opportunities of metaphor, as I illustrate below. It seems more plausible to me that, as Lorde was writing about her experiences with cancer, she was gradually discovering the multiple meanings of warfare, and in exploring the metaphor and what it could convey about her experiences, she learned how to negotiate its opportunities and limits.

Challenging the Concept of War

In section 2 of *The Cancer Journals*, entitled 'Breast Cancer: A Black Lesbian Feminist Experience', Lorde describes how she came to understand her changed body after a mastectomy. Expecting that her body would be a casualty of the war that Lorde and her doctors are waging against cancer, she is surprised by what she finds:

> I looked down at the surgical area as he changed the dressing, expecting it to look like the ravaged and pitted battlefield of some major catastrophic war. But all I saw was my same soft brown skin, a little tender-looking and puffy from the middle of my chest up into my armpit, where a thin line ran, the edges of which were held closed by black sutures and two metal clamps. The skin looked smooth and tender and untroubled, and there was no feeling on the surface of the area at all. It was otherwise quite unremarkable, except for the absence of that beloved swelling I had come to love over 44 years, and in its place was the strange flat plain down across which I could now for the first time in my memory view the unaccustomed bulge of my rib-cage, much broader than I had imagined it to be when it had been hidden beneath my large breasts. Looking down now on the right side of me I could see the curve of the side of my stomach across this new and changed landscape. (44–5)

What is striking about this passage is the sense of surprise and wonder it conveys. The paragraph begins with allusions to warfare, destruction and horror. But then, these expectations transition quickly into a vocabulary that is unrelated to war and even neutral or positively connoted ('unremarkable', 'unaccustomed', 'new', 'changed', 'smooth', 'tender', 'untroubled'). Lorde discovers unexpected qualities about her body and skin. Instead of scars or wounds, the area is 'quite unremarkable', and what Lorde emphasises particularly here is the sense of absence. However, this absence, as Stella Bolaki argues, is not really a hyperbolic narrativisation of loss and trauma (*Unsettling* 215), as one might expect from Lorde's writing that interweaves so poignantly the personal with the political. For Bolaki, 'Lorde seems here to both invoke and refuse the process of identifying absence (or structural trauma) with loss (or historical trauma)' (215). Thus, while there *is* an absence, it is not interpreted or inflated with meaning. Instead of using the typical pattern of illness narratives, in which Lorde's amputation would be 'redemptive' or invested 'with transcendental meaning' (Bolaki 216), Lorde remains literal: the absence of her breast is just that, an absence. This literalness also implies that Lorde is attentive to what *is* there, the manifest quality of her changed body, which Lorde acknowledges with the curiosity of an adventurer who has come ashore a strangely familiar yet foreign continent. After having disproven the battlefield comparison, Lorde compares her body to a landscape. In a sense, she has subtracted 'battle' from 'battlefield' and what remains is a field, plain and simple.

A critical reconsideration of the aptness of the warfare metaphor is a crucial strategy for Lorde to navigate the risks of metaphor and comparison more generally. Lorde explicitly turns away from the overdetermined warfare metaphor when she finds that it does not resonate with her experiences. This strategy demonstrates that Lorde is not tied to or constrained by the warfare metaphor, as Khalid argues. Instead, Lorde consciously dismisses and replaces a problematic metaphor when it fails to describe her reality. In doing so, she points out the gaps and incommensurabilities of the comparison.

Stretching the Concept of War

A second strategy that Lorde employs is that of stretching, which is her version of what Lakoff and Turner call *expanding and elaborating* (see Chapter 1). Stretching is a concept that Lorde repeatedly evokes in her illness writing. For example, in the introduction to *The Cancer Journals* and six months after her mastectomy, she writes on 30 May 1980: 'I feel like another woman, de-chrysalised and become a broader, stretched-out me, strong and excited, a muscle flexed and honed for action' (12). Similarly, in the epilogue of 'A Burst of Light', she maintains that living with cancer has taught her to distrust 'the myth of omnipotence' and to engage, instead, in an 'open-eyed assessment and appreciation of what I can and do accomplish, using who I am and who I most wish myself to be. To stretch as far as I can go and relish what is satisfying rather than what is sad' (133–4). In foregrounding elasticity, pliability and softness, Lorde uses the idea of stretching to bend the meanings of warfare, which typically emphasises hardness and rigidity, so that she finds room within it for herself. By stretching, she can insert her own experiences and identity, her 'history and particular passions' (70), into this language, which is, indeed, masculinist and binary. Alan Bleakley (2017) and Per Krogh Hansen, among others, have argued that in the Western model of standardised medicine cancer is considered a hostile enemy attacking the body.[3] In this line of thinking, medical treatment is a weapon, cure is a victory, and death is a defeat. Thus, when Lorde speaks of warfare and battle, she uses a language that is not of her own making and that, at times, jars with her beliefs and experiences. But by using this language nonetheless, she pays attention to differences and incommensurabilities and explores how this language can be redefined and used so that it expresses Lorde's particular experiences and passions.

This approach to language, Lorde's strategy of stretching language like a rubber band until it spans her own needs and experiences, is particularly significant when Lorde reflects on the meanings of victory and survival. In 'A Burst of Light', when she does not yet know that the cancer has returned, she says:

> I am determined to fight it [the possibility of liver cancer] even when I am not sure of the terms of the battle nor the fact of victory. I just know I must not surrender my body to others unless I completely understand and agree with what they think should be done to it. I've got to look at all of my options carefully, even the ones I find distasteful. I know I can broaden the definition of winning to the point where I can't lose. (61)

A day later, on 10 June 1984, Lorde continues to 'stretch' the meanings of winning:

> We all have to die at least once. Making that death useful would be winning for me. I wasn't supposed to exist anyway, not in any meaningful way in this fucked-up whiteboys' world. I want desperately to live, and I'm ready to fight for that living even if I die shortly. Just writing those words down snaps every thing I want to do into a neon clarity ... For the first time I really feel that my writing has a substance and stature that will survive[4] me. (61)

In redefining the meanings of winning, Lorde imagines a victory in the battle against cancer even if, following the conventional meaning of the metaphor, she 'loses' that battle by dying.

Stretching allows Lorde to continue to argue from within the warfare discourse while she simultaneously undermines its origins and history. Lorde expands and broadens the roles of the actors and the setting of the battle. In fact, Lorde turns the tables on who and what is actually attacking and trespassing the body: it is not the disease but the doctor whose 'intrusive action' consists in cutting her open and, possibly, activating 'a questionable mass into an active malignancy' ('Burst' 114). What is potentially rendering her sick are the actions of the doctor. Therefore, the war Lorde has to fight is not only against the disease but also against her doctor. The default meaning of the warfare metaphor is thus turned on its head. The front line has shifted, and Lorde destabilises any certainties about who is her friend and who is her enemy.

Importantly, this turn towards holistic treatment and her resistance to standard medicine do not inspire a change of language: when Lorde chooses homeopathy and anthroposophy as 'soft' alternative treatment options, she does not blindly reject standardised medicine, but she scrutinises it for its probability of success. Lorde does not feel heard and understood by the medical establishment, which she experiences as racist, sexist and heteronormative. As a result, she turns to other forms of treatment and sources of inspiration, and these alternative options allow her to resist the hegemonic treatment of the 'american medical establishment' (*Cancer* 73). Interestingly, she continues to use the language of battle. This is possible because she has begun to stretch and redefine its meanings. This stretching involves a reimagination of roles and attitudes: instead of drawing on aggression, destruction and hardness, Lorde's warriors foreground stoicism, perseverance, self-care and self-knowledge. For example, on 20 April 1986, Lorde writes:

> As warriors, our job is to actively and consciously survive it for as long as possible, remembering that in order to win, the aggressor must conquer, but the resisters need only survive. Our battle is to define survival in ways that are acceptable and nourishing to us, meaning with substance and style. Substance. Our work. Style. True to our selves. ('Burst' 98–9)

Survival, for Lorde, comes to signify quality rather than quantity, authenticity rather than denial. I will come back to this idea at the end of this chapter.

Combining War and Music

Besides stretching and expanding the warfare metaphor from within, Lorde's third strategy of engagement is to *combine* it with other metaphors, such as that of music. Combining one metaphor with others is an important strategy for several reasons. First, it recognises that the war metaphor, though pertinent in medical discourse and in Lorde's thinking, is not the only way of thinking about illness. In exploring other concepts, Lorde draws attention to the social and cultural contingency of the warfare metaphor, which is, even though it has come to seem natural, a construct. Second, combination yields new perspectives and insights on the meaning of war and illness. In using other comparisons for experiences of illness and combining them with the notion of war, she can identify which dimensions of 'battle' are imperfect or lacking and need replacement or further stretching.

For example, Lorde repeatedly mentions a concert of different voices and her attempts of orchestrating the diverse ideas she has. When she has to make a decision about her treatment, she hears a 'concert of voices from inside myself, all with something slightly different to say, all of which were quite insistent and none of which would let me rest' (*Cancer* 30). Lorde embraces these different voices as part of herself. They are not (or not primarily) a sign of chaos or a sign of a confused, unreasonable mind. Instead, the image of the concert locates Lorde in her experience of contemplating divergent views and options. The concert evokes an accrual of energy and volume from being joined by other 'instruments'. Similarly, a few pages later, she declares:

> And I orchestrate my daily anticancer campaign with an intensity intrinsic to who I am, the intensity of making a poem. It is the same intensity with which I experience poetry, a student's first breakthrough, the loving energy of women I do not even know ... I make, demand, translate satisfactions out of every ray of sunlight, scrap of bright cloth, beautiful sound,

delicious smell that comes my way, out of every sincere smile and good wish. They are discreet bits of ammunition in my arsenal against despair. ('Burst' 123)

While the concert signifies a polyphony of voices and a solidarity among women, it is also relevant as a metaphor for dealing with illness. In combination with the warfare metaphor, which surfaces in the form of ammunition and arsenal, the notion of orchestration adds a different connotation: Lorde's battles and the ammunition she uses are carefully orchestrated in the symphony of her life. In likening this process to the creation of music and poetry, Lorde's battle is not only informed by destruction and resistance but also by acts of creativity, the emergence of something new that is affirming and aesthetically appealing.

Combination – in this case the extension of the warfare notion with music metaphors – is a significant strategy in Lorde's engagement with metaphors. First, it decentres the pertinence of the warfare metaphor and, by way of contact and juxtaposition with other concepts, it allows her to tease out complementary ways of thinking about illness as war. Second, when necessary, combination functions as a supplement to stretching. When stretching comes to its limits, or turns into overextension, that is, it can have devastating effects, as Lorde suggests in the epilogue of 'A Burst of Light' (131): 'Overextending myself is not stretching myself', she proclaims, and comes to realise that she 'had to accept how difficult it is to monitor the difference' (131). Stretching, she argues, is a form of self-care and self-preservation (131); to care for herself, as she concludes, is 'an act of political warfare' (131). Overextension means to ignore the boundaries of her body and psyche. From this perspective, combination diverts the risk of overextension and allows her to zoom out of the tunnel vision of a single conceptual domain, such as warfare, mitigating some of the risks that comparison inevitably entails.

The Affordances of Engaging with the Warfare Metaphor

Before we discuss the risks of comparison, however, let us turn to its affordances. In Lorde's use of the warfare metaphor, she continuously broadens her experience to connect it to a larger cause. She argues, for example, that constant battle is her lived reality as 'a black woman warrior poet' (*Cancer* 19) because the horror of her cancer is aligned with 'the barbarity' of other forces on a more global scale, including social norms, environmental crimes, and the 'tyrannies of silence' and suppression (15, 19). Lorde decides to take 'joy in that battle' (15), claiming that she is 'not only a casualty' but also 'a warrior' (19). To this end, Lorde refuses to fight against her own body and turns the fight outward, away from her individual body, towards an unjust system of patriarchy, racism and a medical establishment complicit with those evils. For example, Lorde recounts how her doctors tried to blackmail her into a biopsy and an array of standard medical treatments, suggesting that if she does not follow his advice, she will suffer ('Burst' 112–14). 'I felt the battle lines being drawn up within my own body,' Lorde confesses (112), suggesting also that her doctor's racist and sexist remarks contribute to her feeling like 'a total failure' (114). Lorde decides to draw her own lines of the battlefield: as I discussed above, Lorde considers the possibility that the doctor's 'intrusive action' of cutting her open might be the event that turns 'a questionable mass into an active malignancy' (114), thus suggesting that the aggressor is no longer the cancer but the doctor's knife, as well as the racist and sexist system he represents.

In relating her personal illness to the struggles against other evils in the world, Lorde stretches her experiences beyond the individual and idiosyncratic. She creates a larger-than-life vision of herself in which she becomes a 'super-woman' (Wu 250).[5] With *Zami: A New Spelling of My Name* (1982), Lorde even creates a new genre for this kind of work, the biomythography,[6] which provides her with 'a larger space for her myriad selves', a space for her collaged self-construction (Alexander 696). As a biography of 'the mythic self', Lorde's biomythography conjures up a self that is multiple as well as connected and shaped by a community of other women (Smith and Watson 263). As Sidonie Smith and Julia Watson argue, Lorde draws on 'cultural myths, dreams, fantasies, and subjective memories' (12) and thus expands the 'ingredients' of life writing and self-formation. As a consequence, Lorde constructs a mythological vision of her struggles: her individual experiences with cancer transcend the personal, idiosyncratic and socially contingent situatedness. As a result, she fashions herself as 'a scar, a report from the frontlines, a talisman, a resurrection. A rough place on the chin of complacency' ('Burst' 59).

Such mythologising is typical of illness narratives, says Anne Hunsaker Hawkins in her work on pathography. As a reconstructive endeavour, mythologising helps writers extrapolate from their individual experiences and offers more general lessons and advice. Importantly, as Hawkins maintains, such strategies often align the singular experience with the dualistic worldview of ancient myths, in which the world is organised around an agonistic distinction between 'light and darkness, life and death, good and evil' (62). Following

Bolaki, self-mythologisation also feeds into narratives of American exceptionalism (*Unsettling* 222). Indeed, Lorde emphasises how it is her destiny to transform and improve her dire situation through exceptional willpower and actions, and the warfare imagery she employs lends a heroic vibe to her extraordinary battle. However, as Bolaki argues, drawing on Deborah Madsen's work, narratives of exceptionalism are not necessarily oppositional to other narratives, such as narratives of resistance: in fact, the grand narrative of exceptionalism 'can be adopted as "a counter-discourse" and a strategy for "writing back" by ethnic writers' (222). In such a frame of resistance, the exceptionalism that Lorde ascribes to her asymmetrical body and her situation as a 'black woman warrior poet' (19) is noteworthy to Bolaki, as it 'seems both to evoke this mythology and turn it against itself' (222). The ambivalent nature of Lorde's mythologisation also affects her engagement with the warfare metaphor. I agree with both Bolaki and Jeanne Perreault that, paradoxically, Lorde celebrates this additional meaning of her illness while laying out her deepest fears. Therefore, to Perreault, Lorde's writing represents a contradiction: she 'lives close to the vulnerable and uncertain flesh, and yet enjoys rhetorical authority, sureness and even righteousness' (30).

Thus, while Lorde is challenging normative discourses and prescriptive assumptions, she is also, one might object, imposing norms herself. One could also criticise Lorde for overstretching the significance of her singular experiences in her attempt to connect the personal to the political, an individual experience to those that are larger-than-life, universal. What is at stake when comparison – a defining characteristic of metaphor – is used for political purposes?

THE RISKS OF METAPHOR AND COMPARISON

Like Audre Lorde, Eve Ensler, the acclaimed author of *The Vagina Monologues* (1996), uses metaphors to connect her individual experiences of uterine cancer with her political activism. In her illness narrative *In the Body of the World* (2013), Ensler merges her own story with that of women in the Democratic Republic of Congo, Sarajevo, Pristina and Port-au-Prince, among others, and thus with women who have experienced misogynist violence. In doing so, Lorde's and Ensler's articulations sound surprisingly similar. For example, in 'The Burst of Light', Lorde claims that her battle to save her own life is 'inseparable' from the fight against South African apartheid by the African National Congress (59). Likewise, Ensler finds that her 'Cancer, a disease of pathologically dividing cells, burned away the walls of my separateness and landed me in my body, just as the Congo landed me in the body of the world' (7–8). There are more similarities in the vocabulary Lorde and Ensler employ. Lorde notices that her poems become infused by the images she sees in the news: 'My poems are filled with blood these days because the future is so bloody. The blood of four-year-old children in Soweto ...' (59). Similarly, Ensler suggests that the stories she hears from violated and raped women of the Democratic Republic of Congo start to saturate her cells and nerves (4), maintaining that 'All the stories began to bleed together' (4). And when Lorde considers racism, patriarchy and homophobia carcinogenic, Ensler echoes a similar understanding when she describes her illness as 'the cancer that is everywhere' (7):

> The cancer of cruelty, the cancer of greed, the cancer that gets inside people who live downstream from chemical plants, the cancer inside the lungs of coal miners. The cancer from the stress of not achieving enough, the cancer of buried trauma. The cancer that lives in caged chickens and oil-drenched fish. The cancer of carelessness. The cancer in fast-paced must-make-it-have-it-own-it-formaldehydeasbestospesticideshair-dyecigaretess-cellphonesnow. (7)

To Christine Marks, Ensler's use of metaphor is highly problematic: 'While Ensler's metaphorical poetry of connection demands that readers become aware of being agents in interlocking global systems, her push toward this global awareness ... posits a universality of suffering and pain that erases considerations of positionality and cultural difference' ('Metaphor, Myth' 15). For example, Ensler, as Marks analyses, likens the effect of her uterine cancer with the effect of rape for the women in Congo, suggesting that their suffering is commensurable and that the pain Ensler feels in her body is an expression of the pain the Congolese women feel (18). As Marks contends, metaphor is particularly useful for Ensler's endeavour because metaphor functions as a 'counter agent to the fragmenting forces of illness, trauma, and violence' (14) as it bridges the gap between two distinct phenomena and foregrounds commonality (20). However, in using metaphor to create connection between her own suffering and that of women across the world, as Marks convincingly argues, Ensler homogenises and colonises the diversity and contextual specificity of women's experiences of suppression. As a white, privileged US-American woman, Ensler thus silences other voices, glosses over differences and 'posits a universality of suffering and pain' (15). Not only is this act of appropriation 'a self-aggrandizing gesture' (Judith Butler qtd in Marks 21), it also (mis)uses metaphor as 'a centripetal force organizing the events of the world into a unified whole centered on Ensler's embodied self' (18). Therefore, metaphor acts as an agent of transformation through which a narrative of incongruous events and experiences is jelled into 'a single triumph narrative' (Marks 19).

Ensler has been criticised for her colonialist and essentialising gestures before her illness narrative *In the Body of the World*. In the acclaimed and controversial *Vagina Monologues*, for example, Ensler problematically links a woman's vagina with her identity, which entails that the trope of the vagina becomes naturalised and 'loses its figurative status, cultivating a literal equivalence in the play' (Cooper 732). In expanding this metaphor to woman around the world, Ensler commits an 'epistemological violence', Cooper finds, because it erases all difference and 'flattens out, if not denies, diversity of experience within populations of women and across them, too' (738). Difference, however, is 'a critical imperative' (749), and in ignoring or belittling the epistemological importance of difference for the feminist cause, Ensler's feminism remains locked in second-wave agendas of 'consciousness-raising practices' (728).

Ensler's case illustrates an important point when it comes to the ethics of engaging with metaphors. Even though a writer's intentions with a particular metaphor may be worthy, the effects of her metaphor use can still be questioned and even found unethical. In other words, metaphors can also be abused – even after they have been reclaimed from abusive contexts. In Ensler's case, the flickering ambivalence of de/familiarisation that defines metaphor is replaced by a straightforward familiarising gesture. What bears resemblances (and differences) is presented as same and identical. Such a use of the connecting potential of metaphor thus erases (other voices, differences, gaps, translational problems) rather than builds (bridges, connections, resonances). The sense of triumph and personal healing is constructed at the expense of others and, partly at least, forged out of the pain of others. In 'Why Not Compare?', Susan Stanford Friedman (2011) lists the problems that comparing can entail:

> comparison decontextualizes: that is, it dehistoricizes and deterritorializes; it removes what are being compared from their local and geohistorical specificity. Consequently, one reason *not* to compare is the potential violence such removals can accomplish, the damage they can do to the requirements of a richly textured understanding of any phenomenon in its particularity. (754–5)

Drawing on Gayatri Chakravorty Spivak, Friedman argues that comparison is deeply interwoven with value-judgements and power structures because it 'presumes a normative standard of measure by which the other is known and often judged ... The known then operates as measure of the unknown, standing in unequal relation to it' (753–4). From this perspective, comparison appears as an instrument of domination. Tied to the history of colonialism and inextricably impacted by 'the imperial traces it carries within it' (Mignolo 100), the practice of comparison is built on and continues the problematic power of 'isms', such as Eurocentric, sexist and racist paradigms (also see Felski, 'Comparison' 754). In comparing two disparate things, metaphor risks erasing difference, 'imposing false equivalences and oppressive forms of homogenization' (Felski, 'Comparison' 747–8). In doing so, comparison flattens and reduces what is actually complex and ambiguous. It lumps together diverse, individual and contingent experiences and risks perpetuating hierarchies and systematic violence.

Such unethical effects are implied but not problematised in Laurence Kirmayer's suggestion to creatively misuse a metaphor (see Chapter 1). The possibilities of misuse and abuse require further exploration in the context of illness metaphor. While misuse is an improper use or mistake, abuse is a systematic, intentionally wrong use that involves damage. In a short essay published in a special issue of *Critical Inquiry* in 1978, Ted Cohen usefully, but only briefly, hints at ethical concerns when he describes metaphors as a means to cultivate intimacy, which, similar to jokes, can create connection but can also ostracise and be cruel and hostile (10–12). Cohen concludes with the defensive and provisional statement that 'there can be no effective procedures for dealing with metaphors' (11). While I agree with Cohen that we should not look for definite rules for metaphor, I propose that a joint reading of Ensler's and Lorde's metaphor use is informative and helps describe in a more nuanced way how metaphor and its homogenising effects might be mitigated. Lorde's academic work is particularly relevant here because, in it, she demonstrates a great sensitivity to the misuses of comparison. In a keynote address at the Women's Writing Conference in Melbourne in August 1985, Lorde spoke about 'the language of difference' in response to the commemoration and recognition of the genocide of the Black Aboriginal women of Australia:

> When language becomes most similar, it becomes most dangerous, for then differences may pass unremarked. As women of good faith we can only become familiar with the language of difference within a determined commitment to its use within our lives, without romanticism and without guilt. Because we share a common language which is not of our own making and which does not reflect our deeper knowledge as women, our words frequently sound the same. But it is an error to believe that we mean the same experience, the same commitment, the same future, unless we agree to examine the history and particular passions that lie beneath each other's words. ('Burst' 70)

In drawing attention to difference and in calling for a language of difference, Lorde leads the way to a more capacious understanding of the affordances of comparison and metaphor.

A NEW LANGUAGE OF DIFFERENCE?

Throughout her academic work, Lorde is acutely aware of the dangers of erasing difference and assuming sameness. In her famous essay 'The Master's Tools Will Never Dismantle the Master's House' from 1984 (*Sister Outsider* 111), Lorde criticised the organisers of the Second Sex Conference in New York in 1979 for their arrogance in excluding the voices of 'poor women, Black and Third World women, and lesbians' and in assuming that they speak for all women (110). She invokes a metaphor of slavery and compares dominant paradigms (racism, patriarchy) with the master's house and dominant meanings of words (such as *difference is to be feared* and *difference implies separation*) with tools. Lorde's central argument revolves around difference: feminists need to redefine the meanings of difference if they want to effect change. Similar to her strategy of stretching the meanings of warfare and survival, Lorde argues that feminists need to detach difference from the implication of insurmountable separation or unavoidable friction and understand it instead as a source of empowerment, creativity and solidarity. If feminists manage to use a patriarchally defined language in new ways, Lorde argues, they will be able to dismantle patriarchy and racism and overcome binary paradigms. 'Difference', Lorde claims, 'is that raw and powerful connection from which our personal power is forged' (112).

In foregrounding the importance of difference in opposition to sameness, Lorde seems to echo Paul Ricœur's notion of tension which he sees in metaphor where '"same" and "different" are not just mixed together, they also remain opposed' (*Rule of Metaphor* 232). This 'clash' and open conflict does not fuse one thing into the other but keeps both sameness and difference in tension (232, 234). Similarly, to Lorde, difference bears many opportunities when it is 'seen as a fund of necessary polarities between which our creativity can spark like a dialectic' (*Sister Outsider* 111). It enables the nurturing, creative and redemptive powers of interdependency between women, as diverse and singular as they may be (111).

To further illustrate Lorde's nuanced approach to difference, I return to a comparison of Lorde's and Ensler's use of metaphors. The concepts of weaving and spinning are used by both Lorde and Ensler. Lorde uses the metaphor of a tapestry when she reflects on the 'lessons of the past

18 months' in *The Cancer Journals*. She gives a list of questions and asks herself among others: 'How do I give voice to my quests so that other women can take what they need from my experiences? How do my experiences with cancer fit into the larger tapestry of my work as a Black woman, into the history of all women?' (15). By asking questions rather than making statements, Lorde is concerned with conceptualising how her experiences relate to those of others. Rather than imposing the tapestry of her experiences and work onto others, she wonders how her experiences fit within a larger scheme. Importantly, the image of a tapestry suggests that the singular threads of the design will remain intact and distinct even if they are interwoven.

Ensler also uses a metaphor that draws on the notion of handcraft, spinning and weaving. But in Ensler's vision, those singular threads seem to blend into one another and dissolve into something else, 'a flesh monument', that is

> spun out of the stories of women, made of tears, silent screams, rocking torsos, and the particular loneliness of violence. A flesh creature birthed out of the secrets of brutality, each blood vessel a ribbon of story. My body has been sculpting this tumor for years, molding the pieces of pain, the clay residue of memories. It is a huge work and it has taken everything. (27)

The central agent and significant location of this hideous object is Ensler's body, which 'uses' other women's experiences to produce 'a huge work', a homogenous monument. Ensler's writing is declaratory and aggregates diversity into one entity, namely Ensler's body (Cooper 753; Marks), in which all stories 'bleed together' (Ensler 4). By contrast, Lorde's writing is meant to be shared 'for use' by other women. It remains open and invitational and is conveyed in a set of questions. Of course, there are many places where Lorde's voice is declaratory and powerful, too. Yet, unlike Ensler, Lorde does not homogenise nor does she consider herself the ultimate centre of experiential authority. She keeps foregrounding her multiple roles and fragmented selves, and therefore, the connection and solidarity Lorde seeks and experiences is infused by a dialogic nature, by interdependence and relationality. Lorde's use of metaphors thus attends equally to what is similar and what is different.

How to Compare Well

In *Comparison: Theories, Approaches, Uses* (2013), Rita Felski and Susan Stanford Friedman suggest 'a renewed focus on comparison' (2), asserting that 'acts of comparing are … crucial for registering inequalities ... [and for] the analysis of world systems, transcontinental connections, and interculturalism' (2). Drawing on actor–network theory, Felski maintains that practices of comparison and translation are basically modes of relation: comparison is not 'a one-sided or intrinsic nefarious technology of power. Rather, it is a form of relational thinking that can be deployed to many different ends' ('Comparison' 754). Through comparison, ties are created and co-created, and for this reason, comparison harbours many possibilities. It can

> deliver a sobering jolt to consciousness and a brake on narcissism, initiating a humbling sense of the limits of one's own perspective. Without implicit comparison, it is hard to see how one could ever escape, for even a moment, the confines of one's own experience and become aware of alternate ways of conceiving or inhabiting the world. ('Comparison' 754–5)

Walter D. Mignolo, too, emphasises the many positive effects of and legitimate reasons for comparison. To Mignolo, power and political agendas are not the only motivations for comparison. People compare to effect change, correct views, to find out what to buy or endorse and to improve understanding (100). In fact, 'All living organisms, plants, and animals need to compare what among all the options of the environment is convenient to their survival – comparing is then knowing, and knowing is living' (Mignolo 99). In this light, comparison is a heuristic strategy that creates insights and knowledge.

Such a gain in knowledge through comparative practices is also noticed by Lorde who describes in *The Cancer Journals* and in 'A Burst of Light' how comparing her fight with cancer and oppression provides her with a new access to her experience and allows for different forms of knowledge that are grounded in relational thinking. For example, Lorde finds that on the recurrence of cancer, her relationship to it has changed. Juxtaposing her different battles, she observes in November 1986:

> Racism. Cancer. In both cases, to win the aggressor must conquer, but the resisters need only survive. How do I define that survival and on whose terms?
>
> So I feel a sense of triumph as I pick up my pen and say yes I am going to write again from the world of cancer and with a different perspective – that of living with cancer in an intimate daily relationship. ('Burst' 111)

Lorde continues to explore the notion of an intimate relationship with cancer two days later. She considers her vigilance to not miss any treatment a positive experience because it 'keeps me in an intimate, positive relationship to my own health' (116). Another two days later, she describes how this relationship is defined by urgency and how it fosters new insights. She maintains that her awareness of the recurrence of cancer 'exists side by side with another force inside me that says no you don't, not you, and the x-rays are wrong and the tests are wrong and the doctors are wrong' (117). Each feeling, she says, has a different kind of energy – intensity, purpose, urgency, feisty determination to continue – and these 'tensions created inside me by the contradictions' are a 'source of energy and learning' for her: 'I have always known I learn most lasting lessons about difference by closely attending the ways in which the differences inside me lie down together' (117–18). In paying careful attention to what difference yields, Lorde gains new knowledge about herself.

Friedman expands the usefulness of comparison from self-knowledge and political activism to theory building. Following Friedman, it is 'the possibility of conceptual thought that comparison fosters [which] moves knowledge beyond pure particularity and thereby enables theory' ('Why' 756). Any systematic thinking naturally requires comparison. 'If the danger of comparing is the potential erasure of the particular and nonnormative, the danger of not comparing involves the suppression of the general and the theoretical' (756). Friedman suggests a methodology of juxtaposition which

> sets things being compared side by side, not overlapping them as in a Venn diagram, not setting up one as the standard of measure for the other, not using one as an instrument to serve the other. Juxtaposition can potentially avoid the categorical violence of comparison within the framework of dominance. The distinctiveness of each is maintained, while the dialogue of voices that ensues brings commonalities into focus. (758)

Juxtaposition thus attends to both similarity and difference and fits perfectly with Lorde's writing and her use of metaphors. 'Racism. Cancer.' appear side by side, as do her conflicting feelings about them: 'Battling racism and battling heterosexism and battling apartheid share the same urgency inside me as battling cancer', Lorde maintains in 1986 ('Burst' 116). Moreover, she describes her approach as 'juggling' and 'balancing' (125), and it seems that there is no hierarchy: all causes and concerns are on an equal plane.

Juxtaposition resonates in a similar way on the narrative level. As scholars have emphasised, Lorde's writing is characterised by a polyvocal collage and non-linear narrative, which mirrors her fragmented and non-linear self-construction (Alexander 696–7). Even though she, like Ensler, strives for the reintegration of fragmented selves and embodied wholeness (Marks 16–18), Lorde's notion of identity continues to be grounded in fluidity and difference (Alexander 710, 713). Lorde's self-description as 'a black woman warrior poet' (*Cancer Journals* 19) and as a 'Fat Black Female' (40) erases all punctuation and stresses the fluidity and erasure of boundaries between these dimensions of her multiple selves (Alexander 710). In claiming these different parts of herself but refusing to be divisible, Alexander argues, Lorde manages to speak 'through difference' (713) and 'configures the self as simultaneously fragmented and reassembled' (699), 'simultaneously multiple and integrated' (696). Perreault also comments on the particular form Lorde chooses – the journal fragments along with other genres such as speeches, manifesto-like essays, retrospective accounts, epilogue, and 'informal conversational passages' (29) – and considers it a hallmark of Lorde's writing through which she reconstructs, textually, her sense of self and gives an account of her transformation (18).

Lorde's language, too, takes various forms: passages with 'the flavor of kitchen-table intimacies', sections that are 'formal, ritualized, carrying the echo of the preacher' as well as 'plain expository prose, informative with few flourishes of lyricism or exhortation' (Perreault 29). This collage of different genres and styles produces a text that 'spirals' (29):

> Lorde writes layer after layer of the experience, no single issue allowed to dominate the others: death, cancer, surgery, and the attendant fear and pain; repetitions of hope, feminist support, and understanding; the cycles of relationship of selves in her body and in the world and as a representative of other women and their experience; and consistently, her refusal to 'waste' the experience, that is, her self, in privacy, in silence. (29)

From such a polyphonic, dialogic stance, the practice of comparing as juxtaposition yields ever new insights and new ways of knowing. The last pages of 'A Burst of Light', as I explore below, are particularly remarkable in that sense. First, they foreground Lorde's attempt to describe what she has *found* rather than *lost* in living with illness. In doing so, Lorde exemplifies what Havi Carel describes in *Phenomenology of Illness* (2018) as 'well-being in illness'. Second, they showcase how Lorde's writing on illness is shot through with aesthetic pleasure – a pleasure that complicates any reading of her work as either primarily personal or primarily political.

Well-being and Aesthetic Pleasure in Illness

We tend to think of illness as a catastrophe, as a devastating experience and, most importantly, as loss (Carel, *Phenomenology* 36). That illness can be existentially but also epistemically transformative (Carel et al. 1152) and that it can prompt many gains is often viewed with suspicion. Such scepticism is certainly in order when claims about the gains of illness mandate – from a third-person perspective and a priori – how an individual patient *should* understand and experience illness, namely as valuable, redemptive and influenced by the right habit of mind. While positive experiences of illness *can* be and often *are* true,[7] the problem with positive thinking or 'bright-siding' is that it is normative and prescriptive (see Ehrenreich 2001, 2010). To Carel, such bright-siding misrecognises the diversity, fluidity and richness of illness. Instead, and similar to culturally acknowledged narratives, such strategies can quash or minimise the singularity of a perception. As a consequence, narratives of redemption, which are often associated with illness and are deeply ingrained in American cultural history, can become expected frames for interpreting subjective experiences as 'atonement, emancipation, recovery, self-fulfilment, and upward social mobility' (McAdams and Cox 197). For Carel, however, the focus should lie on subjective experiences in all their diversity, and not on assumed objective truth claims or 'the reality of things' (*Phenomenology* 20). When Carel considers well-being in illness, she draws on studies about adaptation and resilience which have shown that suffering *can* be 'morally or spiritually rewarding and edifying' (140). Linking these studies to her own experiences, she recalls that her illness led to a 'flourishing in unexpected ways' (143): surprising discoveries, new insights and self-knowledge. Carel suggests that 'adversity reveals hidden abilities; it "makes good relationships better"; and it changes priorities in a way that provides focus and peace of mind' (140). She also lists 'central positive themes' that are associated with illness, such as 'being courageous, regaining control over an altered life course, reshaping the self, self-transcendence, empowerment, and discovery' (145). Given that illness can be such a changeable, unpredictable experience, it is, for Carel, 'an invitation to philosophize' (142).

Lorde's writing, too, emphasises the positive aspects and unexpected insights of her illness. Particularly the endings of both *The Cancer Journals* and 'A Burst of Light' are saturated with a sense of gratitude and serenity. In *The Cancer Journals*, she lists the gains of her experience, and she keeps emphasising on these last pages that both her sorrow and her joy are part of her. In the last sentence, she claims: 'I would never have chosen this path, but I am very glad to be who I am, here' (79). Lorde stresses that she has not become someone new nor that she is unchanged. Rather, she points to 'here', this moment, the concentrated point of the present, that is both within time (the end of a journey) and outside of time (a status she has always held). Similarly, in 'The Burst of Light', there is a conspicuous serenity in many of her entries, and this brightness becomes increasingly dominant in the last entries. This is not to deny or ignore the many entries that are suffused by despair, anger and powerlessness. However, it is impossible to overlook that Lorde also describes some of the positive dimensions of her experiences. For example, she recalls the many lessons she has learned, and she repeatedly ties her experiences to a newly awakened sensuous perception, such as the feeling of the bedsheet against her heels, the sounds of animals, the waves of the ocean in Anguilla, and the quality of the light. Her poetic sensibility and her attention to detail and beauty have been sharpened by illness. Moreover, Lorde's writing illustrates that the aesthetic and the political are not mutually exclusive, but rather that they exist side by side and inform one another. I want to use these final paragraphs to explore some of the aesthetic dimensions, the moments of elation and aesthetic pleasure, that are crucial to her work on illness.

From a phenomenological perspective, illness and aesthetic pleasure are not diametrically opposed. Carel defines illness as

> a 'deep phenomenon', an encounter with [sic] which reveals the lack of autonomy of rational subjectivity, and as such exposes the limits of this subjectivity. Another example of a deep phenomenon is art; Merleau-Ponty writes about Cézanne's paintings as showing us a world in which subjectivity recognizes its limited capacity to organize and structure experience (Merleau-Ponty 1964a). This experience of vulnerability, but also illumination, is fundamental to the experience of illness.[8] (15)

The comparison that Carel makes here between the perception of illness and the perception of art is intriguing: both are described as encounters that reveal something *to* the individual. Like art, illness is inherently varied, rich and unpredictable. It is therefore impossible to say a priori what such an encounter will yield and which quality the encounter will have.

Ted Cohen links the multi-sense apprehension of art to metaphors. In fact, he considers metaphors 'peculiarly crystallized works of art' ('Cultivation' 7) which can create opportunities for intimacy. While this notion of intimacy is not unproblematic, as I discuss above, there is something intriguing in what Cohen proposes: in emphasising that metaphors generate intimacy and draw the maker and appreciator of a metaphor 'closer to one another' in their effort to understand a comparison (8), Cohen suggests implicitly that such an intimacy can also accrue between the maker of a comparison and the object or condition she tries to describe. Appreciating a metaphor then does not only imply that we *understand* something better or differently, we also develop different *affective* relationships because we feel about and care for the thing we express via metaphor ('Metaphor' 375). Therefore, metaphor 'offers a novel way of seeing something, and that novel sight brings a feeling with it' (375). Such affective dimensions of the use of metaphor may offer an additional explanation for the strange fact that Lorde continues to use the battle metaphor – even within the most serene and peaceful journal entries. Following Cohen's concepts of metaphor appreciation and intimacy, I want to suggest that Lorde cares for the ideas behind battle and that she feels a deep connection to what has practically become her way of being, a lifestyle that is inseparable, as she maintains repeatedly, from the multiple selves that constitute her identity. Fighting connects the different dimensions of her self, and as she evolves and is transformed by illness, so does the way she carries out her fight.

This battle is not only fuelled by negative emotions, it is also sustained by aesthetic enjoyment. For example, on 17 November 1985, Lorde maintains that her everyday living has added a 'terrible and invigorating savor of now – a visceral awareness of the passage of time, with its nightmare and its energy' ('Burst' 124). This visceral, sensory relation with her illness adds an organic fluidity to what it means for her to fight. In the same entry, she maintains: 'If living as a poet – living on the front lines – has ever had meaning, it has meaning now. Living a self-conscious life, vulnerability as armor' (125). In this peculiar reversal of the metaphor, it is not the armour that protects the vulnerable poet-warrior; rather, the poet's vulnerability becomes a form of protection. In addition, vulnerability assumes a new meaning: it does not (only) imply weakness and defencelessness but also encompasses the opposite – strength and power. Following Carel, vulnerability is indeed not only a negative experience:

> Vulnerability also suggests a relationship of openness to the world. Without investing in and caring about transient and vulnerable things, like people, the environment and works of art, we would not be able to flourish. In order to flourish we must let ourselves be vulnerable. ('Reply' 218)

The conventional and overused metaphor of fighting against illness, of shielding one's vulnerable human condition against malicious attacks, assumes new connotations. In order to live fully, vulnerability cannot be hidden behind a shield but must be exposed and actively used. Under these altered circumstances and with a newly defined set of armament, the battle can be generative and replenishing. For Lorde, the 'black woman warrior poet' (*Cancer* 19), fighting is therefore inseparable from who she is. By connecting the fight against cancer with her long experience of fighting on other fronts as well as her skills as a poet and artist, she derives strength and meaning from this integrative strategy and she can claim: 'It takes all of my selves working together to fight this death inside me. Every one of these battles generates energies useful in the others' ('Burst' 99). The war metaphor continues to provide Lorde with a useful and productive language, but rather than following the antagonistic and oppositional constellations inherent in battle and war, Lorde stretches the meanings of these concepts: she sets different activities side by side and highlights the connections and ties that characterise her life and her identity. Lorde's 'battle' against illness thus does not only wish to destroy, disrupt and resist. It is also generative of a new kind of knowledge; it is a source of power and repair and grounded in attentive perception, desire and love.

Besides the continued use of the battle metaphor, a new metaphor emerges in the last pages of 'A Burst of Light': spatial concepts increasingly replace the temporal organisation of 'before' and 'after', cause and effect, of assuming that after one fight is won, 'real life is waiting for me to begin living again' (132). Lorde begins to stress intensity, fullness and breadth rather than duration and longevity, arguing that it is her duty to live 'fully' and with 'maximum access' to her experience and power (130). She is fuelled by the resolve to 'print [herself] upon the texture of each day fully rather than forever' (127). She also expresses the wish 'to live whatever life I have as fully and as sweetly as possible, rather than refocus that life solely upon extending it for some unspecified time' (130). Elsewhere she repeats: 'Living fully – how long is not the point. How and why take total precedence' (126). Thus, instead of hoping to extend time, Lorde finds intensity and pleasure in attending to the moment. It 'gives a marvelous breadth to everything I do consciously' (132), she says. Moreover, Lorde notices that

> another kind of power is growing, tempered and enduring, grounded within the realities of what I am in fact doing. An open-eyed assessment and appreciation of what I can and do accomplish, using who I am and who I most wish myself to be. To stretch as far as I can go and relish what is satisfying rather than what is sad. (134)

Stretching herself as far as possible without risking overextension is thus not only a strategy to explore and expand the meanings of words, it becomes a new insight and theory from which she deals with the uncertainty and fragility of her situation. The notion of space over time captivates Lorde: she keeps mentioning this new conceptual insight in her entries from November and December 1986, and she returns to the notion of breadth in her epilogue, written in August 1987. It seems as if this new metaphor, like a burst of light, reveals something important to her and opens up a new way of conceptualising life lived in an intimate relation with cancer. Therefore, when Lorde resolves to take up as much space as possible, to stretch as far as she can go and to focus on breadth rather than duration, she finds herself living a conscious, alert and attentive life.

Lorde takes up the tapestry image again when she considers how the mundane and the apocalyptic are 'laced together' and how she tries to 'weave together' her treatments with other aspects of her life (131). Rather than pursuing a 'single-minded concentration upon cure', her aim is now to move easily between the different strands that make up her life, to attain a swiftness and fluidity between the exceptional and the average, the dramatic and the everyday. Breadth rather than duration allows her to locate herself in her experience and bring together the different dimensions of her experience:

> My most deeply held convictions and beliefs can be equally expressed in how I deal with chemotherapy as well as in how I scrutinize a poem. It's about trying to know who I am wherever I am. (132)

Audre Lorde's engagement with metaphors illustrates a great variability and flexibility. As I have tried to show, Lorde's writing on illness is deeply informed by her political activism as well as her personal quest for meaning making. Lorde's use of metaphor is grounded in her appreciation of language and in her creative and joyful reclaiming of a language that is not of her making. I agree with Rita Felski who argues in *Literature after Feminism* that we need 'a double vision' to understand the varied usability and meanings of texts by women writers (21–2). Feminist criticism, Felski maintains, tends to foreground negative options, such as the way that feminist artwork subverts, fragments, disrupts and exposes existing norms. Resistance is thus both advocated in the texts and required as a reading stance from which critics make their claims. Felski criticises that such political readings tend to ignore (or dismiss as naive) the aesthetic dimensions that also inform the objects of feminist criticism. The double vision that Felski suggests is also useful for approaching illness metaphors. Similar to the texts discussed by feminist critics, Lorde's writing has an 'aesthetic, moral, and political force' (108). On the one hand, it aims at disrupting the status quo and raises questions about morals and ethics. On the other hand, it is also reparative, aesthetically nourishing and an important emotional resource. Lorde's work illustrates that metaphors destroy as much as they repair, they afford resistance as much as they help generate new insights, solace and aesthetic pleasure.

The concurrence of intellectual critique and aesthetic enjoyment is also prevalent in the illness writing by Anatole Broyard, who further develops Lorde's reparative approach to metaphor by proposing and modelling a style of living with illness that is informed by lightness, playfulness and exaggeration.

NOTES

1. Inspirations for this chapter in its current form came from presentations by Christine Marks and Alfred Hornung during a Narrative Medicine symposium at Johannes Gutenberg University in Mainz, June 2019. I am very grateful for the generous feedback I received on this chapter from Christine Marks and my colleagues in the 'Uses of Literature' group at the University of Southern Denmark.
2. In fact, a footnote in *The Cancer Journals* references only the West African warriors of the eighteenth and nineteenth century who were also called warriors of Dahomey (now Benin) (also see Alpern; Dash). Lorde's footnote explains that the Amazon women cut off their right breast to be better archers (*Cancer* 34). However, the alleged self-mutilation is mythological and a case of folk etymology.
3. Following Alan Bleakley's diachronic account of medical metaphors in *Thinking with Metaphors in Medicine*, the poet John Donne is often quoted as an early prominent writer who used the war concept in relation to illness in 1627 (36ff.). The physician Thomas Sydenham, too, used the warfare idea in the mid-seventeenth century. Fighting illness, however, did not become a dominant discourse until microbiologist Louis Pasteur introduced a militaristic language in the mid-nineteenth century to describe how illness attacks the human body.
4. Lorde's conclusion – namely that it is her work that will survive her – is, of course, an insight or desire that she shares with other writers who face death and oblivion. For Lorde, 'survival' is a more loaded term, however. Since she, as a Black woman, was 'never meant to survive' in the first place, the fact that she lives makes her into 'an anachronism, a sport, like the bee that was never meant to fly' (*Cancer* 11). Survival, to Lorde, implies 'learning how to stand alone, unpopular and sometimes reviled, and how to make common cause with those others identified as outside the structures in order to define and seek a world in which we can all flourish' ('Master's Tools' 112).
5. Following Wu, Lorde reacts to the mastectomy in peculiar ways: Lorde '"super-feminizes" her body into that of a "super-woman"' in spite of what is often considered to be a de-feminising alteration of the body (250).
6. Lorde first mentions this genre in relation to her semi-fictional, semi-autobiographical novel *Zami: A New Spelling of My Name* (1982).
7. See studies on adaptation and resilience in Carel's *Phenomenology* (136, 140–6).
8. Carel here cites M. Merleau-Ponty, 'Cézanne's Doubt', in M. Merleau-Ponty, *Sense and Nonsense*, translated by P. A. Dreyfus and H. L. Dreyfus. Northwestern University Press, pp. 9–25.

4. Anatole Broyard: A Style for Being Ill; or, Metaphor 'Light'

Anatole Broyard (1920–90), the US-American writer, bookstore owner, literary critic and editor of *The New York Times Book Review*, was an important cultural figure in New York City's literary scene.[1] He wrote daily book reviews for fifteen years and published his reflections on literature and everyday experiences in two anthologies – *Aroused by Books* (1974) and *Men, Women and Other Anticlimaxes* (1980). Broyard's memoir *Kafka Was the Rage* focuses on life in Greenwich Village in the late 1940s and was published posthumously in 1993. After his death, it became known that Broyard had concealed his mixed-race origin and passed for white (B. Broyard; Gates). In Medical Humanities and Narrative Medicine, Broyard's writing about his own and his father's illness has become a standard reference, anthologised in *Intoxicated by My Illness and Other Writings on Life and Death* (1992). In *Intoxicated*, Broyard describes his dissatisfaction with the reductive ways with which evidence-based medicine considers prostate cancer. He diagnoses an impoverishment and blandness that is at odds with the richness and depth that Broyard, to his own surprise, experienced when he got sick. Broyard claims in *Intoxicated* that the technical, matter-of-fact approaches of modern health care should be fundamentally rethought so that the boundary experience of illness become more fully resonant. Thus, rather than depriving illness of meaning, as Sontag polemically urges in her critique of illness metaphors (99), Broyard wishes to add *more* meaning, *more* options of sense-making and *more* capacious understandings of what it means to be sick. Metaphor is a crucial instrument in this endeavour.

In *Intoxicated*, Broyard makes a compelling case for metaphor over narrative by modelling a playful use of metaphors as an expression of his individual style. Like Susan Sontag and Audre Lorde, Broyard applies the battle metaphor to illness and creatively imagines different scenarios for his fight. However, the battle metaphor is only one of many that Broyard uses for illness. Moreover, instead of being primarily driven by an adversarial or resistant motivation, Broyard's approach is best understood, I suggest, in terms of its reparative or even joyful qualities. In fact, Broyard directly calls for a 'style for illness' (*Intoxicated* 25), which he associates with self-love and self-care and which is informed by exaggeration, vanity and pleasure. To tease out the many gains of this style, this chapter will turn to concepts such as reparative reading, camp, hyperbole, light comparison and collage to demonstrate that Broyard's use of metaphors is not only an act of self-care, it is also an intriguing style for his readers.

NEW BATTLEFIELDS

Compared to the writers discussed in previous chapters, Broyard uses warfare and battle metaphors in a more indirect way. For example, Broyard relates only implicitly to the concept of battle when he describes a recurring dream:

> With this illness one of my recurrent dreams has finally come true. Several times in the past I've dreamed that I had committed a crime – or perhaps I was only accused of a crime, it's not clear. When brought to trial I refused to have a lawyer – I got up instead and made an impassioned speech in my own defense. This speech was so moving I could feel myself tingly with it. It was inconceivable that the jury would not acquit me – only each time I woke before the verdict. Now cancer is the crime I may or may not have committed, and the eloquence of being alive, the fervor of the survivor, is my best defense. (*Intoxicated* 5)

In comparing cancer to a crime, Broyard echoes the common associations of illness as an offense or aggression that is also central to the illness-as-battle metaphor, suggesting that this offense requires a (violent) counteraction and needs to be fought.[2] Moreover, Broyard's imagined courtroom is a place where arguments are presented, which, as I discussed in relation to Sontag's adversarial style, we tend to conceptualise as battles: we hear *indefensible* claims, we *attack* weak points in an argument, and a criticism is *right on target* (Lakoff and Johnson, *Metaphors* 4). Moreover, many of the central terms of warfare, including weapons and attacks, are often used figuratively. Second, but no less important, the basic values and attributes of warfare – self-reliance, bravery, heroism, passion – are retained in Broyard's version. This impression is sustained by Alexandra Broyard, Broyard's wife, who describes her late husband in the foreword as some kind of war hero when she maintains that her husband 'did not conquer his cancer, but he triumphed in the way he lived and wrote about it' (*Intoxicated* xviii). While Broyard engages with the battle metaphor only indirectly, he remains invested in keeping and intensifying the established meanings of triumph, heroism and strength.

Broyard's use of this implied battle metaphor makes a number of important shifts, which – similar to the strategies I identified in Arthur Frank's use of the metaphor – can be described with narrative criteria. For example, Broyard changes the *setting* from a battlefield to a courtroom with attorneys, judges and jury members as the main *actors*. The central props or instruments are different, too: instead of guns and missiles, the weapons of a courtroom are words and arguments, eloquence and knowledge of the law. While in both lawsuits and wars the *action* is related to strategising, rules and timing one's 'attack', war combat is often physical and life-threatening. In contrast, a courtroom battle is primarily intellectual and cognitive, and no lives are directly at risk. Similarly, emotions are central in both military warfare and courtroom battles, but military war is often driven by destructive affect, such as fear, anger or hatred, whereas battles in courtrooms (while not free from such emotions) tend to aim for *preservation* – of precedent, of process and of orderly civic life. By invoking a courtroom battle, Broyard thus expands the warfare comparison, activating new mappings and recontextualising the fundamental notion of opposition.

Broyard recontextualises the battle metaphor once again when he invokes a sports game and compares his cancerous prostate to 'a worn-out baseball' (47).[3] This comparison is remarkable because it introduces the notion of play on the one hand and a sense of decline on the other. The game element twists the type of action: the fight in a baseball game is lighter and associated with entertainment and leisure time. Similar to the courtroom battle, a sports game features opposing teams in a contest from which winners and losers emerge – but the battle is not militaristic, and the consequences of losing are less dramatic. Importantly, while Frank uses his reference to a marathon in order to suggest a more tender relationship to his body and its capacities, Broyard's recontextualisation continues to stress the conventional associations of warfare, such as heroism, triumph and hardness. The deplorable condition of the baseball and, analogously, his prostate is the result of having played vigorously and thus having lived intensely and passionately. As Broyard's imagined doctor says: 'you've worked the prostate of yours pretty hard' (47), and for Broyard, the statement implies that the decline is a worthy, honourable one. In comparing his prostate to a worn-out baseball, he alludes to the status of baseballs as cultural icons and collectibles, objects of worship and awe that speak of triumphant battles in the past.

Broyard elaborates these positive connotations of decline when he imagines a doctor who uses metaphors to personalise Broyard's illness and tie it to his life and identity:

> The doctor could use almost anything: 'Art burnt up your body with beauty and truth.' Or 'You've spent your self like a philanthropist who gives all his money away.' If the patient can feel that he has *earned* his illness – that his sickness represents the grand decadence that follow a great flowering – he may look upon the ruins of his body as tourists look upon the great ruins of antiquity. Of course I'm offering these suggestions playfully, not so much as practical expedients but as experiments in thinking about medicine. Just as researchers play with possibilities in laboratories, medical thinking might benefit from more free associations. (48; original emphasis)

In this short paragraph, Broyard re-evaluates in perceptive ways the notion of decline as part of an illness experience. By invoking the ambivalent comparison of the body to an economic system or business – a concept that Sontag, Frank and Joan Didion also grapple with – Broyard does not see the decline of the body as a sign of bad management, failure or punishment. Instead, in mentioning a 'grand decadence', Broyard seems to summon the literal meaning of decadence – namely decline, decay, a general 'falling away' (Desmarais and Weir 3) – as well as the stylised aesthetics of *decadence* in literature and art. Jane Desmarais and David Weir argue that decadence is not only a descriptor of artworks from a particular period such as the Roman Empire, French libertine Enlightenment or nineteenth-century anti-bourgeois modern literature à la Baudelaire and Wilde; decadence is also 'a means of expressing the new and hitherto unknown feelings produced by the experience of historical decline' (2).[4] Decadent artists are intrigued by what is repulsive and immoral, and they find the symptoms and experiences of decline to be surprisingly generative and inventive. For this reason, as Desmarais and Weir argue, decadence can be a 'a major cultural trope with broad explanatory power' for the experience of decline and decay, death and dying (7). Broyard, similarly, is intent on considering his personal decline as an opportunity: in the quotation above (and in his writing more generally), he does not abhor it, nor does he avoid the unsavoury topics – defecation, blood clots, pain – it entails. Instead, he celebrates decline as proof of a life lived to the fullest. Life's possibilities have been burnt up and spent. What follows is a different kind of flowering. Following this logic, the 'ruined' body or worn-out prostate are not primarily waste, nor are they shameful remains. Instead, the body changed by illness is reframed as a place of wonder, an indicator of a life well lived, calling for worship and respect rather than disgust and rejection.

The baseball metaphor thus personalises and intensifies Broyard's experience of illness, and this is a significant and positive function of metaphor for Broyard: metaphor inflates illness with meaning so that what is otherwise abstract, technical and distant becomes personal. If 'the patient can feel that he has *earned* his illness', Broyard suggests, the patient may feel proud of the illness and even accept it as a sign of personal achievement (48; original emphasis). With this approach to illness and metaphor, Broyard deliberately positions himself in direct opposition to Sontag: while she advocates a language of illness informed by objectivity, matter-of-factness and reduction, Broyard uses a register defined by imagination, indirectness and abundance. Broyard's reading of his illness embodies different values, such as intensity and an aesthetics of accretion and thickness.

Broyard's approach and celebratory attitude may be admirable, but they are also perplexing. Broyard fashions the condition of his prostate/baseball as the result of a tough, heroic fight. Similarly, the allusion to the courtroom is based on the notions of triumph and bravery. Like Lorde's powerful and proud use of the warfare metaphor, then, Broyard's use retains some of the common meanings and underlying values of the warfare concept. In other words, the elaborations of the basic metaphor, the new scenarios that are imagined, do not fundamentally change the underlying cultural narrative of 'illness is war'. The narratives of triumph and heroic overcoming as well as the focus on individualism, self-reliance and responsibility remain basically undisturbed. In contrast to Sontag, Lorde and Frank, whose counter-metaphors are couched in counter-narratives that challenge some of the problematic dimensions of the warfare idea, Broyard's reimagination seems to reinforce this darker underbelly. This is surprising in so far as Broyard expresses a wish to change medical care and prompt reform through his writing. For example, Broyard lists a number of additional competencies and sensibilities that doctors should bring to medical care, such as close reading skills, a personal style and philosophical sensibilities (40ff.). Moreover, he calls for systemic reform when he speaks against the sterile, laboratory-like atmosphere of clinical encounters: 'the sterility went too far', Broyard complains (55).

> It sterilized the doctor's thinking. It sterilized the patient's entire experience in the hospital. It sterilized the very notion of illness to the point where we can't bring our soiled thoughts to bear on it. But the sick man needs the contagion of life. Death is the ultimate sterility. (55–6)

Given such fiery claims we may wonder if Broyard's appeal for reform and change fizzles out because he (inadvertently?) undermines these propositions via his chosen figurative language that perpetuates problematic notions of triumphant warfare and battle? How can we understand this paradox?

BAD BOY BROYARD

Broyard's critics have discussed the ethical consequences and contradictions of his proposals, portraying his expectations as unrealistic; they have also problematised both the form of his argument and the persona making it. For example, William Major maintains that Broyard leaves unchallenged the flawed ideological values inherent in the battle metaphor. According to Major, Broyard embodies a romantic version of the American hero, a lonesome cowboy who detaches himself from the social context and fashions himself anew in isolation (Major 98, 110). In doing so, as Frank adds to the critique, Broyard 'treats his ordeals with an off-handedness that places him above his fate. His myth is his lightness, but this lightness remains his alone' (*Wounded* 124). Major identifies a Romantic idealisation of art and the artist underlying Broyard's writing: the search for the sublime and godly, the glorification of loneliness and isolation, and a deliberate detachment from social context and ties (98–100).[5] This stance itself would be peculiar but not problematic, Major argues, if Broyard were not espousing a social and political agenda, namely his wish to free medical practice from its technocratic and style-less paradigms by introducing a humanistic vision in which art is redemptive and potentially reparative (Major 103–4, 109). In light of this agenda, however, Major concludes that '*Intoxicated* squanders its opportunity to build a community of politically-engaged readers' and 'fails as a practical ethics for others' (99, 119).

Broyard himself admits to this lack of practicality, stating straightforwardly that his approach is 'irresponsible' (67) and warning readers that he is only offering thought experiments. From an ethical, application-oriented perspective, however, his suggestions are still problematic. For example, in one of his last pieces in *Intoxicated*, Broyard cautions against capitulation: 'You mustn't surrender to illness: Shave, comb your hair, dress attractively, be aggressive, not passive. It's the change in the sick person that embarrasses his friends, and the whole inhibition begins there' (66). Broyard does not seem to care for the effects of propositions like these. The connotations of the battle metaphor, which frames surrender as a shameful act, do not bother Broyard.

In this sense, one might argue, Broyard is very American. Following Siri Hustvedt, American culture

> does not encourage anyone to *accept* adversity. On the contrary, we habitually declare war on the things that afflict us, whether it's drugs, terrorism, or cancer ... The person who lies back and says, 'This is my lot. So be it', is a quitter, a passive, pessimistic, spineless loser who deserves only our contempt. (*Living* 24; original emphasis)

In continuing to invoke the conventional connotations of the battle metaphor, Broyard perpetuates normative views of how patients should behave, thus undermining his call for a change of medicine. Recommending a form of 'business as usual', Broyard clearly offers a very different form of resistance compared to Lorde, for example, and her critique of the strategies of concealment in relation to breast prostheses (see 'Breast Cancer: Power vs. Prosthesis' in *The Cancer Journals*). Similarly, when juxtaposed with Anne Boyer's illness narrative 'What Cancer Takes Away' (2019), which details the devastation of Boyer's breast cancer experience and makes a plea for retiring the cultural expectations of cheerfulness, bravery and feistiness, Broyard appears to be trapped in a limiting and prescriptive understanding of appropriate patient behaviour.

Given these paradoxes, Major identifies a 'narrative schizophrenia' in Broyard's writing (98): by using the trope of intoxication, Major maintains, Broyard suggests that his illness liberated him from petty, ordinary worries and provided him with a surprising sense of elation, a reckless and joyful abandonment of control. However, Major argues, Broyard also confirms a sick person's profound need to overcome the shock of illness and, as Broyard claims himself,

> try to bring it under control by turning it into narrative. Always in emergencies we invent narratives. We describe what is happening, as if to confine the catastrophe ... Just as a novelist turns his anxiety into a story in order to be able to control it to a degree, so a sick person can make a story, a narrative, out of his illness as a way of trying to detoxify it. (*Intoxicated* 19–21).

In other words, on the one hand, Major finds Broyard celebrating the loss of control that illness brings; on the other hand, Broyard wishes to exert control (Major 116). For this reason, Major rightly observes that Broyard 'circumvents the intoxication he glorifies' and questions the adequacy of 'the figure of intoxication as a narrative strategy' (98).

Still, the comparison of illness experiences to intoxication is more ambivalent than Major acknowledges, as it contains a flickering of contradictory associations. Like alcohol or other drugs, Broyard's illness is both euphorigenic *and* dangerous. While it seduces him with unexpected moments of elation and pleasure, intoxication also contains the harsh reality of sobriety, the toxic nature of his condition and the side effects of flying high. These experiences are not mutually exclusive but interwoven. Broyard finds this entanglement in his illness: his sick body is *both* a site of pain, shame and discomfort (even though Broyard does not describe these aspects at great length) *and* it is, for him, a site of surprising energy, unpredictable reactions and funny incidents (e.g. 46). These incongruous associations of intoxication are central to Broyard's writing.

There is a risk, I think, in taking Broyard too seriously. Or, to put it differently, there is a risk in not taking him seriously enough when he cautions us about the playfulness of his suggestions. He argues, after all, that what he proposes are merely 'experiments in thinking' (48). It is in the nature of experiments that they can go wrong, run astray or produce dead ends. To foreground the mistakes and failures does not do justice to the many achievements of Broyard's experimental thinking.[6] Following Henry Louis Gates, Broyard was a 'virtuoso of ambiguity and equivocation' who constantly used 'distance and denials and half denials and cunning half-truths' (n. pag.). Oliva Banner, too, emphasises the 'double modes of signification' in Broyard's writing as well as the recurring tropes of imposture, misidentification and deception, which she links to the pervasive structural racism that Broyard rightly feared and tried to avoid by concealing his African American identity (34–7, 42). And Kathlyn Conway usefully reminds us that Broyard is writing 'a kind of artistic manifesto' for which he creates the persona of 'the sexual and artistic man' (80–1). Importantly, this persona is a construct that cannot and should not be fully identified with Broyard himself. This persona relishes in extravagant metaphors and uses them, Conway maintains, 'not as an entrance into but as a distraction from his experience in a dying body' (81). Conway's notion of distraction suggests a diversion from imminent experience and a condition in which the mind is occupied by something else. I want to suggest, in contrast, that distraction can also lay the groundwork for a different point of access. Instead of aiming at distance or oblivion, that is, distraction can sometimes be an intentional drawing away from the immediate in order to let the mind wander elsewhere, creating new associations and flights of fancy. Such distraction or distance is not an end in itself but a momentary, provisional detour that can lead to surprising discoveries, maybe in the form of a hidden entryway.

A STYLE FOR BEING ILL

While it is important to draw attention to the limitations of Broyard's argument, particularly for the practice of medical care, his *style* – and its relation to the varied usability of metaphor – also holds promise. There are many gains to be found in Broyard's indirectness, in his love of experimentation, and in his embracing of mistakes and momentary delusions. One of these is the illuminative, uplifting and refreshing quality of his writing. At the same time, there is a darker underbelly to his style, which Olivia Banner reads as a response to the pervasive structural racism that Broyard faced as a man of African American heritage (34). In other words, Broyard's style is not only an ingenious practice of a self-determining, self-stylising artist-entrepreneur; it is also a strategy of survival in a political and social context structured by racism and discrimination, in which his future employer, *The New York Times*, for example, maintained a whites-only hiring policy in the 1950s (Banner 44). These complexities risk getting lost when we judge Broyard too narrowly on the basis of soundness and logic or according to an aesthetic that values minimalism and practicality. For this reason, it is worthwhile to also examine Broyard's style from supplementary angles that acknowledge his flights of fancy, his distractions and exaggerations, as part of a strategy – one that accepts the theoretical and practical utility of mistakes, delusions and excess. The angles that I will use include reparative reading, camp, hyperbole, light comparison and juxtaposition, all of which bring Broyard's idiosyncratic style into sharper relief.

This style is inherently consistent with the nature of metaphors. As I suggested in relation to intoxication, Broyard's writing is permeated by an oscillatory, flickering sensibility. On the opening page, for example, he invokes but also challenges the genre expectations of the illness narrative when he describes his reaction to his cancer diagnosis as a 'relief, even elation' (1): 'Suddenly there was in the air a rich sense of crisis … It seemed to me that my existence, whatever I thought, felt, or did, had taken on a kind of meter, as in poetry or in taxis' (1). The comparison of his cancer diagnosis to a crisis that becomes structured by 'a kind of meter' is light-hearted and clever due to the pun he makes. At the same time, there is a semantic richness and sincerity to the notion of 'a life on a meter' – this version of life would be defined by structure, rhythm and musicality, but also measured by new criteria, a journey in which every minute counts. It is for this reason that the diagnosis, for Broyard, entails 'a rush of consciousness, a splash of perspective, a hot flash of ontological alertness' that is both elating and grave, euphoric and deadly earnest (7).

In fact, Broyard's *Intoxicated* – from its first pages to its last – holds in suspense both playfulness and sincerity. This is illustrated when Broyard comments on his 'battle' style in the last section of *Intoxicated*. He directly addresses common associations of fighting and maintains: 'It's not enough to be "positive", brave, or stoical. These are too simple, like New Year's resolutions' (61). Instead, he argues that the sick and dying need a style, and he suggests that one way to realise this style consists in patients making 'a game, a career, even an art form out of opposing their illness' (61). Broyard demonstrates here that he is highly aware of the constraints of the battle metaphor and the ways in which it is commonly and often simplistically used. In combining fighting illness with additional concepts of game, career and art, he stretches the meanings of fighting – an approach similar to the paired strategies of stretching and combining that Lorde uses with regard to battle and music. In other words, the triumph of Broyard's fight lies in the activation of other resources, such as eloquence, imagination, playfulness and creativity. Alexandra Broyard's preface to *Intoxicated* underscores this interpretation of triumph: she sees the value of her husband's contribution '*in the way* he lived and wrote about' his illness (xviii; my emphasis). Thus, rather than focusing on matters of fact (e.g. Broyard did not conquer, his fight failed, he contradicts himself), Alexandra Broyard foregrounds his style and habit of thinking – the *way* he fought his fight.

In the following three sections, I explore the unique modes Broyard uses to sustain himself through his illness before asking how practicable those modes might be for other patients.

Be Vain

One particularly useful approach to Broyard's style is through Eve Kosofsky Sedgwick's concept of 'reparative reading'. Sedgwick suggests this concept in *Touching Feeling: Affect, Pedagogy, Performativity* (2003), a collection of essays connected by the aim 'to explore promising tools and techniques for nondualistic thought and pedagogy' (1). Sedgwick proposes a practice of reading in response and addition to the default mode in critical theory, which she denounces as 'paranoid reading'. A paranoid approach to literary texts and cultural artefacts is driven by suspicion and a negative ethos. Drawing on Silvan Tomkins, Melanie Klein and her own background in queer theory,[7] Sedgwick describes a reparative practice as one that aims at maximising positive affect (136). She argues that

> The desire of a reparative impulse ... is additive and accretive. Its fear, a realistic one, is that the culture surrounding it is inadequate or inimical to its nurture; it wants to assemble and confer plenitude on an object that will then have resources to offer to an inchoate self. (149)

Following Sedgwick, 'reparative critical practices' foreground pleasure and hope, creativity and excess of imagination (128). Grounding such practices in queer theory and using the concept of camp as an example, she conceptualises a reparative practice as being driven by love, '"over"-attachment' and a celebration of 'surplus stylistic investments' (149). While a suspicious reading, as Sedgwick argues, sees *through* these important features of camp because it is informed by an aesthetic that values 'minimalist elegance and conceptual economy' (150), reparative reading aims instead at adding something (rather than taking away) and is driven by 'the desire to give sustenance to individuals, communities, and cultures' (Jurecic, *Illness* 113). Importantly, Sedgwick frames reparative reading not in opposition to or as a replacement of paranoid reading. Instead, the two practices are in an 'oscillatory' relationship and are, at heart, 'mutable positions' (Sedgwick 128, 150). In fact, as Jurecic argues, there are many common interests that link paranoid and reparative readings, as 'both positions developed out of awareness and acknowledgement of suffering, loss, and political oppression' (110). As Jurecic and Geoffrey Rees have demonstrated in their scholarship, Sedgwick's notion of reparative reading can be especially generative in a health humanities context because reparative practices offer new ways of approaching texts and clinical spaces not only as *objects* of knowledge but also as *sources* of knowledge (Felski qtd in Jurecic, *Illness* 113).[8]

There are interesting convergences between Sedgwick's reparative practice and her references to camp on the one hand and Broyard's style and his inclination to exuberance on the other. In a sense, Broyard 'reads' his illness as if it were a literary text or cultural artefact.[9] As I mentioned before, style is a significant resource for him, even an antidote, to confront the diminishment of illness. To Broyard, there is a reparative or, as he calls it, a 'therapeutic value of style' (25), and for this reason he is convinced that doctors and patients need to develop a style of their own. Such a style is particularly relevant for the patient whose illness threatens 'to diminish and disfigure' her: according to Broyard, 'only by insisting on your style can you keep from falling out of love with yourself' (25). One of his recommendations to such a patient is to get a new wardrobe, thus nourishing a sense of self-worth and beauty (62). Moreover, he argues:

> If you reflect that you probably helped to bring your illness on yourself by self-indulgence or by living intensely, then the illness becomes yours, you own up to it, instead of blaming something vague and unsatisfactory like fate. Anger is too monolithic for such a delicate situation. It's like a catheter inserted in your soul, draining your spirit. (29)

Broyard's recommendation to personalise one's illness is diametrically opposed to the way that someone like Frank approaches it. As Frank argues convincingly in his memoir, illness is a matter of fate and coincidence; if someone believes that he has brought the illness onto himself, he is indulging in vanity (Frank, *At the Will* 87). For Broyard, however, who deliberately aggrandises and claims ownership of his illness, such vanity is a *positive* choice. Vanity is a strategy of self-care that allows patients to stay in love with themselves even as the illness 'monster' attempts to disfigure them (62). 'And your style', Broyard recommends, 'is the instrument of your vanity. If they can afford it, I think it would be good therapy, good body narcissism, for cancer patients to buy a whole new wardrobe, mostly elegant, casual clothes' (62). Thus, instead of being fully possessed or invaded by an alien force – metaphors against which both Frank and Sontag have warned as well – Broyard suggests that the power structure of the metaphor needs to be reversed, the illness monster repelled. To take ownership and nurture one's body narcissism ultimately replenishes the spirit.

If vanity is part of a therapeutic style, as Broyard proposes, the term 'vanity' itself, paradoxically, also invokes the opposite of positive attachment and self-worth, namely a sense of futility and worthlessness. When something is 'in vain', it is unprofitable, idle and futile. An obsolete meaning of vanity implies 'the quality of being foolish or of holding erroneous opinions' ('vanity'); a 'Vanity Fair' is a place of frivolity and idle amusement ('vanity'). How do these diverse meanings of vanity play into Broyard's concept of style? It holds them in suspense: his style contains both self-love and idleness, pride and foolishness, self-worth and futility – not least because this illness 'style' occurs in the face of death, against which any act is, in the end, in vain.

Dominique Bauby's *The Diving-Bell and the Butterfly* exemplifies these contradictions. As Jurecic explains, Bauby finds a satisfaction in 'wearing luxurious clothing. He explains that he 'sees in the clothing a symbol of continuing life. And proof that I still want to be myself.' 'If I must drool,' he concludes with a mixture of humour and pathos, 'I may as well drool on cashmere' (Bauby qtd in Jurecic, *Illness* 108). Following Jurecic, there is a nourishing, reparative value in sensuality, in tasting, smelling and touching, as vain as they may seem (108). Similarly, Audre Lorde emphasises the importance of beautiful clothes and jewellery as a form of self-love: ten days after her mastectomy, Lorde has a doctor's appointment and makes an effort to dress stylishly even though she still feels depleted. With shining hair, dressed in an African kente-cloth tunic, wearing new leather boots, and with 'the most opalescent of my moonstones, and a single floating bird dangling from my right ear', she feels 'brave' and 'beautiful' and is 'rather pleased with myself, all things considered, pleased with the way I felt, with my own flair, with my own style' (*Cancer* 59–60). To Lorde, such acts of self-care and self-love are not self-indulgent but an essential form of self-preservation ('Burst' 131).

Though it may seem counterintuitive to associate the overtly heterosexual Broyard with Sedgwick's foundation in queer theory,[10] his vain style closely follows Sedgwick's reparative reading of camp. Similar to camp practices, Broyard indulges in '"over"-attachment' and a celebration of 'surplus stylistic investments' (149). In 'Notes on "Camp"' (1964), Susan Sontag describes camp as '"style" over "content", "aesthetics" over "morality", of irony over tragedy' (287).

> Camp is a vision of the world in terms of style – but a particular kind of style. It is the love of the exaggerated, the 'off', of things-being-what-they-are-not. The best example is in Art Nouveau, the most typical and fully developed Camp style. Art Nouveau objects, typically, convert one thing into something else: the lighting fixtures in the form of flowering plants, the living room which is really a grotto. (279)

When Sontag argues that '[t]he whole point of Camp is to dethrone the serious. Camp is playful, anti-serious' (288), the concept seems tailor-made for Broyard.

Before I move on to other modes of Broyard's style, a few clarifications are necessary. My juxtaposition of queerness with illness is problematic, not least because it can be seen to evoke a long history of pathologising homosexuality. To be clear, being queer is *not* like being sick or having cancer. However, a recontextualisation of the queer-based style of camp – like many recontextualisations resulting from comparative practices – can yield a number of gains, as I will illustrate below. Moreover, although I have used reparative reading here as if it were a fleshed-out critical method or theory, this is not (yet?) the case. As a readerly stance, the concept has been used productively by Jurecic, for example.[11] Yet, Heather Love poignantly wonders in her reflection on the enabling potentials of reparative reading: 'I am enabled – but to do what?' (236). I, too, wonder: 'So what next?' (236). With regard to my focus on metaphors, additional questions arise: apart from vanity and a campy pleasure in exuberance, does Broyard make metaphors usable in different ways and for other purposes than repair and sustenance? As I illustrated earlier in this chapter, the concept of decadence is helpful to understand how Broyard's interest in the ruins of his body is associated with acknowledgement and worship rather than disgust and rejection. In what follows, I will draw on the concepts of hyperbole and light comparison to further flesh out Broyard's style and its gains.

Be Tall

In 'The Patient Examines the Doctor', Broyard relates an anecdote that illustrates how his use of metaphor draws on exaggeration:

> I find an irresistible desire to make jokes. When you're lying in the hospital with a catheter and IV in your arm, you have two choices, self-pity or irony. If the doctor doesn't get your ironies, who else is there around?
>
> I was in a hospital room in Brigham. I was there because my catheter kept blocking. When you have a biopsy, a scab forms, and then afterward the scab breaks off, and sometimes bleeding resumes. There are clots, and the clots choke the catheter. The ordinary catheter is about the size of a soda straw. The catheter they put in me was like a garden hose. I was not comfortable.
>
> Finally, they took out the catheter and they said, Now you'll be able to pee again. After a while I felt this Niagara-like rush mounting in me, like the rush of orgasm which you hear approaching in the distance. I leapt out of bed. I did a skip and sprinted toward the bathroom. I didn't make it. I splashed urine and blood all over the floor. My roommate, the hoodlum, who has drawn blood in anger, jumped out of bed with an expression of horror. He began mopping up the floor with a sheet. Illness is not a tragedy. Much of it is funny. (46)

Broyard's comparisons here are clearly overblown and exaggerated. Typical of hyperbole – commonly understood as a 'bold overstatement, or the extravagant exaggeration of fact or of possibility' (Abrams 120) – Broyard inflates the diameter of the catheter and compares the quantity and power of his urine to the water of the Niagara River. After comparing the catheter to a garden hose, Broyard adds, 'I was not comfortable' (46), thus punctuating overstatement with understatement. This juxtaposition increases the paradoxical, ironic, almost humorous effect of his exaggeration and highlights the incongruence of his experiences, which encompass such disparate feelings as pain and relief, shame and joy. Hyperboles, as Sharon Hamilton argues, are often used for comic or ironic purposes, but they also appear in serious contexts so that the exaggeration emphasises the intensity of a feeling (59). Importantly, as Robert Fogelin argues, hyperboles are 'an exaggeration on the side of truth' (17). With hyperbole, 'I say something stronger than what

I have a right to say, with the intention of having it corrected away from the extreme, but still to something *strong* that preserves the *same polarity*' (17; original emphasis). This affirmative quality clarifies that exaggeration, for Broyard, is not an indicator of insincerity, fraudulent intentions, or self-delusion. It is an opportunity to recreate a sense of the intensity he felt during the extreme of his illness experience. At the same time, it allows him to keep a humorous, playful tone.

Broyard's inflations and overstatements echo the American genre of tall tales. Broyard's writing is, after all, informed by a spirit of adventure and curiosity as he embarks on a journey through a 'disturbed country' (*Intoxicated* 21). Similar to early American pioneers, Broyard searches for a new life in an unfamiliar country and, in doing so, pushes the frontiers of what it means to write about illness. Like the larger-than-life heroes described by tall-tale storytellers, who inflate crassly and beyond credibility whatever grain of truth their adventure stories contain, Broyard enjoys exaggerating his experiences in the strange country in which he finds himself and emphasises a distinction between insiders and outsiders to the experience of illness.

The tall tale is, of course, a historically specific narrative genre used by writers such as Mark Twain and many others, and not all features of the tall tale are transferrable to Broyard's writing.[12] Yet the comparison to tall tales brings to light a number of features that help further contour Broyard's reparative strategies. For example, the tall tale's attitudes towards truth and overstatement have been described as a social practice and coping strategy for settlers at the American frontier. As Carolyn S. Brown argues, by telling a tall tale to a cultural outsider, such as a European visitor who was unfamiliar with the specific territory, the storytellers inflated the hardships and circumstances they had allegedly experienced in order to mock the visitor's gullibility and prejudices but also, and maybe more importantly in relation to Broyard, to affirm the specific and hard-won knowledge that had helped them survive (Brown 2). Following Henry Wonham, tall tales served important social functions for the American settlers: 'By exaggerating the conditions that made life virtually unbearable, inhabitants of the frontier were at the same time expressing their defiance and taking refuge in laughter' (18). Indeed, the settlers' exaggerations were 'not a denial of experience; rather, the yarn spinner's exaggerated imagery promotes a renewed acknowledgment of actual conditions that inspired the tale, knowledge of which binds and perpetuates the group' (Wonham 24). Exaggerations thus playfully roam in the borderlands of truth and lie, fact and fiction, for the sake of honouring shared hardship and creating a sense of community.

Comparable to the storyteller's tall tales, Broyard's exaggerations are dialogic and address a particular readership, namely a community of patients who, like himself, may have experienced illness as strangely invigorating, if only for a moment or two. Like Broyard, his implied readers believe in the power of the mind as well as the power of art and are equally driven by a sense of idealism. Thus, while Major sees Broyard primarily as a self-involved solipsist, the tall-tale traditions suggest that Broyard might have a more communal and relational motivation: he is speaking to a group of insiders who share his values, intellectual background and experiences, and are therefore 'in' on the pleasures of exaggeration. In other words, rather than trying to deny or distract from the actual, sordid experiences of illness, Broyard's writing is 'flaunting the peculiar knowledge and experiences' of those who know what he is talking about (Brown, dust jacket). In contrast to the agenda of positive thinking which denies hardship and pain and advocates *one* way of understanding and responding to illness, Broyard's larger-than-life fantasies of super doctors and extraordinary patients are neither prescriptive nor normative. When Broyard finds something funny or remarkable within a painful and embarrassing experience, his cheerfulness places pain and humour side by side, and his outlandishness affirms the same possibility for others.

When Broyard exaggerates – and he does so with abandon – he always signals his awareness of his outrageousness. For example, he self-reflexively calls himself 'an impostor' (33) and identifies his propositions and imaginations as 'delusions of grandeur' (66), thus clarifying that his grandiose trust in the workings of his mind as well as his linguistic prowess are hyperbolised.[13] Broyard also acknowledges completely overdrawing the role of his doctor, whom he wants to be a larger-than-life genius who is not only brilliant in his job but also a literary scholar and general savant. Broyard's awareness of his exaggerations is reflected in his wording: Broyard repeatedly speaks of an 'ideal doctor' (e.g. 36, 41), he offers his thoughts as 'experiments' and playful 'suggestions' (48), and he knows very well that he is imagining 'a heroic model' (36). Broyard also deliberately romanticises the redemptive power of art and literature, which, to him, are like aspirin and thus a form of therapeutic treatment. Following Broyard, illness is 'the parade ground for Romanticism' because illness sounds 'a Romantic note', triggering feelings of exaltation since its diagnosis (23). Being ill is 'like a great permission' which allows the sick person to explore his craziness, if he wants, and 'let it out in all its garish colors' (23). Comparing his writing to the effect of a hallucinogen, he hopes that it will bring him unpredictable moments of joy as well as 'a blaze of revelation' (23).

By Broyard's reasoning, extravagant metaphors are a liberating, absolving *effect* of his illness. At the same time, these metaphors also initiate and fuel the revelatory power he ascribes to illness. In other words, Broyard's metaphors are both a precondition for and a consequence of seeing illness as a parade ground of heightened imagination. Together, these functions become a sort of spiral, lifting Broyard to ever new flights of fancy.

Be Mistaken

Spirals can also lead downward, of course. Rather than causing elation, they can entail confusion, misinformation, humiliation and worse. Broyard is conscious of such dangers when he maintains: 'I'm going to project an ideal, a foolish doctor–patient relationship, the sort of thing that, say, Madame Bovary expected from Rodolphe – a love affair with a doctor' (33). In comparing himself to Madame Bovary, Gustave Flaubert's famous heroine, Broyard makes an analogy that implies a cautionary note: after all, Madame Bovary stands for the worst kind of reader. Married to a good-natured country doctor, she has fallen out of love with him because he is too ordinary, too plain and mundane for her exaggerated and unrealistic romantic tastes. Emma Bovary, like Broyard, is an avid reader, and her hunger for romance stories has distorted her understanding of reality. Unsurprisingly, her love affair with Rodolphe Boulanger, the attractive womaniser, fails tragically and she commits suicide. In Broyard's context, the reference to Madame Bovary alludes to the dangers of mistaking fantasies for reality; yet the reference also invokes the many gains of being enraptured by fantastical, erroneous visions. Madame Bovary's (and Broyard's) sense of elation and enchantment is a relief from the bland and ordinary reality of life (and of illness). In the case of Madame Bovary, her enchantment results from a fatal mistake: she lets herself get carried away, lacks critical distance and is trapped by a sentimental, aestheticising and distorting habit (Felski, *Uses* 51ff.). Making a case for the value of enchantment, Rita Felski proposes that enchantment with literature is not necessarily uncritical or one-sided, nor is it automatically tied to a false sense of reality. Rather than using Madame Bovary as a cautionary example, Felski summons her to defend the value of enchantment in reading, ultimately drawing on this famous literary example to advocate for the possibility of a double vision, a 'mental balancing act':

> Even as we are bewitched, possessed, emotionally overwhelmed, we know ourselves to be immersed in an imaginary spectacle: we experience art in a state of double consciousness. This is not to deny that imaginative fictions

infiltrate and influence our lives, but to note that such a confluence rarely takes the form of a literal confusion of real and imagined worlds. (Felski, *Uses* 74)

Broyard, too, encourages us to get carried away by the spectacular injunctions of his metaphors and claims and, at the same time, draws attention to what he is doing. Not only does he signal explicitly the foolishness of his ideas, the informed reader also knows about Broyard's professional background as a bookshop owner and literary critic for many years who, as we can assume, is very well aware of the discourse around Flaubert's heroine. Thus, in comparing himself to Madame Bovary, Broyard winks at a form of criticism that will spring too quickly at the material implications of his propositions – a lack of plausibility, rigour and logic.[14] Broyard, however, is surely not naive or blind to these implications, and we can assume that, echoing Felski, he engages in 'a mental balancing act ... a state of double consciousness', in which truth and fantasy, earnestness and provocation, are in an oscillatory relation.

This oscillatory quality resonates with the double modes of signification in contexts of structural racism;[15] it is also visible in Broyard's use of crude and faulty exaggerations on the one hand and his self-reflexivity and transparency about what he is doing on the other. In continuously cautioning us that his comparisons are experiments in thinking and that his propositions might be completely amiss, Broyard stresses trial-and-error as a central dimension of his style. Moreover, as I suggested earlier in my discussion of Sedgwick, Broyard's style resonates with queer strategies and camp. Joseph Litvak, for example, whom Sedgwick quotes in her essay on reparative reading, maintains that queer 'practices [are] aimed at taking the terror out of error, at making the making of mistakes sexy, creative, even cognitively powerful' (qtd in Sedgwick 147). Similarly, in *The Queer Art of Failure* (2011), Jack J. Halberstam considers failure a queer style and way of life (3). Failure and stupidity, he argues, are 'counterintuitive modes of knowing' and 'a different set of knowledge practices' that come with many rewards (11–12). In alluding to queer temporalities that challenge heteronormative life trajectories such as 'reproductive maturity' (2), Halberstam argues that failure allows us to escape the punishing norms that discipline behaviour and manage human development with the goal of delivering us from unruly childhoods to orderly and predictable adulthoods. Failure preserves some of the wondrous anarchy of childhood and disturbs the supposedly clean boundaries between adults and children, winners and losers. And while failure certainly comes accompanied by a host of negative affects, such as disappointment, disillusionment and despair, it also provides the opportunity to use these negative affects to poke holes in the toxic positivity of contemporary life (3).

Broyard's writing is certainly not a failure, nor is there fear of humiliation or misery in his triumphalist account. And yet, Broyard's use of metaphors showcases a willingness to 'fail spectacularly' (Halberstam 5) as he flaunts a fearless attitude towards errors, silliness and stupidity, continuously reminding us that his ideas are irresponsible and that his assessment may be delusional (Broyard 66–7).

Broyard's style is highly relevant with regard to metaphors – almost meta-metaphorical – because it resonates powerfully with their nature: metaphors blatantly flaunt their inherent wrongness. They are based on mistakes and *are* mistakes. Juliet, obviously, is not the sun, and Romeo's love-stricken comparison of Juliet to a star and gravitational force in the solar system is, if nothing else, exaggerated. Yet, while to insist that Romeo is wrong and exaggerates is correct, it does not get us very far. What is to be gained from embracing the mistakenness of metaphors? Poet Walker Percy argues in his 1958 article 'Metaphor as Mistake' that the beauty of a metaphor is often 'proportionate to its wrongness or outlandishness' (81). Percy's examples of metaphor-mistakes are based on misnamings, misunderstandings and misrememberings (80): a Blue Darter Hawk, for example, is misnamed as a 'Blue Dollar Hawk', or the record player brand Seeburg is mislabelled as a 'seabird' (79). Despite – or rather because of – their faultiness, these metaphors stimulate the imagination and produce a different kind of knowledge: 'we somehow know it [the target or tenor] better, conceive it in a more plenary fashion, have more immediate access to it, than under its descriptive title' (84). In this sense, metaphor has a 'discovering power' that relies on the 'considerable space between tenor and vehicle' (97); the knowledge it generates is indirect, a 'secret apprehension of my own, which I cannot call knowing because I do not even know that I know it' (89). Importantly, Percy maintains when he draws on R. P. Blackmur, an encounter with a metaphor can entail a 'heightened … excited sense of being' as it offers a possibility of being transported away from the blandness of descriptive names (80). Thus, if we can accept a metaphor's inherent mistakenness, if we can work with its failure to speak an objective truth and allow ourselves to get carried away by distracting, silly associations, we may encounter a different register of meanings and gains: an inkling of the intensity of an experience or perception and surprising visions that bring to our attention new options or entrances to living with illness. In this sense, metaphor, *because* it is wrong and *because* it inflates meaning, can offer sustenance and repair. Broyard's approach is a seemingly 'light' but considered departure from Lorde's urgency, Frank's seriousness and Sontag's critique of metaphor while it offers what Sontag was looking for: an opportunity to 'to *see* more, to *hear* more, to *feel* more' ('Against Interpretation' 14; original emphasis).

BROYARD'S STYLE: MORE STRATEGIES FOR ILLNESS

Describing her own illness experience in an essay on Sontag, Martha Stoddard Holmes models an approach to illness metaphors that bears similarities to Broyard's – as well as some crucial differences. Holmes argues that she would have welcomed

> a spur to transform it [cancer], and myself, through a change in language: the comfort in seeing cancer as a presence, an anchor, an infant, a bubble, a lover, a mosaic, a seedpod, an energy – each metaphor generating a different complement of stories. Or, if not comfort, metaphors could have offered the gift of distraction and curiosity: *what is most like this?* From metaphor might spring story: if cancer were a visitor, a stranger who might change my life in valuable as well as terrifying ways, a host of possible narratives of visitors of strangers – dynamic in time, unstuck – could unfold. (266–7)

Broyard's writing is the result of such a spur to transform illness through a change in language. By enumerating, similarly to Holmes's list, one metaphor after the other, Broyard offers us numerous incentives to think differently about illness. Holmes' quick succession of source domains is bewildering as it lights up one image after the other in an associative, unstructured and incoherent manner. The gains that Holmes invokes – comfort, distraction, curiosity – resonate, partly, with the ones I have described in this chapter. In contrast to Holmes' suggestion, however, Broyard does not pick up the scent and follow the narrative clues his metaphors invoke. For example, in his essay 'Toward a Literature of Illness', Broyard recalls that, during his illness experience, narrative became less and less important to him:

> In the beginning I invented mininarratives. Metaphor was one of my symptoms. I saw my illness as a visit to a disturbed country, rather like contemporary China. I imagined it as a love affair with a demented woman who demanded things I had never done before. I thought of it as a lecture I was about to give to an immense audience on a subject that had not been specified. Having cancer was like moving from a cozy old Dickensian house crammed with antiques, deep sofas, snug corners, and fireplaces to a brand-new one that was all windows, skylights, and tubular furniture. (21)

As he claims here, Broyard is not interested in narrativising his experiences. Although his writing is narrative in some instances, he mainly offers 'mininarratives' or casual anecdotes, which are sometimes tied to metaphors, as in the example above. If Broyard's writing is not a narrative, strictly speaking, what is it then?

Jurecic's term 'illness essay' is useful in this context to clarify the differences between illness essays and illness narratives. Jurecic considers the essay 'a form of writing flexible enough to allow for mental wandering and exploration of the unknown and unknowable' (2). Drawing on Montaigne's work, Jurecic reminds us that the word 'essay' comes from *essai*, the French word for attempt or try. Therefore, an essay has a 'speculative quality ... not arguments or proclamations, but personal reflections that posed variations of the question, "What do I know?"' (2). Quoting John D'Agata, Jurecic finds a particular power in the essay form and its experimental nature: 'less an outline traveling toward a foregone conclusion than an unmapped quest that has sprung from the word *question*' (4).

A good example of Broyard's essayistic style is the chapter 'The Patient Examines the Doctor'. While the first pages indeed recount several events in Broyard's illness history, the later sections do not continue that story. Instead, Broyard presents hypotheses, makes a series of value statements and ponders alternative versions and options of understanding his illness. The anecdotes about Broyard's experiences in the hospital do have a narrative quality, but they do not coalesce into a story with a plot. Rather, they relate condensed insights and moments of revelation. In choosing the essay form, Broyard exploits the capacity of metaphors to invoke moments of elation and surprise. In contrast to Sontag who came to consider the essay limiting and constraining, 'a demagogic activity' even (*Consciousness* 519), Broyard feels freed by the essay genre from some of the constraints of narrative – coherence, linearity and closure. The essay provides a welcoming context for associations, digressions and sudden jolts to consciousness. Metaphor is not entirely free from the constraints of narrative, of course, but it offers a different, lyric aesthetic – see my discussion in Chapter 1 – in which the features of narrative have little or no impact.

Apart from the essay form, Broyard uses additional strategies that impact his use of metaphors. For example, the quote from Broyard I used in the beginning of this section illustrates Broyard's tendency to favour *quantity over quality*. In six sentences, he proposes four new source domains.[16] The individual metaphors are not elaborated or given particular weight; they remain small and appear as suggestions – four among possibly many more. Historian Linda Gordon recommends an approach to comparisons that mirrors Broyard's. Gordon makes a plea for 'small comparisons' – such as thin comparisons and limited comparisons – as a valuable method and epistemological tool for the field of history (321). Like Percy, she foregrounds the benefits of a playful approach to what is flawed, risky, 'misleading and prejudiced' in the act of comparing (333). Gordon praises the value of small or '"light" comparison', which she defines as 'comparison unbalanced, unequal, partial, even reduced to "asides" or parenthetical comments' (333), framing this method as a remedy against possible overreach. To render this method safe and academically rigorous, she advises scholars who use comparison to point out not only similarities but also differences – and to highlight the inconsistencies and incommensurability of the things being compared. In relativising the normative impact of a comparison and by nuancing the inherent suggestion of comparison that this is how things *should* be seen, comparison, in Gordon's view, makes transparent that it comes with blind spots and gains.[17] Illustrating her concept with examples from her own research, Gordon echoes the gains of comparison I have mentioned before: they provide an '"outside" input', a new perspective, and they yield new questions that one might never have thought of otherwise (321, 333).

As a writer and literary critic, Broyard does not need to worry about scholarly rigour. For this reason, his safety measures are slightly different from the ones Gordon mentions. (Broyard does not identify the differences and incommensurability of his comparisons, for one.) Yet, like Gordon, Broyard is eager to note the relative nature of his comparisons and makes transparent his intentions: he is experimenting. Rather than carefully scrutinising each metaphor for its successes or shortcomings, he just offers them. In fact, he offers so many that he almost inundates his readers with comparisons. What this torrent means is that no one metaphor takes centre stage or takes on more weight or significance than another. Broyard's comparisons thus remain small in Gordon's sense because they are not allowed to structure his argument. They appear here and there and are dropped as quickly as they are mentioned. Apart from the war metaphor and the notion of intoxication, Broyard's comparisons are not repeated. They appear as 'asides', as anecdotes or aphorisms. His strategy of 'light comparison' thus consists in a high quantity of metaphors rather than in Gordon's transparent treatment or and scrutiny of them. And yet, similar to Gordon's conception, Broyard's metaphors evoke a 'lightness' that yields surprising associations. His strategy lies in plurality, in the sheer quantity of different metaphors that he lists and which he juxtaposes without claiming that one provides more insight than the other. Though in different ways than in Gordon's method, Broyard, too, relativises his metaphors, thus diffusing the normative power that metaphors can assume.

Broyard uses another strategy that is related to the notion of quantity: Broyard's metaphors bear resemblance to the horizontal aesthetics of a *collage*. The paratactic style of his sentences – 'I saw my illness as a visit ... I imagined it as a love affair ... I thought of it as a lecture ...' – suggests that he is collecting source domains, as if he were making a list of comparisons. Following Susan Stanford Friedman, who sees 'collage as a juxtapositional comparative methodology', collage 'maintains the particularity of each, [and] refuses hierarchy and instrumentalism' (759). The quick succession of Broyard's metaphors indicates that his comparisons are not meant to be scrutinised for their individual appropriateness. If a metaphor does not spark anything useful, it can easily be dropped and be replaced by the next metaphor. In refusing to narratively develop one metaphor rather than another (as Holmes does with the illness-as-visitor metaphor), Broyard does not prioritise or create a hierarchy among his metaphors. They exist side by side on a horizontal plane.

This strategy of collage and juxtaposition can unfold a reparative value that does not invoke the powers of narrative. In *Touching Feeling*, Sedgwick draws on the spatial metaphor of the 'beside' when she describes her methodology (8). She wonders about the ease with which some literary critics claim to reach 'beyond' or 'beneath' an object of investigation (8). Problematically, to Sedgwick, '*beneath* and *beyond* turn from spatial descriptors into implicit narratives of, respectively, origin and telos', entailing 'the linear logics that enforce dualistic thinking: noncontradiction or the law of the excluded middle, cause versus effect, subject versus object' (8; original emphasis). While this definition of narrative is simplistic, I agree with Sedgwick when she proposes, similar to Friedman's argument, that the 'beside' has many gains, such as non-dualistic approaches (8). To Friedman, 'Comparison through cultural collage enables the production of new theories' (759). These strategies are, however, not necessarily more egalitarian or pacific: as Sedgwick clarifies, '*Beside* comprises a wide range of desiring, identifying, representing, repelling, paralleling, differentiating, rivaling, leaning, twisting, mimicking, withdrawing, attracting, aggressing, warping, and other relations' (8). Therefore, rather than privileging one strategy or form over the other, we can understand the gains of Broyard's engagement with metaphor as an aesthetics of accretion, a reasoning of 'both/and' rather than 'either/or' (Felski, *Literature* 124), that holds in suspense exuberant flights of fancy and astute observations about the reality of health care.

A PRACTICABLE STYLE?

To conclude I want to return to the provocative question Heather Love asks about reparative practices and styles. If we agree that Broyard's way of reading his illness promises certain benefits, both for himself and for an implied community of other ill people, what exactly does his style enable him to *do*? And, how can we translate the strategies of his style into a practice – not only in terms of a reading method or knowledge practice – but, quite literally, into a way of doing things differently? Which of his strategies might translate beyond the textual level?

Even though the question of applicability may not be Broyard's mandate, his strategies are, in my opinion, practical and practicable, and I would like to illustrate this proposition with an example from research in health care. Elena Semino has published a leaflet titled *A 'Metaphor Menu' for People Living with Cancer* (2019) in which she uses strategies of collage and juxtaposition. Her menu includes one illness metaphor after another. While Semino's list is numbered, there is no hierarchy among the metaphors. Moreover, in calling the list a metaphor menu – a perceptive metaphor in its own right – Semino evokes the image of dishes offered to a customer in a restaurant. No dish is necessarily better than the other; rather it depends on the customer's personal preferences and appetite which dish is most appealing. Likewise, the preface that introduces the metaphor menu stresses the contingency of metaphors: 'Different metaphors suit different people, or the same person at different times' (Semino, *Metaphor Menu* n. pag.). Importantly, a menu does not impose; it merely invites: the customer chooses and decides which dish makes her mouth water and, analogously, which metaphor tickles her imagination. Semino suggests that people working in health care should make their own list or menu of metaphors so that they can offer to their patients several options. The same strategy, I would argue, can be useful for patients. Broyard's *Intoxicated by My Illness* seems inspired by a similar motivation: in addressing a community of people in boundary experiences, he, too, invites them to use their imagination and collect metaphors. The personal menu he creates illustrates his own flights of fancy that nourished and restored him during his illness.

In *Intoxicated*, Broyard shares with his readers his personal collection of metaphors. Their sheer number is astonishing, and this quantity helps puncture the notion that metaphors are equally good or equally helpful. Rather, the plurality demonstrates a richness that allows readers to choose freely which metaphor is most convincing, surprising or enchanting – and which seems harmful or limiting. Broyard's style is an invitation to test and experiment. This style makes use of metaphor's capacity to generate intensity and elation in the most surprising moments, while it also carefully attends to the flickering nature of metaphor. Such a double vision, as Jurecic argues, is central to a reparative practice: 'When writers or readers hold both rupture and beauty in view at the same time, understanding them to exist in relationship, then they see from a reparative position' (109). Similarly, as Broyard's strategies of exaggeration, light comparison, experimentation and his non-narrative, essayistic writing illustrate, his style is a form of reparative practice that allows him to hold multiple and contradictory experiences in view.

NOTES

1. My thanks go to Elin Abrahamson and Danielle Spencer for the encouraging and invaluable feedback they provided on this chapter.
2. Of course, there are multiple ways to understand Broyard's comparison of cancer to a crime. One could see it as a metaphor in its own right, with no relation to the illness-as-battle metaphor. One could also consider it a classic dream motif. If we follow Lakoff and Johnson's claim that metaphors permeate our ordinary conceptual system and our everyday language, war and battle are foundational to our basic human experiences, and we also use these source domains for understanding how an argument works (Lakoff and Johnson 4–5). Similar to Sontag's strategy of tracing, we can follow the source 'battle' to study how it is applied to vastly different target domains such as illness, argument and courtroom. I am grateful to Danielle Spencer for helping me clarify this point.
3. Again, there are good reasons to see the baseball comparison as a separate metaphor. See my argument in endnote 2.
4. 'Historical decline', in my opinion, does not only reference past eras, it may also describe the diachronic experience of a person's life history.
5. Broyard also has unrealistic expectations towards his doctors, whom he prefers to be heroic and triumphant: in imagining what almost sounds like a physician superhero or superman, the heroic doctor, as Major argues, is 'a reflection of his own romantic and emergent self, the strong man informed by truth and poetry, straddling the two worlds of the redeemed and the fallen' (Major 109).
6. Broyard's work is often celebrated, and his essays are standard references in Medical Humanities and Narrative Medicine contexts. Richard M. Ratzan, for example, describes Broyard's *Intoxicated* as 'a treasure trove of unique material', acknowledging the 'unusually light and clear style' of his writing and adding: 'There are countless sentences that one wishes to include in a course on literature and medicine.' In *JAMA*, Helle Mathiasen

and Joseph S. Alpert praise the 'wisdom and beauty' of Broyard's essays and suggest they should be 'required reading for patients, physicians, and all people who seek a dignified life and death' (2711).

7. Sedgwick locates her observations within the origins and cultural meanings of HIV. Similar to Susan Sontag, Sedgwick is interested in describing what the knowledge about HIV *does* in a culture (124–5). Unlike Sontag, Sedgwick does not seek to denounce or expose the hidden meanings of HIV; she is interested in the performative quality of these meanings.

8. Sedgwick's concept has also caused ripples in literary scholarship and is repeatedly referenced by scholars associated with postcritical approaches to literature (e.g. Best and Marcus; Felski, *Uses, Limits*). In nuancing the criticism that reparative approaches have encountered, Heather Love reminds us that we should not only read reparatively and that there is much to appreciate in the 'energizing force of paranoia' (240).

9. In queer culture, the expression 'reading someone or something' designates the practice of 'pointing out a flaw in someone else (usually publicly and in front of them) and exaggerating it' (see https://www.urbandictionary.com/define.php?term=Reading). Jayme Deerwester, for example, discusses the 'reading challenge' of drag queen RuPaul as an example of such a practice. While this connotation of reading seems fairly recent (it is not listed, for example, in the 2020 edition of the *OED* which features an entry on 'read' that was last updated in 2008), it speaks to the semantic capaciousness of ordinary words. I am grateful to Anna Fenton-Hathaway for pointing out to me these additional connotations and connections to camp and queer culture.

10. Broyard had a reputation of being an 'insistently seductive womanizer' (Linfield). Moreover, in *Intoxicated*, he keeps emphasising his heterosexual desire, for example when he comments on the attractiveness of nurses and his erotic experiences with women (26, 56). Camp per se is, of course, not limited to LGTBQ contexts, as Richard Dyer has argued, and camp has been adopted by straight people, even though such appropriations risk taking away some of camp's sharpness (60).

11. Apart from Dominique Bauby's *The Diving-Bell and the Butterfly*, Jurecic also uses a reparative reading in *Illness as Narrative* for her analysis of Ann Fadiman's *The Spirit Catches You and You Fall Down*.

12. For example, unlike the storytellers of tall tales, Broyard keeps reminding us that we are not supposed to take him too seriously. Tall tales do not provide such clues of warning. Moreover, unlike the tall tale, Broyard is not set on fooling or deceiving his readers. He is also neither inflating the hardships of his illness (even though he does describe some graphic details) nor he is engaging in a deadpan presentation of his suggestions (as the tall-tale tellers did). Instead, he is exaggerating his *idealistic* visions to a point of incredulity.

13. Banner offers another intriguing reading of Broyard's imposture, linking it to his successful passing and the structural racism of medical care (35–7).

14. Gustave Flaubert famously claimed 'Madame Bovary, c'est moi', thus demonstrating a likeness between his heroine and his own abandon in reading. On the cultural and gendered complexities of the Madame Bovary reference, see Huyssen (44–62).
15. Banner's foregrounding of the structural and political implications of Broyard's writing is intriguing in this context because it sheds a different light on the question of agency. As a writer who passed for white, Broyard's use of metaphors is not only a form of resourceful self-stylisation that is grounded in his ingenuity and individual agency. Such a reading risks eluding the social structures to which Broyard responded as well. A different reading informed by the structural constraints Broyard faced would emphasise that Broyard's style of using metaphors responds to a system that leaves him no other choice. In order to survive, that is, he has to use a style informed by concealment, mistakes, pretence, and layers of signification so that he avoids being diminished and downgraded as a human being, a process he experienced first-hand when his father fell ill (Banner 36–43). Broyard himself, however, favoured a concept of identity that consists of 'innate qualities and developed characteristics as an individual' over an identity that is defined by a particular social group (Broyard, 'Portrait'). Broyard championed this view in an article in *Commentary Magazine* on the 'Inauthentic Negro', where he acknowledged that

> Obviously, of course, the Negro cannot develop in complete independence of his situation, but he can resist it in a more useful way; he can react against his reactions, and absent himself from the dialectical process of discrimination until – pushed by progress in understanding – it lamely falls over on one lee. (n. pag.)

Thus, there is an important double vision, too, in this structural approach to Broyard and the strategies that he employs.
16. The disturbed country echoes Susan Sontag's 'kingdom of the sick' (3); likewise, the comparison of the body to a building, such as a house or factory, is a familiar association (see, for example, Fritz Kahn's medical illustrations); and the common nightmare of needing to perform but feeling (and being) poorly prepared seems almost archetypal. Against these well-known metaphors, Broyard's comparison of illness to a love affair seems brand new. The metaphor forges an unusual relation to illness: it is based on infatuation, enchantment and fascination. However, there is also a darker side to the metaphor given that the woman is demented, which implies hardship, sorrow, insecurity and unpredictability.
17. A similar suggestion for an increased transparency is made by Martha Stoddard Holmes in 'After Sontag'. Holmes favours similes over metaphors because similes make the comparison overt. I elaborate on this thought in Chapter 7.

5. David Foster Wallace's Troubled Little Soldier: Narrative and Irony

The US-American writer David Foster Wallace (1962–2008) is associated with postmodernism and a loose group of authors – the New Sincerity Movement – who departed from the stance of irony and parody common in 1990s literature.[1] Wallace's oeuvre comprises three novels as well as several collections of short stories and essays. Compared to the previous authors discussed here, Wallace is not one of the usual suspects referenced in the field of Medical Humanities and Narrative Medicine, even though his writing – especially *Infinite Jest* (1996) – deals with all kinds of human suffering, from drug and alcohol addiction to depression and suicide. The short story 'The Depressed Person', for example, published in *Harper's Magazine* in 1998, deals with a nameless woman who is trapped in a spiral of painful, (self-)destructive thought patterns that represent the agony of her experiences with depression – or claim to do so.[2] In an earlier story from 1984, 'The Planet Trillaphon as It Stands in Relation to the Bad Thing', clinical depression, too, takes centre stage as the narrator, an unnamed, twenty-one-year-old, highly eloquent Brown University student, struggles with the effects of the antidepressant he takes against the 'Bad Thing'. While 'The Depressed Person' uses practically no metaphors to represent 'the impossibility of sharing or articulating' the pain of depression (57), 'The Planet Trillaphon', by contrast,[3] is permeated with comparisons through which its first-person narrator tries to convey the experience of severe clinical depression. These comparisons for depression comprise common source domains for illness (battle, journey) and depression (dark hole, suffocation, glass jar) as well as the narrator's attempt at a metaphor of his own. Like the writers I discussed earlier, Wallace uses these metaphors creatively by questioning, expanding and elaborating them, placing special attention on one consequence of battle, namely defeat. As demonstrated by Joan Didion's writing on migraine, a focus on defeat is not necessarily problematic; Wallace's approach to the often-dreaded side of the battle comparison bears out this insight. His innovation is to invite us to challenge the negative associations of defeat not only via his ingenious use of metaphor but also via narrative form.

In earlier chapters I showed how narrative analysis contributes to metaphor analysis by focusing on the narrative scenarios inherent in metaphor. 'The Planet Trillaphon', however, makes it clear that metaphor can also be bound up with other choices a writer makes, such as narrative voice, characterisation and narrative structure. Indeed, 'The Planet Trillaphon' may even be understood as *meta-metaphorical* in that its narrative form mirrors qualities that are typical of metaphor: contradiction, relationality, and a constant tension among distance, proximity and conflation.

This chapter uses narrative analysis to illuminate Wallace's use of metaphors, arguing that his unique approach to narrative voice and structure might be seen as a remedy for metaphors that seem to close something down. As Wallace's writing illustrates, narrative devices – as well as the employment of another trope, irony – can destabilise too-narrow and too-rigid assertions made via metaphor. Because the text's genre is so difficult to determine – is it autobiographical or fictional?[4] – 'The Planet Trillaphon' extends my discussion of illness writing beyond the illness essay or pathography; because Wallace's writing deals with psychological illnesses, it also extends my discussion of metaphor beyond the somatic.

A TROUBLED LITTLE SOLDIER TAKES A TRIP

Depression is difficult to describe and explain. To Andrew Solomon, it 'can be described only in metaphor and allegory'; prominent metaphors include drowning or suffocation (qtd in Conway 90). According to Kathlyn Conway, however, depression 'cannot be controlled by language', and thus 'defies expression' (89). Although numerous authors – among them Virginia Woolf, William Styron, William James, Edgar Allan Poe, Albert Camus and Sarah Kane – have attempted just that, Conway remains sceptical. Apart from exceptions such as Dante's metaphor of illness as a 'dark wood', she finds the language of depression to be 'surprisingly devoid of evocative images; instead it connotes absence, nothingness, darkness, and confusion' (91). Contrary to Conway's assessment, Jamie Redgate finds in Wallace's 'The Planet Trillaphon' a myriad of metaphors for depression; so many, in fact, that the sheer quantity undermines the purpose: 'no one description of depression is ever accurate: it has to be amended and changed for each individual who reads them' (285). And Wallace's narrator, Redgate argues, is very much aware of this challenge (285).

In an unexpectedly light-hearted, conversational and ironic tone, 'The Planet Trillaphon' tells the story of a young man who is diagnosed with severe clinical depression. The narrator calls this illness the 'Bad Thing'. After a number of critical symptoms and incidents – hallucinations, nausea, crying for no reason, a suicide attempt and a hospitalisation – the narrator starts taking antidepressants, which make him feel as if he were living on another planet, a planet he calls 'Trillaphon'.[5] In interspersed anecdotes, the narrator recounts the incidents that led to his present state on planet Trillaphon. But he interrupts the narration of events with a segment consisting of six paragraphs (28–30), in which he tries to explain what depression is and what it feels like. This segment is different from the rest of the text: it is based around metaphors rather than events, it repeatedly refers to an unidentified 'you', and it makes a series of atemporal propositions and injunctions. Still, two metaphors – journey and battle – can be found both in this segment and in the rest of the text, suggesting these metaphors' prominence and durability across illness and form (Semino et al. 'Online Use').

The journey metaphor is used for the first time when the narrator describes his life as a 'trip' that he has taken from planet Earth to Trillaphon (26), invoking both the notion of a short voyage or journey and, in American slang, a 'hallucinatory experience induced by a drug' ('trip'). This double entendre is clever because, for one, it alludes to the hallucinations the narrator is about to describe and, for another, it circles back to the side effects of the 'drugs', the antidepressants, which the narrator, as he explains in the opening sentences, has been taking for a year and which give him an out-of-body experience, quite similar to the effects of LSD or marijuana. For the remainder of the text, the narrator's 'trip' is defined by different stages, which correspond to an array of symptoms – hallucinations, nausea, crying and so on – and distinct settings – prep school, university, hospital, planet Earth and planet Trillaphon. In organising the story via the journey metaphor, readers are invited to become the narrator's travel companions.

The battle metaphor, too, structures the narrator's account and characterises him. The notion of a war is used a few paragraphs into the story, when the narrator has just conveyed to the reader the early stage of his illness: hallucinations about a gory wound on his face that led to his first incident of serious self-harm. He concludes the anecdote by maintaining: 'I think that year everyone began to see that I was a troubled little soldier, including me' (27). The soldier-metaphor is used seven times throughout the story, but it does not evoke the common image of the heroic, victorious type of soldier. Instead, we are meeting a soldier who seems forlorn, depleted and diminutive. For example, after the narrator has overcome the first symptoms of his disease, the hallucinations, we expect him to come out of the struggle a winner. Instead, painful memories haunt him. Even though he 'survived', he still experiences 'short flashes when I saw mirrors out of the corners of my eyes and stuff' (27). The narrator appears as a traumatised veteran grappling with a lurking fear that the battle is not over yet and that other defeats and losses await him. Indeed, only a few paragraphs later, in the middle of that six-paragraph explanation of his depression experience, he refers to the battle metaphor once more.

> Because the Bad Thing not only attacks you and makes you feel bad and puts you out of commission, it especially attacks and makes you feel bad and puts out of commission precisely those things that are necessary in order for you to fight the Bad Thing, to maybe get better, to stay alive. This is hard to understand, but it's really true. Imagine a really painful disease that, say, attacked your legs and your throat and resulted in a really bad pain and paralysis and all-around agony in these areas ... you wouldn't be able to run for help for those poor legs, just exactly because your legs would be too sick for you to run anywhere at all ... This is the way the Bad Thing works: it's especially good at attacking your defense mechanisms. The way to fight against or get away from the Bad Thing is clearly just to think differently, to reason and argue with yourself, just to change the way you're perceiving and sensing and processing stuff. But you need your mind to do this ... and that's exactly what the Bad Thing has made too sick to work right. (29)

Here the narrator activates some of the typical features of the source domain 'battle': there is a cunning attacker, and the soldier tries to defend himself by warding off dangerous blows. The narrator also activates features of the metaphor that have been discussed as the downsides or limitations of the battle metaphor, such as failure, defeat and shame. For example, we do not get the feeling that the 'troubled little soldier' is really fighting. In fact, what he describes is a situation of feeling paralysed and overwhelmed – 'put out of commission', as he says, by the enemy-illness. We begin to understand that his opponent has incapacitated the soldier by moving behind enemy lines, infiltrating the soldier's system and attacking from within. The boundaries between attacker and victim have blurred. What kind of battle is being described here? A guerrilla war? A Cold War scenario?

In any of these scenarios, we come to see, the soldier does not stand a chance. The narrator has pushed the battle metaphor to its limits: the soldier/narrator is troubled, little and listless, and the act of fighting is one-sided and hopeless. In his attempt to describe depression, the narrator uses the battle metaphor to capture something truthful about his experience, but he also activates some of the dreaded negative sides of the metaphor. Self-destruction and surrender (i.e. suicide) seem like the obvious choices in this unequal fight. Yet surrender need not be a bad thing.

SURRENDERING: JOAN DIDION MAKES PEACE

In her essay 'In Bed', Joan Didion explores how the negative side of battle and warfare need not be quite so harmful or limiting. Indeed, Didion even calls defeat a form of healing that she activated when she was dealing with her own illness, migraine.[6] That Didion associates her surrender to migraine with such positive meanings is astonishing because defeat and resignation are often associated with the opposite, namely shame and lack – of courage, will, the right attitude. As Siri Hustvedt argues on the same topic, a position of resignation is considered 'un-American' and those who do surrender are considered losers (*Looking* 24). And yet, both Hustvedt and Didion find relief in what is socially and culturally shunned.[7]

'In Bed' was written in 1968 and published in the essay collection *The White Album* (1979). In the short, 1,400-word essay, Didion describes how she learned to deal with the debilitating migraines that she has known since she was eight years old. Now thirty-four years of age, she has migraine 'attacks' three to five times a month; this 'physiological error' is, she maintains, 'central to the given' of her life (168). Repeatedly using expressions of war, for example when she speaks of her migraine as 'attacks' or says she 'fought migraine' when she was a student (169), Didion explains that she used to live 'in spite of' migraine, and her fight was characterised by denial (169). In part, this denial was due to the fact that she experienced her migraine as 'a shameful secret' designating a 'chemical inferiority', an affliction associated with 'bad attitudes, unpleasant tempers, wrongthink' (169–70). Migraine is thus fraught with cultural values, judgements and misunderstandings which increase Didion's suffering and spur her fighting attitude.[8]

Didion rethinks the notion of warfare and battle over the course of her essay. The first instance of this rethinking occurs when she relabels her fight with migraine as a 'guerrilla war' (172). In doing so, Didion activates a new, slightly different meaning of warfare: instead of the big, dramatic conflict typical of a military war, a guerrilla war is, literally, a small, irregular series of skirmishes in which the attacks are launched by 'small bodies of men acting independently' ('guerrilla war'). Applied to Didion's life and her fight against migraine, the notion of a guerrilla war implies, as Didion realises, that the triggers for her migraine come from small disturbances and irregularities in her everyday life which are difficult to predict because, like guerrilla fighters, they act by surprise and in small, independent units. Such irregularities include 'small household confusions, lost laundry, unhappy help, canceled appointments ... [and] days when the telephone rings too much and I get no work done and the wind is coming up' (172).[9]

The second instance of Didion's creative rethinking occurs when she recounts, in the two final paragraphs, how she learned to live with migraine. Realising that there is no 'escape' from heredity, she begins to elaborate associations with warfare that are often tacit and implied but rarely addressed in the context of illness. Like Wallace's narrator, that is, she elaborates the possibility of surrender as an outcome of war. Moreover, she makes peace with this possibility. She starts to regard migraine 'as more friend than lodger' (172), and with this personified version of her migraine, she has 'reached a certain understanding', meaning that she has learned to read the signs of when her migraine-friend might be on its way (172). Thus, the migraine-enemy who launches attacks and destroys her health, the lodger who invades her body and mind, is rethought in a different role, as that of a friend. As a result, her relation to migraine shifts into one of peace-making and diplomacy rather than aggression and retaliation. In fact, Didion maintains that she no longer fights migraine: 'I lie down and let it happen' (172). Grasping that surrender, failure and a binary separation into friend or enemy risk further stigmatising the sick, Didion manages to embrace these polar opposites in such a way that they become enabling: in identifying as the loser of the battle, she comes to fraternise with the enemy.

In Didion's use of the warfare metaphor, a deliberate acceptance of defeat is beneficial because it implies acceptance, peace and harmony. While it is not healing in the sense that migraine is overcome, we do witness Didion finding a way of living *with* – not *against* or *in spite of* – her illness. Extending the battle metaphor thus contributes to a pleasant sense of resolution by the end of the essay. This raises a number of additional questions about Didion's strategy.[10] For my purposes here, though, I want to highlight that this pleasing sense of resolution also depends on the narrative choices Didion made – choices that align with sturdy cultural narratives of self-improvement and redemption.[11] For example, the text is informed by notions of personal growth and learning; it features an epiphany and a turning point; and it supplies narrative closure by ending on a positive note – 'I count my blessings' (172). With these final words, Didion, one could argue, meets the standard narrative expectations and (re)creates a balance or harmony.

DEFEAT: CLOSED DOWN AND OPENED UP

There is no such harmonious final image or resolution in 'The Planet Trillaphon'; defeat is and remains a highly unsettled, agonising state for its narrator. His sense of being overpowered manifests in a harrowing uncertainty about how his future life, which started with so much promise, can unfold in the face of an incapacitating illness. Moreover, it becomes actualised in his attempted suicide, which he describes as a way of 'just being orderly' (30). Following the narrator's line of thinking, someone who commits suicide is

> just giving external form to an event the substance of which already exists and has existed in them over time. Once you realize what's going on, the event of self-destruction for all practical purposes exists. There's not much a person is apt to do in this situation, except 'formalize' it, or, if you don't quite want to do that, maybe 'E.C.T.' [Electro-Convulsive Therapy] or a trip away from the Earth to some other planet, or something. (30)

The matter-of-factness with which the narrator considers suicide 'just' a formal act, a logical consequence and imperative, highlights how undesirable the alternatives (E.C.T. or drugs) seem to him. Indeed, we already know that, for the narrator, the use of antidepressants is itself a form of death, given that he describes it as having left the earth. E.C.T. also has a destructive potential because it can erase a patient's memory, such as a person's name and place of residence (26). Rather than opening up new ways of living with depression, as it eventually does for Didion, for this narrator the battle metaphor appears to close down what it means to live with depression.

Yet, the way in which Wallace presents limiting metaphors simultaneously invites us to open them up again. A closer look at the story's narrative features is enlightening in this regard. The battle metaphor and other metaphors are not suspended in a vacuum; they are embedded in a narrative characterised by a distinct structure, perspective and tone. In Wallace's hands, these devices work against the limitations and constraints that these metaphors seem to introduce in the text.

A lack of closure is one of the narrative features that stands out in 'The Planet Trillaphon'. In contrast to Didion's text, Wallace's story provides no such sense of resolution. In fact, the text ends midsentence in yet another attempt by the narrator to explain 'that the Bad Thing is really' (33). With this unfinished sentence, the reader hangs in limbo: Did we miss the last page? Will the narrator find a way to deal with his illness? Will he return to planet Earth? Will he make another suicide attempt? This lack of closure amplifies the sense of failure and defeat that pervades the story: despite the narrator's eloquent attempts to describe what the Bad Thing really is, he has not managed to offer a satisfactory account of what depression is really *like*. Such a failure of (or refusal to) offer closure emerges again in 'The Depressed Person'. In this story, Wallace ends the account with a set of questions, and in doing so, the story echoes the sense of circularity we draw from reading the protagonist's endlessly spiralling thoughts.[12] Moreover, this ending of 'The Depressed Person' returns the reader to the problem raised in the first paragraph, that of an essentially hopeless situation: 'The depressed person was in terrible and unceasing emotional pain, and the impossibility of sharing or articulating this pain was itself a component of the pain and a contributing factor to its essential horror' (57). Thus, in both of Wallace's stories about depression, he displays the narrators' attempts and (alleged) failures to fully convey their experiences.

While a lack of closure can of course be read as a narrative failure, it might also be understood as an invitation to accept the open, provisional nature of the narrator's attempt to describe his illness. That is, the final word on the narrator's fate has not been spoken. In ending mid-sentence, we are prompted to wonder: What other way of describing the Bad Thing was the narrator attempting? Is there another metaphor that would be more apt? The battle metaphor and its notion of defeat is, as we know, just one version of the narrator's experiences; the narrator himself drops the notion of battle at some point to explore other metaphors. Even though 'The Planet Trillaphon' seems to flaunt failure at the level of content and form, it nonetheless stresses the inherent provisional nature of such statements, whether voiced figuratively via metaphor or insinuated via the narrative's open-ended, fragmentary structure. In doing so, the story challenges us to hold off settling the problem prematurely, asking us instead to actively contemplate the narrator's choices.

IMAGINE! SIMILES OF DEPRESSION

Besides the lack of closure, 'The Planet Trillaphon' uses other strategies to question or even reanimate metaphors that seem closed off or limited. For example, when the narrator interrupts his story to describe what depression feels like, he refers to three comparisons he has heard applied to the experience – being underwater, being under a glass jar and falling into a black hole. I will focus on the 'underwater' comparison here to highlight how, first, the narrator refers to these explanations through simile rather than through metaphor, raising questions about the relationship between source and target; and second, how the simile is embedded in a text that changes from first-person narration to a second-person point of view, raising additional questions about the relational dimensions of comparisons in general.[13]

The 'underwater' simile is mentioned after a rather banal description of depression: being depressed, the narrator thought previously, is an intense but temporary sadness. However, as he comes to understand, the Bad Thing is very different, and worse:

> A very glib guy on the television said some people liken it to being underwater, under a body of water that has no surface, at least for you, so that no matter what direction you go, there will only be more water, no fresh air and freedom of movement, just restriction and suffocation, and no light. (I don't know how apt it is to say it's like being underwater, but maybe imagine the moment in which you realize, at which it hits you that there is *no* surface *for you*, that you're just going to drown in there no matter which way you swim; imagine how you'd feel at that exact moment, like Descartes at the start of his second thing, then imagine that feeling in all its really delightful choking intensity spread out over hours, days, months … that would maybe be more apt.) (28)

What happens in this short passage? First, we can observe how the narrator tests the aptness of the comparison and then expands it. He imaginatively unfolds the metaphorical scenario that 'the glib guy' suggested and adds more aspects to it, such as a focus on the individual sufferer, an incidental mentioning of Descartes's *Meditations*, and a comment on the temporal dimension of the suffering. In a sense, the metaphor becomes more alive, more immediate and more his own through these elaborations. It also becomes more harrowing, agonising and constricting. We are trapped.

But we should note that, rather than saying depression *is* drowning or *is* being underwater, the narrator makes clear that depression is *likened* to drowning or is *like* being underwater. In using a simile rather than a metaphor, he makes transparent that he is inviting us to make an act of comparison. This is an important distinction from metaphor, I propose, because the use of simile foregrounds the likeness and similarity between the two domains.[14] While a metaphor would imply a fusion between depression and drowning via the copula 'be' (which is the basic gesture of metaphor), a simile 'leaves both vehicle and tenor visible and distinct, neither incorporated into the other' (Holmes 271). A simile thus emphasises that there is a *relationship* of similarity between the two domains; and this highlighted relationality also manifests in other aspects of Wallace's story.

One intriguing narrative choice Wallace makes is that while the majority of the story is told from a first-person perspective, he sometimes invokes an interlocutor, a *you*, to whom the narrator speaks. While this *you* is also addressed in the first paragraphs of the story, it becomes most prominent in the metaphor segment. In fact, in this segment, the second-person narration takes over for a few paragraphs and replaces the I-narration. Rather than as a single distinct persona, though, the *you* can be understood as representing either the reader or the narrator himself.[15] For example, when the narrator maintains 'I had previously sort of always thought that depression was just sort of really intense sadness, like what you feel when your very good dog dies' (28), he seems to be speaking to himself, thus conjuring up a kind of split or second identity. In this sense, 'the *you* covers up for an *I* of the protagonist in the grip of narrative experience' (Fludernik, 'Second Person' 222; original emphasis). Following Ursula Wiest-Kellner, a you-narration emphasises the otherness and isolation of the protagonist (qtd in Schwibbe 208). But this *you* also seems to address the reader, especially when it is paired with imperative verbs, such as 'imagine'. Following this reading, the narrator appears as someone who trespasses the boundaries of the text by establishing a dialogic communication with the implied reader. This addressee, the reader, turns into an 'actant', who 'instantiates an existential bond with his or her former (discourse) self, positing a subjective verisimilar identity between the address-you and the protagonist-you' (Fludernik, 'Second Person' 221–222). The narrator and implied reader thus blend into a hybrid diegetic creature (Wiest-Kellner qtd in Schwibbe 208). Importantly, in pulling down the fourth wall (Konstantinou 91), Wallace makes us aware of our function as readers; we are prompted to self-reflexively consider our position towards the claims made in the text. The uses of the *you*-address, second-person narration and imperative verbs thus produce an ambivalent effect on our relationship with the text: on the one hand, we are invited to immerse ourselves in the narrator's imaginative journey; on the other hand, the text invokes a meta-discourse entailing detachment and critical distance – the opposite of immersion. Thus our relation to the narrator and the narrator's relation to us is one of oscillation: even though (or in spite of) the narrator's continuous attempts both to close the gap between himself and his illness and between himself and the reader, we are also pushed away, made to observe all of these attempts at a critical distance.

What does this juxtaposition of simile on the one hand and narrative discourse on the other imply for the uses of metaphor? It offers a way out. I suggested that the narrator has driven a comparison into an impasse: in elaborating on the notion of drowning, he intensifies the situation by adding more and more factors that increase the feeling of hopelessness. In inviting us, via his narrative choices, to follow his imagination, we are just as trapped as the imagined person with depression. This is a clever, highly effective move which demonstrates that the strategies for handling metaphor and simile, such as questioning, elaborating and expanding them, can actually make a metaphor more dangerous and more limiting. However, we are also given an escape path, a way of breathing air into a metaphor that seems hermetically sealed: in foregrounding the *relationality* between source and target, narrator and reader, via second-person narration and the use of similes, the story leaves room for us to step back, to resist the affective pull of the story and wonder if the simile that is suggested is really 'more apt', as the narrator claims.

While my attention to the story's complex destabilising effects may seem theoretical or academic, I have found that many readers with whom I discussed 'The Planet Trillaphon' describe these very effects when asked to characterise the story. For example, when I ask students (some of whom are medical students with little or no specific training in close reading) to reflect on their reading experiences, they typically convey a wide range of emotional involvements: they were annoyed, could not finish the reading in one go, skipped passages because they had had enough, felt overwhelmed and shaken by what they read, sympathised with the narrator, considered the comparisons compelling and apt or blown-up and exaggerated, and so on. The students' diverse responses suggest to me that they were thrown off balance by the story's way of unsettling certainties and questioning fixed meanings. These effects are, I think, caused by Wallace's narrative choices: in keeping the story open-ended (thus frustrating our expectations of closure and resolution) and in confronting us with a narrator who shamelessly tries to pull us into his world of pain and suffering while simultaneously alienating us, he puts us on a vector of relationality where we shuttle continuously between distance and proximity. The way relationality is problematised in the story is echoed, too, on other levels. Not only does the story repeatedly use spatial metaphors (think of the narrator who speaks from outer space), the story also self-reflexively comments on relationality in its title. 'The Planet Trillaphon As It Stands in Relation to the Bad Thing' foregrounds the relationship between the effect of the antidepressant and the illness itself. And these two elements, as we gather quickly, do not stand in a good relation because either causes loss and incapacities.

The question of relationality – How close is okay? How much distance is necessary? – is eventually pushed to its extreme when the narrator proposes his own metaphor for depression.

THE ILLNESS IS YOU

After Wallace's narrator has presented and expanded three similes for depression – being underwater, being in a glass jar, falling into a black hole – all of which he has heard elsewhere, he describes what *he* thinks 'the Bad Thing is like' (29):

> To me it's like being completely, totally, utterly sick. I will try to explain what I mean. Imagine feeling really sick to your stomach. Almost everyone has felt really sick to his or her stomach, so everyone knows what it's like: it's less than fun. OK. OK. But that feeling is localized: it's more or less just your stomach. Imagine your whole body being sick like that: your feet, the big muscles in your legs, your collarbone, your head, your hair, everything, all just as sick as a fluey stomach. Then, if you can imagine that, please imagine it even more spread out and total. Imagine that every cell in your body, every single cell in your body is as sick as that nauseated stomach. Not just your own cells, even, but the e. coli and lactobacilli in you, too, the mitochondria, basal bodies, all sick and boiling and hot like maggots in your neck, your brain, all over, everywhere, in everything. All just *sick* as hell ... Just imagine that, a sickness spread utterly through every bit of you, even the bits of the bits. So that your very ... very *essence* is characterized by nothing other than the feature of sickness; you and the sickness are, as they say, 'one.' (29; original emphasis)

In the paragraphs that follow, the narrator reiterates and intensifies the point he has just made: the illness pervades body and mind. Then, he rephrases and clarifies what he calls above the oneness or unity of sickness and patient:

> *you're* the Bad Thing yourself! The Bad Thing is you. Nothing else: no bacteriological infection or having gotten conked on the head with a board or a mallet when you were a little kid, or any other excuse; you are the sickness yourself. (29; original emphasis)

This conflation of illness and self is certainly the emotional climax of the narrator's attempt to describe his agony. The source has been extended to such a degree that it now contains additional features, summing up the entire body and mind. Conversely, the target (person with depression) is entirely structured by the source (sickness or illness). Source and target have become interchangeable; they are the same. Following Paul Ricœur, a 'living metaphor' is constituted by 'a tension grounded in contradiction at the literal level' (253). In a dead metaphor,[16] however, this tension has disappeared (253). Has the narrator 'killed' his metaphor? Has he sucked out all its life by suspending its essential tension? Are we even dealing with a metaphor anymore? And how can we understand this conflation, in which dissimilarity and otherness between source and target – the essential features of metaphor – are swallowed up whole?

The US-American writer Siri Hustvedt argues that the full identification of illness and self is particularly prominent with neurological and psychiatric illnesses: while people *have* cancer, they *are* schizophrenic or bipolar (*Shaking Woman* 7). Similarly, linguist Suzanne Fleischman maintains that the possessive construction 'I have' posits illness as an external object, thus creating distance between patient and pathology (8–9).[17] The 'I am'-construction, however, is an existential statement in which a pathology is incorporated as part of a suffering individual (8). Such an identification with illness is often felt to be very real. Problematically, it may increase a patient's sense of isolation, otherness, failure and likelihood for self-blame.[18] Yet such identification with an illness is not *necessarily* problematic. Instead, it may represent an effort to integrate an illness into the story of one's life, or to make peace with it. For Hustvedt, who lives with migraine and a mysterious shaking disorder, identifying as a migraineur (and not a person with migraine) – despite all the problematic aspects of such an identification – chimes with her becoming 'curiously attached' to her migraines (*Shaking Woman* 189): 'I cannot really see where the illness ends and I begin; or, rather, the headaches are me, and rejecting them would mean expelling myself from myself' (189). For Hustvedt, her illness is thus not (or no longer) a mysterious Other or a hostile invasion from outside. 'The shaking woman', as she has named her other symptoms, moves from the third person into the first person and becomes part of the self. In her case, full identification is not a symptom or a problem to overcome; it is the result of living *with* (rather than constantly struggling *against*) a chronic disease. From this perspective, full identification may foreground a collaborative relationship between self and illness and need not imply erasure or closure.

In 'The Planet Trillaphon', however, full identification with the illness does not have such benign effects. On the contrary, it conveys (and successfully so) the totalising power and destructive nature of depression. This is depression viewed as complete usurpation, leaving no escape route, no fresh air, no distance. As with the previous metaphors, I want to suggest that the narrator's ingenuity (and problem) lies in the fact that he elaborates and expands the source domain to such a degree that he can relentlessly explore depression's darkest corners and parade its ugliest sides. At the same time, as shown above, readers are invited to unsettle and question the narrator's use of metaphor. Fully exploring this dynamic demands a close reading of both the story level and the level of discourse. What this double vision reveals is how Wallace uses narrative devices as strategies to reconsider a metaphor that his narrator has creatively elaborated – but whose wings he has brutally clipped in the process. Narrative analysis – particularly in such a rich case as Wallace's – can restore metaphor's potential to fly.

Consider the quotations above. The perspective of the first-person narrator is limited in so far as he is the centre of consciousness through whose eyes we see and perceive. This is a distinct choice, as Wallace could have chosen a different mode of narration. In 'The Depressed Person', for example, the story is focalised through the depressed person but narrated in the third person, allowing us some distance from her perspective. In that story, too, the narrator intersperses expressions or thoughts that provide comic relief in a narrative that is otherwise suffocating in its emotional tightness. 'The Planet Trillaphon' furnishes possibilities for distance as well – but via different means. When the first-person perspective changes into a you-narration, we may notice that it is not the 'I' that is fully identified with illness but the *you*. In other words, the narrator has removed himself from the equation and projects onto *you* – the reader? – a range of assumptions about how it feels to be depressed. While this information is of course grounded in the narrator's own experiences, it is useful to think of this information as assumptive or propositional: for one, because of the move from *I* to *you*, and for another, because similar projections and assumptions matter a great deal in the course of the actual story the narrator is telling us.

The narrator's problematic conflation of distance into sameness climaxes when the narrator relates the events that led to his suicide attempt. The narrator travels home to his parents for the holiday season, and an accident occurs during the bus ride for which the bus driver is fully responsible. Injured and afraid of losing his job, the bus driver starts crying, and the narrator cannot help but empathise with the bus driver's predicament.

> I felt unbelievably sorry for him, and of course the Bad Thing very kindly filtered this sadness for me and made it a lot worse. It was weird and irrational but all of a sudden I felt really strongly as though the bus driver were really me. I really felt that way. So I felt just like he must have felt, and it was awful. I wasn't just sorry for him, I was sorry as him, or something like that. All courtesy of the Bad Thing. (Wallace, 'The Planet Trillaphon' 30)

This collapsing of boundaries between the narrator and the bus driver – the full identification between these two very different human beings and consciousnesses – is presented as a symptom of the narrator's alarming condition: 'that's when the Bad Thing really got [the narrator] by the balls', Dr Kablumbus, the narrator's psychiatrist, maintains (31). The narrator can no longer distinguish between himself and the other, and this overidentification leads him to make a terrible mistake: In an attempt to help the bus driver, the narrator secretly places money and marijuana in the bus driver's pockets. Later, he realises that this clumsy effort to relieve some of the bus driver's worries via marijuana will very likely exacerbate his desperate situation. But there is no going back; the damage is done. At home, the heartbroken narrator pulls 'about three thousand electrical appliances' into his bathtub. He survives, is hospitalised and sent to 'the Troubled Little Soldier Floor' (31).

The narrator's inability to distinguish self from other and his tendency to project onto others what *he* thinks *they* feel are revealed as symptoms of his illness. This realisation raises specific questions about the story itself: to what extent we can trust the narrator's version of events? Is he a reliable source of information? Such doubts about the narrator's reliability are amplified by the fact that he presents himself as an ironist and describes the most harrowing experiences with lighthearted diction.

Trust and reliability are, of course, relative terms.[19] There is no absolute reliability, no single final version of events. Moreover, the narrator is frank with us from the start: we know that he is ill and seriously troubled; he never hides these facts from us. Our suspicion need not completely undermine the truth value of what he is telling about his illness, and indeed, there is good reason to take him seriously when he describes his subjective experiences. However, the text also *does* encourage us to be cautious, to take a step back and critically question the narrator's assumptions and projections. This tension prompts a number of questions: If the narrator fails to understand the dangers of overidentification in his own life, how trustworthy is the full identification he suggests when he describes his illness? And, if his overidentification with the bus driver is a symptom of his disease and thus pathological, what does this say about *our* degree of identification with the narrator?[20]

Empathy and identification are dominant themes across Wallace's works.[21] According to Kathleen Fitzpatrick, Wallace was critical of unthinking overidentification, not only when it

> promotes an essentialist model of selfhood – assuming an identity between self and Other – but [also when] it runs the risk of colonizing the Other's experience as one's own, whether by taking over the Other's perspective or by projecting one's own perspective onto the Other. (185)

Colonisation, essentialism and the appropriation of Otherness are issues that Audre Lorde, too, struggled with in her writing and which, in my discussion of Lorde, I show to be at the heart of comparison and metaphor. How does Wallace handle metaphor with respect to these risks? Does he suggest any solutions? I have argued so far that we can take Wallace's narrative choices as strategies to mitigate the harmful effects of overidentification. Fitzpatrick foregrounds Wallace's use of a rhetorical device – irony – to foster both a critical awareness of the risks of overidentification and to allow readers a safe space to explore their own affective responses, attitudes and subjective biases when reading a story about human suffering (185). In this view, rather than dismissing transferences, identifications and projections for their many risks, Wallace seeks a nuanced approach to (over)identification that would still enable human connection. If irony is a tool for readerly connection, as Fitzpatrick implicitly suggests, how does it work? And how does it reflect on metaphor?

ISN'T IT IRONIC?

Definitions of irony typically foreground a mismatch between two things that are brought together.[22] Verbal irony is commonly defined 'as a statement in which the meaning that a speaker implies differs sharply from the meaning that is ostensibly expressed' (Abrams 135). In other words, an ironic statement or text plays with the friction between what is directly said and what is unsaid or implied. Irony requires careful attention to clues so that the ostensible, literal statement is not taken for the only or actual thing (135–6). Scholars who work on irony's effects and functions often associate negative attitudes and purposes with ironic statements, such as derision and superiority. Linked with other, potentially malign styles of humour such as sarcasm, irony can be aggressive and destructive, manipulative and belittling. This form of irony 'jeopardizes social relationships and self-worth' (Scheel 18) in part by undermining common beliefs and the accepted usage of terms. It can be 'socially irresponsible' when, in grabbing for unconventional truth, it obfuscates and confounds its audience, leaves nothing but a gap (Colebrook 731–2). For this reason, irony has been associated with an attitude of distance and aloofness (Colebrook 732). If someone is ironic, she is exposing another's ignorance and creating exclusionary in-groups (Hutcheon 51). In short, while irony may inject ambiguity and complexity into a text, it also has many problematic functions and effects.

In 'The Planet Trillaphon', irony is everywhere. For example, when the narrator calls his suicide attempt a 'silly incident' or a 'really highly ridiculous incident' (26), both descriptions seem misplaced given the severity of the situation. He also summarises his distressing experiences of crying, nausea and hallucination as 'all this extremely delightful stuff' (28) when they clearly are not. Is he making light of what happened? Or making fun of himself? The narrator also claims that he does not want to elaborate on 'the silly incident', but then he does; he says he is not glib, but he flaunts his cleverness and eloquence throughout his writing; and he struggles to find adequate metaphors, even though, as he claims, the fight is over. Besides these implicit ironies, the narrator also explicitly mentions the irony he found in two situations. First, he considers it 'highly ironic' that the imagined wound in his cheek becomes 'a *real* wound' through the hands of the doctors at the hospital because they had to open up the stitches after an infection prevented the healing process (26; original emphasis). Second, by the end of the text, the narrator returns to the notion of irony when he speculates about a larger, underlying structure or design in his experiences that would link together the antidepressant, the name of the girl he meets in the clinic – May Aculpa – and the name of the bus driver via the initials of the M.A.O. inhibitor. It 'would be incredibly ironic', he says, if 'the bus driver I more or less killed had the initials M.A.' (33). And shortly before that he observes: 'May's initials are M.A., and when I think about her now I get so sad I go "O!"' (33). Why does Wallace use so much irony in 'The Planet Trillaphon'? And what does irony add to our understanding of the story and its metaphors?

As one of the hallmarks of early postmodernist texts, irony holds an ambivalent status in Wallace's thinking. He was intrigued by how postmodernists used it to debunk illusions and ridicule hypocrisies, and much of Wallace's own writing adopts an ironic tone. In an interview with Larry McCaffery, Wallace acknowledged irony's power: 'it splits things apart, gets up above them so we can see the flaws and hypocrisies and duplicates. ... Sarcasm, parody, absurdism and irony are great ways to strip off stuff's mask and show the unpleasant reality behind it' (McCaffery n. pag.). In Wallace's essay on television, 'E unibus pluram' (1993), however, he is also critical of what he calls the 'aura of irony' and offers a sweeping critique of the tyranny that irony has come to imply (174, 183): for ironists, he writes, 'expressions of value, emotion, or vulnerability' are naive and compared to 'a crime' ('E unibus pluram' 181, 183). As Wallace came to believe, irony's strengths are ultimately less than its harms, for the gaps it creates (between explicit and implicit meaning; between speaker and audience) exacerbate loneliness and isolation. In other words, irony has nothing to offer readers who seek solace, redemption or healing.[23] For this reason, Wallace argued that, at best, irony works to diagnose and liberate; at worst, it ridicules or even enslaves by creating a climate of detached weariness in which irony has become an end in itself and any effort at changing things for the better is condemned as pointless or sentimental (McCaffery). Given this view, Wallace's biographer D. T. Max maintains that Wallace became increasingly committed to 'single-entendre writing', that is, to forms of expression that meant what they said (Max, *Every Love* 158).[24]

Wallace, however, never completely abandoned irony but rather continued to struggle with understanding and exploring its potential. Lee Konstantinou describes Wallace's relationship to irony as 'postironic', suggesting that Wallace wanted to 'discover and develop a viable postironic ethos for U.S. literature and culture' and that, to achieve this aim, he used techniques of metafiction (84–5, 90–1). In Fitzpatrick's view, irony has a pro-social effect in Wallace's work. She argues that Wallace used irony not as a space of protection 'from the pain of connection but rather as a means of allowing those readers a safe enough space within which they can explore their own feelings of loneliness, of inadequacy, of duplicity, of failure' (185). This space, placed amid such a harrowing subject, may in fact enable intersubjective connection as it allows us to become aware of our own opacities, gaps, biases and desires (Fitzpatrick 186). But how can this side of irony be activated?

Linda Hutcheon's work on irony offers one answer. To her, the common definition of irony, the binary of 'said' and 'unsaid', is too simple and ultimately limiting because it considers irony a direct inversion in which what is said is rejected and substituted by what is unsaid (58). Hutcheon proposes a more capacious understanding of irony, one with nine social functions and effects including irony's ludic, complicating, reinforcing and self-protective functions (44–53). The distancing function of irony seems particularly relevant in the case of 'The Planet Trillaphon', which plays so conspicuously with proximity, distance and overidentification. To distance oneself via irony is, as Hutcheon argues, a double-edged sword: it might mean that the ironist becomes detached, uncaring and non-committal; but it may also allow for a new, and broader, perspective (36, 47). In the latter understanding, distancing can become an oppositional strategy against 'the tyranny of explicit judgments' and being 'pinned down' (47). 'The Planet Trillaphon' is, as I demonstrated earlier, replete with oppositional strategies as its narrator keeps evading and undermining overly narrow definitions of depression and illness identity. Irony, I want to suggest, is yet another strategy in Wallace's toolbox, allowing readers to distance themselves and destabilise seemingly fixed meanings. Juxtaposed with the narrative strategies I discussed, the question arises if and to what extent irony is different? Does it offer something in addition to destabilisation, resistance and critique?

There is, indeed, more to irony. In Hutcheon's study, irony is defined as relational, inclusive and differential (56),[25] and it is particularly the inclusive feature that seems relevant to my inquiry. Ironic meaning is inclusive, Hutcheon maintains, because it operates within a 'both/and' paradigm: rather than focusing on the two poles of said and unsaid, what matters is the 'perceptual or hermeneutic *movement between*' these poles, the 'simultaneous perception of more than one meaning' (57–8; original emphasis). In other words, 'ironic meaning is *simultaneously* double (or multiple), and ... therefore you don't actually have to reject a "literal" meaning in order to get at what is usually called the "ironic" or "real" meaning of the utterance' (58; original emphasis). This inclusive feature of irony resembles the definitions of metaphors that I am using – its tensional dynamic, the double vision it invites, the flickering simultaneity between the figurative and the literal. Metaphor and irony then make a similar gesture: they involve a double vision built on a gap, a disparity or incongruence.[26] If irony, as Hutcheon argues, has such inclusive potential, might it intensify a metaphor's capacity to expand our perception of the world? Could irony help us – to reiterate Sontag's phrasing – 'to *see* more, to *hear* more, to *feel* more' through a metaphor?

To test this hypothesis, I return to the journey metaphor in 'The Planet Trillaphon'. I discussed above the inherent double meaning of the narrator's word choice in calling his journey a 'trip' – it can be read as invoking the classic metaphor that 'illness is a journey' or it can be read as a hallucinatory experience. In many ways, the narrator's trip is more like the latter, as hallucinations are not only a symptom of his illness but also, as we learn by the end of the story, part of what it feels like, for the narrator, to be on Tofranil, the antidepressant he is taking. On Tofranil he is constantly sleepy, he has the impression that the ground is slightly tilted, and he hears 'a sort of electrical noise' that makes life on planet Trillaphon appear as 'a more electrical way of life' (33). We also find out that the narrator is smoking marijuana regularly because it helps him with another symptom, nausea. Marijuana plays a crucial role in another journey the narrator takes, the fateful bus ride, which is both an actual journey and a figurative one because it marks a stage in his illness journey. His illness progression and intermittent hallucinations are intersected with other – actual and figurative – journeys and departures: 'travelling' from life to death in his attempted suicide and relocating to the 'Troubled Little Soldier Floor' in the clinic (31). Three additional 'journeys' are evoked in 'The Planet Trillaphon': first, we learn that May, a girl the narrator meets during his stay at the clinic, has died in a car accident – during a trip she was taking with her drunken boyfriend (32). Second, when the narrator speaks of 'a trip' for the first time, he associates it with a metafictional comment: 'If someone tells about a trip he's taken, you expect at least some explanation of why he left on the trip in the first place' (26). In commenting on readers' expectations, the narrator alludes to the conventions of storytelling and thus self-reflexively suggests that he is grounding *his* account in such templates, such as the hero's journey. And lastly, in *The Amherst Review*, the college literary journal where the story first appeared, we find this comment in the list of contributors: 'David Wallace '85 is interested in philosophy and creative writing. As far as we know, he has never left this planet' (n. pag.). A student at Amherst College (rather than the narrator's Brown University), Wallace and his narrator both had to leave college for depression treatment (see endnote 3). During Wallace's second leave from Amherst, he started taking the antidepressant Tofranil and wrote 'The Planet Trillaphon' ('David Foster Wallace'). It is unclear who wrote (or suggested) the paratextual comment – the editors of *The Amherst Review*? Wallace himself? Suffice it to say that the comment also, quite obviously, returns to the theme of journey, and does so in a wonderfully ironic way because it discourages readers from drawing a parallel between narrator and author and thus undermines assumptions about the story's autobiographical nature – yet at the same time leaves the possibility of autobiographical correspondence open by pointing to the limited knowledge of the unspecified 'we' and by stating that Wallace did *not* leave a world behind (which he of course did do when he left school). The irony of the paratextual comment affords a flickering simultaneity between *is* and *is not* that builds on the journey metaphor's double vision of literal and figurative meanings.

To summarise, 'journey' is used *literally* to refer to a number of actual trips; it is used *figuratively* to describe the stages of the narrator's illness experience – and his life journey more generally, given that he is a young man who is coming of age; the concept of 'journey' is also used *meta-textually* when the narrator reflects on the conventions of storytelling; and, lastly, it can also be associated with *the reader's journey*, the roller coaster ride of different, even contradictory responses that the narrator courts in us. It is also ironic, on a structural level, that the narrator repeatedly reminds us of the great distance between Earth and Trillaphon when the relationality between distance and proximity is such a crucial topic on the other levels of the story as well. In paying attention to the diverse manifestations of 'journey' in the text, we recognise that multiple meanings are kept in suspense. These meanings do not contradict one another but follow an accretive 'both/and' paradigm, which, to follow Hutcheon's description, holds 'in suspension the said plus something *other than* and *in addition to* it that remains unsaid' or cannot be said (61; original emphasis). Irony here seems to function like yeast or baking soda: it makes a metaphor expand, soften and unfold. Or, to put it less metaphorically, the journey metaphor is refracted and in some of its meanings ironised – but not to the extent that one manifestation or meaning cancels out the other; rather, the metaphor's multiple dimensions exist side by side. Adding an analysis of irony to a close reading of metaphor can thus help tease out *more* in what a metaphor can make us see.

CONCLUSION

The central argument of this chapter (and book) is that metaphors themselves are neither good nor bad, but they do need to be grappled with. Wallace presents a narrator who ingeniously engages with common, existing and new metaphors. However, rather than rethinking the harmful sides of metaphors, this narrator is set on exploring their darkest corners in his attempt to explain what depression feels like. While the previous authors put a positive spin on limiting or constrictive metaphors, Wallace's narrator seeks instead to close down their remaining semantic capaciousness. Wallace's *text*, however, counterbalances the narrator's use of metaphors by unsettling and undermining his strategies via narrative devices such as voice and narrative structure. In other words, in 'The Planet Trillaphon', metaphors are rendered more limiting and more harmful; they are also, simultaneously, opened up again.

Narrative strategies and their analysis are not, however, a magic bullet for all kinds of misuses and abuses of metaphor. In this discussion, I have neatly aligned each problematic use of metaphor with a destabilising, undermining counterstrategy. While this approach has many benefits – helping us, for example, to rectify and balance out the narrator's problematic ways of closing down metaphors – it also risks stalling the power of metaphor in an either/or paradigm. We may wonder: If some narrative strategies can cancel out the harmful effects of a metaphor, what are we left with? To use an example, if we identify that the story in which a metaphor is embedded is open-ended, then the metaphor, too, is provisional, lacking a final ending. Therefore, if the narrator says, 'I lost', we know via the open-ended narrative that the fight may not be over yet. But what do we do with these contradictory pieces of information? Does one negate the power of the other?

Another problem with my juxtaposition of narrative analysis and metaphor analysis lies in the fact that what I suggested as useful strategies may apply only to particular cases. While the illness narratives by patients in health care contexts can be complex and layered – and may even use, for example, an open-ended structure or second-person narration – it is still difficult to compare such impromptu narratives to the self-reflexive, meta-narrative quality of Wallace's postmodernist text. To put it differently, Wallace's dazzling story about depression certainly constitutes fertile ground for combined narrative and metaphor analysis. But does it help us understand how people use metaphor in everyday speech?

In this study, I have chosen to focus on literary texts in order to ask which strategies renowned writers employ when they use, reuse and creatively misuse common metaphors. My analyses are, however, driven by a second, maybe idealistic question: Can we translate these writers' strategies into other contexts? In the case of Wallace's 'Trillaphon', irony may provide that translational link, in part because it is so common in ordinary conversation. Though irony is discussed critically in the context of health care communication (e.g. Berger et al.), it can also have benign social effects and functions, as Hutcheon and others have argued.[27] Imagine a patient who complains to a nurse, maybe with a quipping tone, that the attending physician is 'as kindhearted as a wolf'.[28] Clearly, this is an ironic comparison, suggesting that the physician is like a wolf and that wolves are kind-hearted (when both comparisons are wrong). In this instance, metaphor (or, better, simile) and irony rely similarly on a double vision built on a gap or incongruence between doctor and wolf, between desirable and undesirable features. The irony seems to intensify the metaphor. But what does it mean exactly that the doctor is not kind-hearted? How does the wolf-metaphor inform what is left unsaid? And how should our imagined nurse respond to this ironic comparison?

In the following chapter, I will make suggestions for how insights and methods from literary analysis can be carried over to more application-oriented contexts. The authors I have examined so far have modelled dexterous strategies for grappling with metaphors for their illness experiences. Most patients and clinicians will not engage with metaphors so sustainedly or so idiosyncratically, of course. But knowing how to analyse metaphors and how to apply a range of strategies for their use, reuse and creative misuse can be a valuable tool set in physician–patient communication, connection and understanding.

NOTES

1. This chapter further develops ideas I published in Heike Hartung's collection *Embodied Narration: Illness, Death and Dying in Modern Culture* (2018). I also wrote on 'The Planet Trillaphon' in an article on the pedagogy of narrative medicine, co-written with Anders Juhl Rasmussen ('Brugen'). I want to thank my colleagues at the 'Uses of Literature' group at SDU and my colleagues at JGU (particularly Prof. Dr Matthias Michal as well as the students of medicine, psychotherapy and American studies) with whom I have discussed the story and previous versions of the article and who have made me aware of important details.
2. Critics have suggested that 'The Depressed Person' is not actually about depression but about narcissism and that the original title was supposed to be 'The Devil' (e.g. Redgate 292). Wallace's biographer D. T. Max reads the story as 'revenge fiction' because he sees similarities between the protagonist of the story and Elizabeth Wurtzel, the author of *Prozac Nation* (1994), who allegedly rejected Wallace's romantic advances and lived with depression, too (Max, *Every Love* 241).
3. *Infinite Jest*, too, features metaphors of depression: psychotic depression is described, for example, as 'a large dark billowing shape' (649) or as 'a closed circuit' (696). The latter metaphor is built from the comparison of depression to torture with electric currents which are invisible but still very real. If a person with depression screams due to her invisible pain, the materiality of her pain is misrecognised when she is called psychotic and this in turn exacerbates her loneliness: nobody can see the pain because 'the current is both applied and received from within' (696).
4. Wallace wrote 'The Planet Trillaphon' when he was a student at Amherst College, studying philosophy and avidly reading postmodern writers, such as Thomas Pynchon and Donald Barthelme. The story was his debut as a writer, and the text was published in *The Amherst Review*, a year after Wallace had withdrawn from school for the second time to get treatment for his depression. This autobiographical background prompts Wallace's biographer D. T. Max to conflate author and narrator when he finds that 'the authorial "I" and the "I" of the narrator parallel each other in the story in a way they would never again in Wallace's fiction' (*Every Love Story* 34). However, it is difficult to determine Wallace's relation to his first launch into (creative) writing. Max suggests that Wallace may not have been very proud of this early story or may have found it 'too revealing' (*Every Love* 310n9) because Wallace never republished 'The Planet Trillaphon', as he did his other stories. Interestingly, after Wallace's suicide in 2008, the story continues to be read. In Germany, for example, it was translated by Ulrich Blumenbach and published by Kiepenheuer & Witsch in 2015. In the same year, an audiobook was released with Lars Eidinger, a renowned German actor, reading the story.

5. In fact, we learn that the narrator is taking 'Tofranil', an existing antidepressant. Trilafon is also an FDA-approved drug (a type of perphenazine), which is used in the treatment of psychoses, involving symptoms such as hallucinations, nausea and vomiting (see https://en.wikipedia.org/wiki/Perphenazine). The narrator explains that he changed the name to 'Trillaphon' because it resonates more with what he experiences: the word, he says, 'is more truly and electrical, and it just sounds more like what it's like to be there [being on anti-depressants]' (33).
6. Depression and migraine are very different illnesses, of course, but they share a recurring nature and are often associated with the psyche and mind rather than the body, even though both have physical causes, too.
7. To interpret surrender as a form of defeat is, of course, a binary conceptualisation of battle, in which there are only two options: winning and losing. A non-binary understanding also includes compromise or ceasefire as viable options that go beyond an either/or construct.
8. Didion also explores the material side of her migraine by referencing research on the chemical and physiological processes in the body and by exploring the dimensions of heritage and the predisposition to migraine that was passed down to her by her family. She also mentions psychological dimensions of migraine and the assumed personality traits that encourage migraine attacks. Even though her doctor initially misdiagnoses Didion by identifying her as a perfectionist housewife (which she denies she is), Didion accepts, to some degree, this explanation when she identifies as a compulsively perfectionist writer.
9. Guerrilla warfare and migraine medication bear similarities, too: in a guerrilla war, the standard weapons of the medical commanders and warlords no longer hold sway over the enemy-migraine. Likewise, migraine medication, as Didion reports, has many contraindications and is used only 'in the most incapacitating cases' (170).
10. We may wonder, for example, to what extent the sense of closure, which the essay provides, matches the ongoing quality of her chronic situation. Moreover, the notion of purging that Didion associates with surrender seems to problematically imply sin and shame. One may also wonder how 'In Bed' fits with Didion's other writing, such as the essay 'The White Album', which so overtly mistrusts the power of narrative and simple resolutions.
11. See, for example, the work on redemption narratives by McAdam as well as Ehrenreich's critique of the way the redemption narrative is problematically warped in what she calls the breast-cancer 'pink ribbon culture' (*Smile or Die*, 'Welcome to Cancerland'). For research on self-improvement narratives in health care contexts, see, for example, Gygax and Wohlmann ('Illness Narrative').
12. Some of my students read the ending of 'The Depressed Person' in a much more positive light, suggesting that the death of the therapist and the terminal illness of a close friend trigger an important change in the depressed

person. The final questions signal to them that she is ready to move on with her life even though her struggles may not be over.
13. For a discussion of the other two similes, see Wohlmann ('The Illness is You').
14. For a more elaborate discussion of the differences between metaphor and simile, see Chapter 7 and my article titled 'Symbol or Simile? Sylvia Plath's Poem "Tulips" and the Role of Language in Medicine' (2019).
15. In his discussion of Wallace's short story 'Octet' which also uses you-narration, Lee Konstantinou proposes that the 'you' can be understood as Wallace himself. This interpretation suggests, to Konstantinou, a metafictional dimension of the story (96).
16. For example, when we speak of a table leg, the figurative nature of the comparison is no longer transparent, and the fundamental difference between source (a part of the body used for walking and standing) and target (a supporting pillar on which a tabletop is placed) has disappeared due to usage. Over time, the source (leg) has been expanded and now also includes other objects.
17. Fleischman draws here on the work of medical semiotician Kathryn Vance Staiano.
18. Such processes have also been observed in the context of HIV/AIDS. In the early days of the virus, it felt utterly real and consistent to patients with HIV/AIDS that their illness was a punishment from God (Sontag, *Illness*; Treichler). Socio-cultural values and explanations of a disease were equated with a patient's personality. Indian American physician-writer Abraham Verghese, who worked with HIV patients in the 1980s, is convinced that such dead metaphors can kill: 'I lost two of my patients to suicide at a time when the virus was doing very little harm to them. I have always thought of them as having been killed by a metaphor, by the burden of secrecy and shame associated with the disease' ('Hope'). As Verghese's example illustrates, the full identification with illness can imply that social and cultural ascriptions, values and norms associated with an illness take on a material reality.
19. See, for example, James Phelan ('Estranging Reliability') and Dan Shen.
20. Another narrative device to be mentioned here is the namelessness of the narrator. Rather than giving us his proper name, the narrator refers to himself as a 'troubled little soldier'. This gap is also used in 'The Depressed Person', where not only the main character but also all other characters are defined by their functions: the therapist, the Support System, father and mother. The characters are types rather than rounded figures, which emphasises that they are completely swallowed by their function and that there is no room for anything else. Similarly, in 'The Planet Trillaphon', the narrator is absorbed by his illness. Yet, other characters in 'Trillaphon' do have names, such as Dr Kablumbus and May, the girl he meets on the psychiatry ward. Withholding one's name, we can speculate, is a strategy that leaves a secret. We are confronted with our limited knowledge about

the narrator, who remains distant and 'other'. Is this a warning that we cannot fully know the narrator? That we should be cautious about making assumptions and question his reliability? Should we trust someone who calls himself 'a troubled little soldier'? And, as a consequence, can we trust his use of metaphor?

21. For a more in-depth discussion of the role of empathy in Wallace's oeuvre, see Fitzpatrick (2012). In the context of Narrative Medicine interventions, I discuss empathy in relation to 'The Planet Trillaphon' in an article with Anders Juhl Rasmussen ('Brugen', only available in Danish) and in relation to 'The Depressed Person' ('Empathie und ihre Grenzen'; only available in German).

22. The term 'irony' goes back to Greek comedy where a character was 'a dissembler, who characteristically spoke in understatement and deliberately pretended to be less intelligent than he was' (Abrams 134). Over the years and centuries, irony's function to deceive was replaced with a focus on the rhetorical or artistic effects that irony adds to a text (135).

23. In *Infinite Jest*, for example, Wallace compares irony and recovery with oil and water, suggesting in the context of alcohol addiction that irony is counterproductive. For this reason, Leslie Jamison argues that, in Wallace's fiction, irony seems incompatible with a positive ethos of repair and healing (*Recovering* 349).

24. Wallace became increasingly committed to exploring the ways that literature can create and sustain human connections (see Fitzpatrick). Inspired by the New Sincerity Movement, with which Wallace is often associated, Wallace developed an approach to literary writing that 'actively courts an affective response' and wishes to establish an authentic connection with the reader (Fitzpatrick 184–6).

25. Irony is relational, Hutcheon argues, because it navigates a relation between the said and unsaid as well as a relation between ironist and interpreter (56).

26. For Hutcheon, irony and metaphor are markedly distinct. In introducing the third feature, irony's differential nature, Hutcheon foregrounds that irony is defined by difference whereas metaphor posits a similarity between source and target. Hutcheon's distinction is based on Paul de Man's definition of irony, who argued that in an ironic statement 'the sign points to something that differs from its literal meaning and has for its function the thematization of this difference' (de Man qtd in Hutcheon 61–2). I agree with Hutcheon's and de Man's distinction. In foregrounding their similarities here, I am interested in understanding how the effects and functions of irony and metaphor may speak to and intensify one another.

27. Following Berger et al., humour can be harmful and ostracising, but it also provides a sense of relief and community.

28. I found this example at https://literarydevices.net/irony/ (accessed 5 August 2020).

6. From Theory to Practice: A Method for Using Metaphor

How can the insights from the previous chapters be translated into everyday contexts and ordinary health care practice more specifically? How can practitioners and patients alike explore and evaluate the varied usability of metaphors? These questions are echoed in the calls for greater metaphor competence, metaphor literacy and metaphor reflexivity from the field of Medical Humanities (e.g. Bleakley 204; Holmes 272; Reisfield and Wilson; Semino et al., 'Online Use' 6).[1] While a number of studies do answer these calls, few ground their recommendations in established metaphor theory and analysis. This chapter departs from these studies by using metaphor theory and analysis and by spelling out five concrete steps. Each step is tied to specific actions and illustrated by metaphors used in clinical practice and health care. In the last section, I make a short excursion and add the role of symbols and similes to this book's privileging of metaphor.

The method[2] I am proposing here is not a new invention. By contrast, it heavily draws on established methods such as close reading and metaphor analysis. And yet, these methods have largely remained exclusive to textual or cultural analysis. In other words, the value of this chapter does not lie in novelty but in laying out as clearly as possible a method of how metaphors can critically and mindfully be engaged with. That this method may result in a more skilled and reflexive use of metaphors seems reasonable, but, at this stage, it is a hypothesis that requires empirical research.

In shifting my focus from literary writers to the ways metaphors are used by patients and health care providers in everyday contexts, I suggest that a creative engagement with metaphors is not unique to professional writers or literary critics. Rather, as the following examples show, creative uses of metaphor take place in non-literary contexts, too, and therefore this chapter addresses readers who are engaged in health care – as practitioners, patients, relatives and researchers.

METAPHORS IN PRACTICE: GUIDELINES AND RECOMMENDATIONS

A critical, creative and mindful engagement with metaphors has many benefits. For one, a health care practitioner who pays close attention to a patient's language can use this information to build an interpersonal relationship with the patient. As Kristine J. Harrington explains, when a doctor or nurse picks up on a patient's metaphor and develops, collaboratively, 'a common language between patient and care provider', he or she can prevent isolation and miscommunication and signal that the patient is being heard (411). Striving for a common language, in other words, can be a strategy for 'enriching and deepening the therapeutic relationship' (Harrington 411). For another, Gary M. Reisfeld and George R. Wilson observe that attention to patients' metaphors helps practitioners better understand 'the cognitive and affective underpinnings' of each patient's illness experience – and their idiosyncratic behaviour in facing illness (4027). Moreover, recent studies suggest that an awareness of metaphors might even have a transformative effect on medical culture, for example by improving patient care and safety.[3] It comes as no surprise that scholars have weighed in on how these beneficial effects might be achieved.

Recommendations for a mindful use of metaphors come in different shapes and forms. In *Thinking with Metaphors in Medicine*, Alan Bleakley offers up lists like 'Ten things ... that medical educators should know' about metaphors (205–6), '9 Ways in which metaphors in medicine "work"' (208–13) and 22 'ways of looking at metaphor', which are derived from Richard Nordquist's classification (216–20).[4] He also supplies a table to visualise three ways in which metaphors perform (namely sinister, dexter and neutral) (204) alongside two main uses of metaphors in medicine: (1) to think with and (2) to communicate with (204–5). Bleakley's lists describe and summarise pertinent information about metaphors in health care. For example, we learn that 'doctors and patients may use metaphors positively, as transformative devices for opening up communication' (206). But how exactly this creative and generative potential of metaphors can be activated requires, in my opinion, a more detailed explanation.

Elena Semino and her colleagues also use the list form in their *'Metaphor Menu' for People Living with Cancer*, which I discussed previously in my chapter on Anatole Broyard. The document compiles seventeen metaphors, based both on common and new source domains, that help describe what it means to live with cancer. The menu is meant to provide patients (and health care workers) with a range of options to choose from, allowing people's personal preferences and mood to determine the metaphor that is most apt for them.

A more prescriptive recommendation appears in *The Chief Concern of Medicine*. Ronald Schleifer and Jerry B. Vannatta suggest a list of 'simple questions and comments' that can be used as a response to a patient's figurative language:

> 'What do you mean by that?'
> 'Can you describe that in other words?'
> 'Why do you describe your illness as a site of warfare?'
> 'It sounds like your job performance is creating stress.'
> 'It sounds like you feel guilty about your illness.' (242)

These questions are presented as part of a 'schematic response' (385), which, as Schleifer and Vannatta argue, promotes 'thoughtfulness and action' and 'make[s] physicians and health care workers mindful of aspects of humanistic understanding in their interaction with patients' (382). Schleifer and Vannatta maintain that such skills can be taught via careful close reading of literary texts, a conviction they share with Rita Charon, who links close reading with narrative competence (*Narrative Medicine*, 118–19; *Principles*, 200–5).

Another guideline aimed at practitioners is suggested by Vyjeyanthi S. Periyakoil, who distinguishes between two kinds of responses to a patient's metaphor:

1. a basic response which consists in 'naming, mirroring, validating, exploring' the patient's metaphor. This engagement with metaphor allows the doctor to 'vocalize the possible discrepancies' of a metaphor, for example when the comparison does not adequately represent an illness; and
2. an advance response, which implies that the doctor enters into the patient's metaphor and continues to provide new information and corrects misperceptions *through* the metaphor that the patient has used himself or herself. (843)

This recommendation enumerates specific actions, such as naming and mirroring, which echo the wording in other studies. For example, Bob Spall and colleagues advise 'direct questioning' (i.e., asking the patient what they mean or asking the patient if the metaphor is appropriate) and suggest 'record keeping' and thus making notes of the metaphors a patient uses and returning to these metaphors in the next meeting

(352).⁵ Such record-keeping can help create a sense of continuity for patients who realise that they are being remembered.

While these lists, menus, recommendations and guidelines contain useful information, I see two problems with them. First, many remain vague on how exactly 'metaphor competence' can be achieved. Reisfield and Wilson's otherwise excellent study is instructive in this respect. They conclude that '[s]imply by being mindful, physicians can develop an awareness of metaphorical language' and 'can tailor their use' of metaphors to the multiple variables that impact doctor–patient encounters (4026). Yet such attention only makes sense, in my view, when physicians and health care professionals more generally know what to be attentive to. Identifying a metaphor is not as easy as it seems, especially when the metaphor is so conventionalised and internalised that we no longer recognise it *as* a metaphor. Take, for example, anatomical expressions such as the chambers of the heart, the roof of the mouth and the floor of the pelvis, which are all based on the body-as-house metaphor (Verghese, 'Linguistic Prescription'). While the conventionalised house metaphor can be rendered visible again with close attention to and a basic knowledge about metaphors, metaphor awareness is not a self-evident undertaking.

Besides conventionalisation, metaphor identification is complicated by another challenge: Not all figurative language is a metaphor. Symbols, idiomatic language, sayings and colloquial expressions may draw on metaphors, but they function quite differently. A patient who vigorously refuses to be treated for a serious illness, for example, uses a symbol when he reasons that 'So much has happened with syringes – my mother died of it and three acquaintances as well' (Wohlmann and Michl). Of course, the syringe can also be taken as a metaphor (suggesting, for example, that both syringes and medicine get under one's skin and can hurt while bringing relief). In this context, however, the syringe seems to stand for (and is thus symbolic of) the patient's fears and negative experiences.

It might be objected that such distinctions matter only to literary scholars and that in everyday language and especially in a health care context such subtleties are beside the point. I do not insist on these distinctions for distinction's sake; but if the goal is a more reflective engagement with *metaphors*, metaphor identification is part of the game.

The terminological vagueness of existing recommendations correlates with a second problem: the guidelines tend to be too general. On closer scrutiny, they also apply to ironic statements or jokes or any expression that can cause misunderstanding. The recommendations are thus very helpful for health care communication in a broader sense, but I wonder: How can they be concretised so that they factor in the specificity of metaphoric communication? What is missing, in my opinion, is an emphasis on metaphor analysis and thus specific instructions for how to identify, break down and evaluate a metaphor. In order to better understand metaphors, we need to take metaphors seriously *as metaphors*.

In the following sections, I describe five steps which draw on the close readings of the previous chapters and expand on the strategies I identified there. In each step, I demonstrate the relevance of these strategies with examples from medical practice. The five steps are:

1. to identify an expression as a metaphor
2. to name the salient features of a metaphor
3. to evaluate a metaphor
4. to analyse the context of a metaphor
5. to activate the generative potential of a metaphor.

Though listed numerically, these steps do not necessarily form a linear sequence. While some steps build on one another, others benefit from intermittent revisiting.[6]

A METHOD FOR USING METAPHOR

1. *Identify an Expression as a Metaphor*

Identifying a metaphor is often a matter of intuition: we sense a gap between a literal meaning of a word and an implied, figurative meaning. Tom Furniss and Michael Bath call this the 'acid test': 'We know that a word, phrase or statement is figurative *when it cannot be taken literally in the context in which it is being used*' (146; original emphasis). When a doctor says to a patient, 'The dendritic cells are the scriptwriters of your immune system', the context makes it impossible to take the scriptwriter reference literally (Casarett et al. 258).

It is helpful to identify what exactly is being compared in a metaphor: in our example, a specific type of cells of the immune system is compared to scriptwriters. In the terminology of metaphor analysis, features from the source domain, the writers, are mapped onto or carried over to the target domain, the cells.

The acid test works well with metaphors that surprise us with their unconventionality. Applied to conventional and 'dead' metaphors like the fight metaphor for illness, however, it is far less precise. Many patients, after all, feel that they are *literally* fighting against illness, and they consider their psychical and physical wounds to be injuries from very real battles. And yet this is nonetheless a metaphor, a figure of thinking and speaking in which features from a source domain (battle) are mapped onto a target (illness).

The 'Metaphor Identification Procedure', developed by the Pragglejaz Group, an association of ten metaphor researchers, recommends three steps for identifying a metaphor: (1) establish the contextual meaning of a word or phrase, (2) determine if the word or phrase has a more basic meaning in other contexts (a glance at the dictionary can be informative) and (3), if there *is* a more basic meaning, decide if the basic and contextual meanings contrast with one another but are comparable (Kövecses, *Metaphor* 5; Pragglejaz Group). If there is a contrast and if the relationship between basic and contextual meaning – or source and target domain – is one of comparison, we are dealing with a metaphor. Imagine, for example, a health care team that describes a patient's serious condition with the following words: 'He is walking on thin ice.'[7] This is a common idiomatic expression. But what is the metaphor? The contextual meaning indicates that the patient is in a fragile situation. His vitals might suddenly crash, putting his life in danger. The more basic meaning of the expression refers to a quite different scenario or concept: someone risks their life by (maybe recklessly?) stepping on the frozen surface of a lake. This more basic meaning and the contextual meaning are comparable: a life is at risk, and a condition is unstable. The metaphor maps features from the source domain (walking on thin ice) to the target (a patient's fragile health status). At the same time, it may map a value judgement, such as unfairly blaming someone for irresponsible behaviour, which can be appropriate in one context but not in the other.

Applied to the fight metaphor, the 'Metaphor Identification Procedure' prompts certain initial questions: Does the battle refer to a patient in actual trenches, equipped with ammunition and weapons, fighting against a real enemy such as another soldier or a foreign state? Is the patient in a fistfight, exchanging punches and leaving with a black eye or a broken arm? But the procedure also suggests a more critical line of inquiry: Can we think about dealing with illness without using the battle domain? The last question is important for identifying expressions that have achieved a high degree of conventionality yet remain metaphorical. In this case, we should recall that sick bodies are also compared to other source domains, such as a crime scene (when illness is considered a crime to be solved by a doctor) or a broken machine (when healing is considered a form of repair by a doctor-mechanic) (Mattingly, *Paradox*

57ff., 76ff.). The fact that we can think of other source domains is a sure sign that illness-as-fight is a metaphor. Moreover, as Arthur Frank reminds us in his chapter 'The Struggle Is Not a Fight', the fight metaphor is not applied to all illnesses; heart troubles and high blood pressure are not said to be fought against.

Identifying a metaphor also involves the ability to recognise when a figurative expression like 'you have to fight' is being taken literally. For example, Richard T. Penson and his colleagues describe a situation when the mother of a six-year-old patient told her daughter to keep fighting in order to beat cancer (711). The child started to kick and hit the nurses and doctors. In doing so, she did literally what her mother asked her to do; she was being a good girl. At the same time, had no one recognised that she was taking a metaphor literally, the girl would have been considered a difficult patient.

As this example indicates, identifying metaphor also demands the ability to perceive a potential lack of metaphor awareness in *others*. Children, for example, develop metaphorical thinking around the age of four or five (Carriedo 2).[8] And this process is a gradual one: children develop their ability to understand a metaphor as their knowledge about the world expands.[9] And there are other reasons why someone might not be aware that a metaphor is used: people with brain injuries or schizophrenia, for example, can lose the ability to understand metaphor (Frommelt; Karabanowicz et al.). A traumatised refugee might take references to battle and war literally because they represent very real and fresh experiences. Lastly, someone might not be *willing* to consider an expression to be figurative and thus as theoretically flexible and negotiable in its meaning. In illness, so much of what we took for granted suddenly becomes uncertain, unpredictable and open to interpretation; it is a tall order to expect someone to be open to the ambiguities of language when everything else seems to be falling apart. Metaphor identification, in this sense, also includes that such multiple contingencies are taken into consideration.

2. Name the Salient Features of a Metaphor

After identifying a metaphor, the mappings between source and target can be explored by defining the salient features that are being transferred. Paraphrase can be a useful first step. The elephant metaphor, for example, that a doctor was using to explain 'bone marrow' (see Chapter 2) was accompanied by a form of paraphrase when he elaborated that 'It has a long memory. It remembers everything it has ever seen before' (Casarett et al. 258). The paraphrase clarifies what exactly in the elephant creates the link to bone marrow: the elephant's memory (and not its size, skin texture or colour).

Let's use another example we have encountered before. Cheryl Mattingly observed in her field studies how a health care team compared a seriously sick baby to a vegetable ('Machine-Body' 377). I summarised the complexity of the case in Chapter 2, and I am returning to it once more because the term 'vegetative' is so salient in medical contexts for cognitive impairment.[10] To analyse the vegetable metaphor, we identify Darrelanna as the target and *vegetable* as the source domain. To the nurse who used the comparison, the salient feature transfers from one domain to the other like this:

Source: Vegetable **Target: Darrelanna**
a. Vegetables lack cognitive capacities   Darrelanna lacks cognitive capacities

In this view, the target domain (human being) becomes structured or equipped with certain elements from the source domain (vegetable). The mapping is complicated by the fact that Darrelanna's condition is (or is close to) a vegetative state. According to the *Merriam Webster Medical Dictionary*, 'vegetative' refers to a range of meanings:

1. 'growing or the power of growing',
2. 'relating to the plant kingdom',
3. 'involuntary bodily functions', and
4. 'a state in which there is a total loss of cognitive functioning' (n. pag.)

This range of definitions points out additional characteristics of 'vegetative' that the nurse may not have thought about – but which Darrelanna's parents found entirely salient when, in their response to the nurse's metaphor, they invoked the image of a garden that they care for:

Source: Vegetable **Target: Darrelanna**
a. Vegetables lack cognitive capacities   Darrelanna lacks cognitive capacities
b. Vegetables are cultivated   Darrelanna is nursed and cared for
c. Vegetables grow when properly cultivated   Darrelanna will grow when adequately cared for

The mapping of these three diverse features raises another question: Are those the only possible mappings? What other, additional knowledge might be brought to bear on this comparison, either actively or intuitively? Kövecses calls this dimension 'metaphorical entailment', which he defines as the 'rich additional knowledge about a source' that we map onto a target' (*Metaphor* 122). If we consider our personal knowledge of vegetables or consult a dictionary or encyclopaedia to find additional meanings or usages of the word, we may come up with more potential mappings. For example, vegetables are immobile: they stay in one place. This entailment matches Darrelanna's situation: she is unable to move on her own. But even though immobility is coherent with the structure of the target, it is not the main focus of the metaphor and is thus not activated or mapped by everyone. Only some features seem salient to some people, whereas others remain unutilised (Kövecses, *Metaphor* 91–5).

Other metaphorical entailments may simply not map onto the target. For example, we know that vegetables are often cultivated in order to be eaten by people and animals. The food notion, however, jars with this target: Darrelanna is not and will never serve as food. This feature is blocked, and no mapping will occur. However, if we elaborate on the notion of food and nourishment, we might argue that plants do not eat in the way that humans or animals consume food; similarly, Darrelanna does not eat regular food. Because food conveys affection and love in many cultures, we may ponder what this might imply for the care that Darrelanna receives.

As this scenario illustrates, mappings are neither totally stable nor totally predictable, and there is always a potential for new features to be activated. Being able to name salient features of a metaphor is relevant for two reasons, then. First, it is the foundation for comparing one person's salient features to another's, which can help establish a common language with patients or colleagues and, ideally, prevent miscommunication. Second, it helps clarify what unspoken or subtle features a metaphor might entail. In this regard, it is a crucial factor in the generativity of metaphors, as I discuss below.[11]

A critical analysis of salient features was applied during the early phase of the COVID-19 pandemic, when warfare metaphors were popular. However, many of the salient features of warfare – such as mobilising the populace and gathering of secret intelligence – do not actually match reality. Rather, as Anders Engberg-Pedersen observes, 'people are demobilizing by sheltering in place' and 'there is a widespread international cooperation and open sharing of information and statistics' in order to solve the problem together (n. pag.). Such inadequacies require careful evaluation because warfare metaphors elicit 'a suppressed nostalgia' for quick solutions, a desire for what was once imagined (or declared) as a 'simple, manageable, and perhaps even heroic' war (n. pag.). The decades since 9/11, however, brought other features of war to the foreground: the war against terror has been a long-winded, seemingly endless and hopeless undertaking (n. pag.). *These* features of war are indeed salient in a pandemic.

3. Evaluate a Metaphor

Once the salient features and mappings have been identified, we can examine what a metaphor is doing, or trying to do: What is the function of a specific metaphor? And what are its effects? The second question necessarily prompts self-reflection, demanding that we explore the resonances that a metaphor may have with us on both a personal and a professional level.

The following criteria are useful for evaluating a metaphor:

- *In/adequacy*
  All metaphors are ultimately inadequate, but we can ask: Where does a metaphor work well and where does it fail?
- *Function*
  Does a metaphor function as explanation, description or prescription?
- *Effect*
  To what extent does a metaphor empower or disempower? Does it express an affective state? If so, whose? Does it clarify something or obscure it?

Admittedly, these criteria are interrelated and dynamic. The following three cases acknowledge that interplay yet nonetheless illustrate their utility.

In science communication, explanatory metaphors are often used to familiarise a lay public with abstract research findings. Researchers on resilience, for example, chose two metaphors – dandelion children and orchid children – to assert that some children thrive under almost any circumstances, 'the same way that dandelions seem to prosper irrespective of soil, sun, drought, or rain'; orchid children, by contrast, are more susceptible 'to the nurturant or neglectful characteristics of the ambient environment' (Boyce and Ellis qtd in Kendall-Taylor and Haydon 577). The explanatory function of these metaphors is successful in so far as the sources are familiar and their salient features easy to identify. At the same time, the comparison of children to flowers is inadequate: it is 'only a *partial* distillation of the science of resilience' and narrows down the complexity of the field significantly by suggesting, for example, that resilience is an inherent trait rather than a process or positive outcome (Kendall-Taylor and Haydon 577–9). The metaphor thus clarifies some aspects while it muddies others. Moreover, the entailments of orchids and dandelions may prompt objections or even indignation. Orchids are considered fragile, fastidious, even difficult; they are thought to need an abundance of care. Dandelions are considered robust and tough, but they are also typically considered to be weeds. Transferred to children, either comparison might well offend the parents. Thus, while these metaphors may indeed communicate research findings in an engaging way, they risk evoking misunderstanding and resistance. Here function and effect undermine one another.

My second example is from the context of organ transplantation. The metaphor comes from an interview with a patient who describes his chronic kidney disease in the following way:

> I don't think that I am sick, I have an organ that does not work properly. There are blind people whose eyes do not work, and they do not think that they are sick. At first, they are maybe disabled in their way of life. Okay. The kidney is, if I may say so, an auto repair shop. Three times a week, I have an oil change done, and that's it. Apart from that, I am very healthy. (Wiebel-Fanderl 357; my translation)

The patient is invoking the common metaphor of the body-as-machine by comparing dialysis to an oil change. Mapping the salient features highlights the similarities between the fluids of oil and blood, which can deteriorate over time, and the benefits of replacing them if necessary. Moreover, oil changes are performed periodically as part of a maintenance regimen. Likewise, a dialysis procedure is needed at regular intervals. In mapping these salient features of the oil change onto dialysis, the patient suggests that dialysis responds to a broken body in need of fixing. This comparison works well for the patient: the metaphor's function, it seems, is to convey that dialysis is not troublesome, life-changing or frightening, but routine. For this patient, who we learn is a technical clerk, the idea of seeing his body as a machine or engine fits within his worldview. The metaphor also summons expectations of repair and a quick fix.

Additional entailments can be activated to further evaluate the metaphor. Machines have no emotions; they do not feel pain and they do not suffer. It is easy to imagine why such a body concept is appealing. Yet its inadequacy is also potentially limiting. The comparison prescribes a specific and narrow role to patients' bodies (considered passive and unfeeling) as well as to health care professionals (who are compared to mechanics). In using this metaphor, the patient rules out that his condition might affect his psychosomatic state in subtle or unexpected ways (through tiredness, anxiety, nightmares or other constraints). An evaluation of the metaphor thus requires a recognition and assessment of what the metaphor accomplishes and what options it limits or neglects – both in terms of its functions and its effects.

In palliative care, metaphors are also used to navigate difficult conversations. For example, a nurse described her interaction with a dying patient, a woman in her late fifties, in the following way:

> She had not yet acknowledged dying. She was silent about her diagnosis and her future. One night, during the routine of evening care, we were discussing the challenges and struggles of raising children as single parents. She stated, 'I thought that now with my kids raised, I was out of the woods.' I replied with the metaphor, 'Till this cloud on the horizon.' At this point she could have selected any number of meanings: her pain, her cancer, the admission, her future. Instead, she took a leap and blurted out 'Till this *big black* cloud on the horizon!' Before I could decide how to respond she raced on: 'I know what's happening and I can't talk about it and I can't tell my kids either.' (Hutchings 283; original emphasis)

What is the metaphor here? 'Out of the woods' is a common idiomatic expression to indicate that one is 'no longer ... in danger or difficulty' ('be out of'). The 'cloud on the horizon', too, is an idiom, suggesting 'something that threatens to cause problems or unhappiness in the future' ('cloud'). The expression contains a symbol, the cloud, that, as Hutchings identifies, could stand for a number of different things, such as pain, cancer or death. The metaphor is nestled in the idiom and the symbol: it is the comparison between the patient's impending death (target) and a weather phenomenon, a cloud (source). The salient features of the 'big black cloud' echo the idiomatic meaning: a storm or weather front indicates that turbulent times are ahead, entailing difficulty and sometimes danger. According to the nurse's interpretation, her patient is indirectly acknowledging through this metaphor that she is aware of her approaching death, even though the patient insists she 'can't talk about it'. The function of the metaphor thus consists in retaining a sense of vagueness and ambiguity; it serves as a veil or shield, protecting the patient from the harsh 'glare of reality' (Hutchings 282). This indirectness allows the two women to confront what is otherwise inexpressible. In this sense, the metaphor is empowering for the patient even though (or because) it is ambiguous and vague.

The cloud metaphor also has some limits. It associates death with frightening features, such as darkness and danger, which might contradict certain values in palliative care. Yet its entailments are well worth exploring: a cloud is condensed watery vapour that floats in the air ('cloud'). It can bring much-anticipated rain or vanish as quickly as it came, leaving the earth dry. In exploring these additional mappings, nurse and patient can further develop the common language they have established, without sacrificing the ambiguity that seems to comfort the patient.

As these examples indicate, metaphors often fall into several categories at the same time: They can be empowering and disempowering, explanatory and prescriptive, adequate and inadequate, clarifying and vague, revealing and elusive. The identification of salient features and additional entailments helps to evaluate these multiple roles in specific contexts. Sometimes, however, a broader sense of context must be brought to bear.

4. Analyse the Context of a Metaphor

Context can mean many things. I will focus here on three, interrelated dimensions of context: historical, cultural and narrative (that is, the sentences in which a metaphor is immediately embedded). This analytical step comprises specific strategies for discerning the relationship between metaphor and context. The writers I discuss in the previous chapters model how such context-specific strategies may look. Susan Sontag, for example, traces metaphors across multiple manifestations over time and compares how the same source domain has been applied to different targets. Audre Lorde, too, collects additional information about the battle metaphor and juxtaposes it with other metaphors which help her challenge and resist the metaphors she finds questionable. As these examples show, context analysis benefits from time-consuming methodologies, such as archival research. My suggestions for context analysis combine the results of historical and anthropological research with the close reading approach I have been using so far.

Historical

To analyse the historical roots of metaphors can be significant for two reasons: not only are these roots a testament to the deeply entangled nature of metaphors in a culture's way of thinking, they also remind us that languages change over time and acquire new meanings in new historical contexts. The metaphor 'illness is war', for example, has been traced to the mid-seventeenth century, when poet John Donne and physician Thomas Sydenham used references to cannon shots, sieges and rebellious fever when they described illness (e.g. Bleakley 36, 39, 61). Military metaphors have also structured the practice of health care more generally (see Penson et al. 713). Its long history in Western culture thus explains, to some extent, why the metaphor feels so natural to us.[12]

A historical contextual analysis of the metaphor 'surgeons are butchers' exemplifies how a metaphor's meaning changes over time. The metaphor can be traced to a time when it was butchers and barbers who performed surgeries because only they had sharp knives.[13] While history books are an important resource for learning more about earlier periods, a quick look into a dictionary can be useful, too. If we want to collect historical information about the source domain 'butcher', for example, the *Oxford English Dictionary* lists a number of obsolete meanings, such as: 'An executioner; a person who inflicts capital punishment or torture' or 'a scourge' ('butcher'). Since the mid-nineteenth century, 'butcher' has also been used for 'A person who is reckless or incompetent in making cuts or alterations' and, since the mid-eighteenth century, 'butcher' has described 'A doctor or surgeon, *esp.* one who is incompetent or too readily inclined to operate on patients' ('butcher'; emphasis in original). The salient features of this metaphor – such as to cut brutally without care or to cut poorly, sloppily and incompetently – can be quickly identified. However, the assumption that butchers are brutal or incompetent is not a universal or absolute characteristic of the profession.[14] A more neutral definition in the *Oxford English Dictionary* clarifies that a butcher is a 'person whose trade is the preparation and selling of meat'. And yet, incompetence and brutality are salient features which disparage the trade and which we seem to activate intuitively in the mapping, suggesting both their long-ingrained nature and their power as stereotypical ascriptions. In evaluating a metaphor like 'the surgeon is a butcher', the historical information helps activate additional salient features or entailments. It also clarifies that the implied value judgements have been shaped over time and are not intrinsic to either profession.

In health care, such a nuanced analysis can become relevant if the butcher metaphor appears in the context of human organ donation and transplantation, for example. Which salient features *exactly* are implied? Incompetence? Brutality? Or is it something else? Another entailment of butchering is the use of meat as a commodity – both for profit and for consumption. All three mappings should prompt concern if applied to human organ transplantation; and each mapping requires a different response. What the 'butcher' examples demonstrate is that historical context can help untangle the layers that are nestled in a common, conventionalised metaphor. It reminds us that a metaphor's associations are neither static nor absolute.

Cultural

In metaphor theory, two theories compete with one another: one considers metaphors universal; the other considers them culturally specific. Taking the former view, Lakoff and Johnson have argued that many metaphors are inextricably connected to our human body and our experiences as human beings. The metaphor 'intensity is heat' is for them an embodied, universal metaphor: when we do an activity intensely and vigorously, our bodies respond with an increase of heat. This physiological response is common for all human beings and, for this reason, its related metaphorical expressions are similar across cultures. Other metaphors are contingent on specific contexts; this contingency accounts for the great variation of metaphors both cross-culturally and within cultures. For example, while many cultures share the notion that 'the body is a container for emotions' and the associated metaphor 'the angry person is a pressurized container', in Japanese anger is located in the belly while in Zulu it resides in the heart (Kövecses, *Metaphor* 207–8). Cultural context also comes to bear when we think about dominant metaphors such as 'time is money' and 'age is decline', both of which are pervasive in Western cultures. Metaphors thus reveal a culture's norms and values in significant ways; for this reason, both need to be analysed together.

A culture's gender hierarchies, for example, can inform the metaphors used for reproductive organs. Emily Martin examines medical textbooks from the 1980s and finds that male and female reproductive organs are often compared to 'systems for the production of valuable substances' ('Egg' 486). That is, the processes of ovulation and spermatogenesis are likened to the production processes in factories and enterprises (486).[15] In comparing the same source domain of production for different targets, namely male and female bodies, Martin makes an astounding observation: whereas spermatogenesis is celebrated as a 'remarkable' and 'most amazing' process due to the 'sheer magnitude' of sperm produced, the female organ is cast in terms of low productivity: it 'sheds only a single gamete each month' (486), does not produce any new follicles after a woman's birth, and most of those follicles are said to 'degenerate' until menopause (487). Thus, whereas spermatogenesis is valued for high, continuous production throughout a man's lifetime, ovulation is considered inferior in output and duration (488). If in these terms ovulation does not really 'produce', we might pose the question: is a system of production really an adequate source domain for this target? We might further challenge the production metaphor by juxtaposing it with related metaphors that are dominant in the West. For example, Lakoff and Johnson identify a number of metaphors that structure our everyday thinking, such as 'significant is big' (*Metaphors* 50) and 'high status is up/low status is down' (16). These concepts explain why the description of spermatogenesis is so admiring: high quantity carries favourable value judgements of industriousness and success. In this light, the production metaphor does not simply explain a universal biological process, it evokes cultural values and norms that need to be interrogated and challenged. Resistance to such gendered metaphors can be achieved in numerous ways: by identifying the patriarchal lens and calling out the inherent double standard, by refusing to use the source domain, or by continuing to think with the metaphor and turn it on its head (see, e.g., Wohlmann, 'Termites').

Our orientation towards mainstream cultural metaphors need not always be one of suspicion and resistance, however. These metaphors also have an affirmative value when they help frame a situation that is experienced as extraordinary and destabilising. Culturally legitimised metaphors may supply a sense of security, offering a shared common language through which unfamiliar experiences are made intelligible to the self and to others. Martha Stoddard Holmes describes how her refusal to use the mainstream battle metaphor after her breast cancer diagnosis led to a kind of silencing. The battle metaphor 'didn't fit. But without a fitting metaphor,' she acknowledges, 'I had no story' (266). In other words, to *not* have a metaphor at one's disposal might be as challenging as a metaphor that does not fit or is fraught with problematic cultural values.

Narrative
The immediate context in which a metaphor is used is pertinent, too. As the previous chapters illustrate, a metaphor's function and effect can be impacted by the narrative in which it is embedded. I am suggesting here a broad understanding of narrative which also encompasses the analysis of voice, tone, tropes and rhetorical devices, such as irony and exaggeration. Such contextual information is important for understanding a metaphor more fully. The following example is taken from a thread in an online cancer support group, where a blogger describes the side effects of living with a colostomy bag. The blogger invents a Cold War fantasy scenario:[16]

> Since my bowel cancer operation in January I have met a Russian Schitt called Bagov Schitt. Bagov Schitt has become very attached to me, but I think he could be a spy because he leaks things occasionally. Bagov needs constant attention and can be a real drain on me, to be honest I want to get rid of him as soon as I can. At least Bagov Schitt is not a pain in the bum. (Semino et al., *Metaphor* 233)

The metaphor in this example is a personification that compares a stoma bag to a Russian spy. In the elaboration of the metaphor, the blogger spells out the mappings: both stoma bag and spy 'leak', both follow the blogger constantly, both are related to drain or draining, and both involve 'secrecy, underhandedness and untrustworthiness' (Semino et al., *Metaphor* 233). Clearly, some of these mappings are based on salient features whereas others are merely implied. What adds to the humour of the metaphor is not only the surprising absurdity of the comparison itself but also how the elaboration of the metaphor engages in a playful flickering between literal and figurative meanings: the leaking of excrements *and* information, the physical *and* emotional meanings of attachment, the requirement to drain the bag *and* it being a drain on him. The humour of the metaphor itself is thus amplified by the immediate narrative context.

Moreover, context is relevant in terms of where the blog was published: it belongs to a thread titled 'For Those with a Warped Sense of Humour Warning – No Punches Pulled Here' where bloggers describe their experiences with cancer ('For Those'). In other words, it appears on a site where a community of bloggers comment on each other's posts and, together, engage in humorous banter about their respective illness with a playful and sometimes sarcastic tone. Detached from this specific context, the metaphor itself might be considered funny (or not); through its narrative elaboration and the other bloggers' cheer, its joy is amplified.

The functions and effects of a humorous metaphor are varied. In the example above, it allows the blogger to communicate about a topic that is otherwise taboo and associated with shame (Semino et al., *Metaphor* 233). In making the grotesque and innovative comparison, he is also able to share his thoughts about a negative situation without having to say if and to what degree he is struggling: 'The humorous tone probably makes all this easier to talk about,' Elena Semino and colleagues speculate, 'and in fact, by joking about it, "Sam" might already be feeling better' (233). Metaphor's indirectness allows him to address a taboo topic, and its humour creates a distance to the literal import of the experiences described. This relief might be augmented by the other bloggers who laugh with him and praise this humorous invention.

Laughter can create a sense of a community, solidarity and empowerment (234). It can also have the opposite effect. Not all humorous metaphors are inclusive or beneficial (Cohen, 'Cultivation' 11–12). For example, when an elderly patient with osteoarthritis compares herself to an 'old gray mare', adding that 'she ain't what she used to be',[17] the metaphor is voiced, Jeffrey T. Berger and colleagues maintain, with a tone of irony and self-denigration (Berger et al. 828). Both patient and mare are considered lame and slow in movement; both have their youthful days behind them. The metaphor fits perfectly with the mainstream metaphor 'old age is decline', which scholars in age studies have criticised for privileging a biological understanding of old age and for naturalising what is, in fact, a cultural construct (Gullette). Because the metaphor seems so natural, the old-mare metaphor might be all the more convincing, even though it is uttered as a quip, which leaves open how seriously we should take it. In other words, if the humorous metaphor is meant as 'a call for attention and assistance' – as Berger and colleagues assume (Berger et al. 828) – it might actually achieve the opposite effect and entail misunderstanding: a physician might take the quipping patient literally ('That's just how it is'), or he might ignore the patient's implied call for help ('It can't be that bad if she's making light of it'). Because the old-mare metaphor echoes the commonplace understanding of old age as decline, it augments what we all seem to know: old age involves many hardships. Thus, the humorous metaphor might as well backfire and cause distance and isolation.

Such negative effects might also result from misreading another option that ironic statements supply: it is likely that the patient does not actually mean what she says. In irony, we say something false and expect that it will be *recognised* as false because we *intended* it to be false (see Paul Grice qtd in Fogelin 2). If such a mutual recognition between two speakers takes place, irony holds another promise: it can create a subtle bond between patient and physician, inviting a mutual appreciation of irony's inclusive, relational and ludic potential to express *both* what is meant and not meant, said and unsaid (Hutcheon 56–8). In this sense, the old-mare metaphor might as well express the patient's stoicism and serenity – rather than her despondency and worry – suggesting she knows very well that she is not, of course, what she says she is. This is just another option though. Ironic statements, like metaphors, often muddy the lines between truth and falsity. A patient might use irony to say something intentionally false and still believe that there is a grain of truth to it.[18]

Context can help analyse how a metaphor is impacted by and responding to historical, cultural and narrative dimensions. Such contextual information is also being applied to burnout syndrome,[19] which has become a prevalent term to describe emotional exhaustion, disengagement and compassion fatigue in, among others, physicians.

The term was coined in the second half of the twentieth century by psychologist Herbert Freudenberger who used 'burned out' in a self-diagnosis. He came up with a metaphor that compared high-achieving, stressed-out people like himself to a burned-out house: they look intact from the outside, but 'their inner resources are consumed as if by fire, leaving a great emptiness inside' (Freudenberger qtd in Carter). This metaphor has been criticised for being fatalistic and misleading: since gutted buildings are often beyond repair and need to be torn down, the comparison obstructs the possibility that people with burnout syndrome can be restored (Barron et al.). The history of burnout also harbours another dimension which associates the term with the metaphor *life is war*. Freudenberger worked with many drug-addicted Vietnam War veterans who were diagnosed with combat fatigue and later post-traumatic stress disorder (Lepore). When Freudenberger coined the term 'burnout', he also related it, in a literal sense, to the addicts whom he had observed staring, with empty eyes, at a cigarette burning out in their hands. What then does the term 'burnout' imply when we know about this specific contextual information? If we indeed feel that life (or work) is a battlefield with many causalities – a notion, as Jill Lepore argues, that is often used to describe conditions of late capitalism – then it makes sense to compare, let's say, an exhausted physician to a war veteran: both are 'worn down, wiped out, threadbare, on edge, battered, and battle-scarred' (Lepore). Within such a cultural context, burnout becomes a 'combat metaphor', suggesting that we are 'engaged in a Hobbesian battle for existence, civil life having become a war zone' (Lepore). Whether this is an appropriate and productive comparison is a question that everyone needs to answer for themselves.

5. Activate the Generative Potential of Metaphors

Generating new meanings from existing metaphors is a creative act. Metaphor creativity, however, is not the special talent of a lucky few. Indeed, our rich (if unacknowledged) practice with metaphorical thinking may mean we simply need to 'have the courage to be "absent-minded"' and let our intuition, our subconscious, do the work (Bolton 128). Still, springboards can be helpful in this regard. Accordingly, this last section compiles strategies suggested by Helen Sword and Gillie Bolton and illustrates how these strategies, together with steps 2–4, can help unlock metaphor's generative potential.

Helen Sword suggests the DEEPER rubric as a tool for 'testing the breadth and depth' of metaphors (42). The rubric prompts writers to answer six questions about the metaphor of their choice: Does the metaphor deal with

1. the natural world or human experiences?
2. a process or a product?
3. negative or positive emotions?
4. the self or other people?
5. some form of agency or learning?
6. a form of personal or universal resonance? (42–4)

Answering these questions is a way to analyse an existing metaphor, but it also reveals where a metaphor has potential for being developed. For example, if we conclude that a metaphor is product-oriented, how can that same metaphor be imagined as process-oriented? The question relies on binaries – negative/positive; product/process – but those can nonetheless be put to interesting uses, especially because they work both ways. We can tease out, for example, the 'shadow sides' – the negative connotations – of a metaphor like 'illness is a journey', so commonly considered to be neutral if not outright positive. While the metaphor inspires many favourable connotations (e.g. adventure, new experiences and insights), it might also invoke a sense of homelessness and instability; imagine the journey-maker as a person who is exhausted and prefers the quiet of living in one place. Such binaries, as I have argued in this book, are not mutually exclusive and can exist side by side.

In *Reflective Practice: Writing and Professional Development* (2018), Gillie Bolton suggests free-writing exercises intended to unlock the creative potential of 'habitual and unnoticed metaphors' (123). Many of her exercises invite readers to develop new metaphors of their own in order to better understand difficult scenarios like a conflict at work.[20] In one exercise called 'Write to Learn', Bolton asks readers to

1. think of 'a picture, object of beauty (for example, a shell), or an element of nature (for example, a mountain, a tree)' they particularly like,
2. describe the qualities they associate with it and
3. 'replace the name of the thing' with the scenario or conflict they are tackling or trying to understand. (134)

The metaphor, in a way, works as a detour: the replacement invites an intentional mapping of features that can illuminate, in surprising ways, problems we think we knew well.

My own experience leading health humanities workshops on metaphor has led to similar insights into the generative potential of metaphors. Here I want to discuss one example of how workshop participants have activated the generativity of a metaphor that was used by a patient. The metaphor comes from an ethnographic study by Richard Gwyn, who quotes a woman he named Yumiko Thomas on her lifelong physical illness. Thomas says: 'my life is my own I want to be ... captain of my *own* ship that ship called Yumiko that's always what I wanted' (219; original emphasis). Strictly speaking, the sentence contains two metaphors: one compares the patient (target) with a captain (source); the other comparison is more ambiguous because the ship (source) can potentially refer to several target domains – the patient's life, but also her body and her illness. The features of the source domain 'captain' are numerous. The most salient mapping is probably the notion of a captain who is in power and makes decisions. The metaphor thus expresses a desire for control, autonomy and leadership. Such leadership is a privilege, but it also implies responsibilities and duties. The ship comparison may work at odds with these more directive connotations, however, in that it also evokes connotations of floating and going with the flow.

How might this dual metaphor be elaborated and extended, combined and further explored? We can, for example, consider what is *not* immediately activated in the ship/captain metaphor, such as the crew that a captain works with and depends on. In other words, we might activate new meanings or valences if we add a cast of different characters to the metaphor: a captain, for example, depends on her crew and needs a mate, a mechanic, an engineer and a cook. The metaphor can also easily be combined with the metaphor of a journey: the ship might be imagined sailing from island to island, with each island representing a different stage of the illness. Since the type of the ship is not specified by the patient, we can imagine any kind: a sailboat, a naval ship, a bulk carrier, a steamship, a cruise ship, a yacht, or any other vessel that floats on water, like a raft. Each type of ship adds a different flavour to the metaphor, for example by emphasising different purposes of and experiences during the journey. Where does it take place – on the ocean? On a lake or river? How might each setting inflect the experience of the journey, its obstacles and vistas?

In one workshop session, a participant shared that Yumiko's ship made him think of spaceships. Once he had this type of ship in mind, he said, he could not help but think of the Kobayashi Maru test featured in the *Star Trek* universe. In the episode, the test is designed to find out how James T. Kirk's crew reacts in a desperate, no-win situation.

To my mind, this association testifies to the imaginative potential of the allegedly simple and overt metaphor of the ship and her captain.

While exercises like these foreground the positive, creative potential, this type of engagement should be treated with great care in medical settings. The risk of metaphor creativity is that it may be carried too far or too zealously; a patient might feel like her metaphor is being appropriated if a practitioner imposes her own creative vision too strongly.[21] To avoid alienating or silencing patients, one preventative measure is to withhold one's subjective elaborations of a metaphor. This restraint, I believe, does not nullify the creative mental work that has been done; even if the results of that creativity are not shared, the work creates a tie, a connection, between practitioner and patient, or between one colleague and another. That tie may deepen understanding, or it may simply make the patient more memorable and distinct. The exact nature of the tie is not predefined. This unpredictability is also true of the earlier steps. Still, each may lead to a useful opening-out, a refresh curiosity and new perceptions.

BEYOND METAPHOR: SIMILES AND SYMBOLS

Having identified, mapped the salient features, evaluated, contextualised and creatively explored metaphor proper, we are now better equipped to:

- understand 'the cognitive and affective underpinnings' of the patients' illness experience (Reisfeld and Wilson 4027)
- name and mirror a metaphor, 'vocalize possible discrepancies', and try to correct and redirect misperceptions (Periyakoil 843)
- develop a common language (Harrington 411)
- keep a record of the metaphors used in a consultation to develop a common language with a patient (Spall et al. 352)
- collect metaphors. As Elena Semino and Anatole Broyard implicitly suggest, the wider the choice, the less we are stuck with and limited by single metaphors and the more we can consider other options, depending on circumstance, interlocutor, topic, and mood.

Before I conclude this practice-oriented chapter, though, I want to expand its scope a bit. Figurative expressions, after all, comprise symbols and similes as well as metaphors. I have not included them in my treatment of metaphors for two reasons. First, in analysing symbols, we cannot use the same approaches we use for metaphors. Mappings between source and target domains, for example, do not work. Second, the effects and functions of similes and symbols are quite different from those of metaphors. In this section, I want to highlight some of these differences and outline some practical implications that follow.[22] I mean this focus on symbols and similes as an invitation and a spur to other scholars, as there are many other forms of figurative language to be explored for their use in health care.

Both similes and metaphors establish a resemblance between two dissimilar things, with similes adding a 'like' or 'as' to what would otherwise be a metaphor. There is an ongoing controversy about how to categorise simile in relation to metaphor: Is metaphor simply an elliptical simile (Fogelin 28)? That is, are they basically the same, differing merely in their length? Or is a simile somewhat inferior to metaphor because a simile's expression is not 'enough', and a metaphor goes 'further' and does more (Donoghue 6)? Or does the addition of 'like' or 'as' impact a simile's function and effect so decidedly that both must be treated as distinct entities? I am less interested in answering such ontological questions, and, as I mentioned previously, in this book, I too sometimes disregard the differences between metaphors and similes. Yet I want to briefly lay out here why such differences may indeed matter.

To Julie Carlson, for example, there are ethical implications that distinguish similes from metaphor. In saying that illness is *like* a journey, a simile does not hide its comparative gesture but instead makes it transparent. 'Whereas metaphors, in equating two things, have the potential for colonisation through conceptualisation, ... simile teaches us "to perceive in relation not to *is*, which often conflates identities, but *likeness*"' (Carlson qtd in Holmes, 271). In this way, similes avoid the source/target hierarchy of metaphor: a simile 'leaves both vehicle and tenor visible and distinct, neither incorporated into the other' (Holmes 271).

Similes also have a different relation to truthfulness than metaphors. All similes are true because 'everything is like everything', and therefore,

> we use a simile ordinarily only when we know the corresponding metaphor to be false. We say Mr. S. is like a pig because we know he isn't one. If we had used a metaphor and said he was a pig, this would not be because we changed our mind about the facts but because we chose to get the idea across in a different way. (Davidson 41)

Choosing between the use of a simile or a metaphor thus indicates how we – and the person we talk to – relate to a comparison: 'What matters is not actual falsehood but that the sentence be taken to be false' (42). Thus, if a comparison is patently false and if we know that the absurdity of the comparison is also apparent to others, the comparison is understood as a figure of speech and not as literal statement (42). This is of obvious relevance for health care: When the falsity of a comparison is not crystal clear to everyone involved – due to different knowledge bases or cultural contexts, for example – the effect of a metaphor may undermine a speaker's intentions and result in a misunderstanding. The risk of miscommunication increases when a comparison is novel or unconventional. Indeed, research shows that people prefer similes when a comparison is novel and not yet commonly established; by contrast, when the comparison is conventional, metaphors are more frequently used (Zharikov and Gentner).

Should we then conclude that, in health care communication, similes are preferable to metaphors? And is it possible to make a metaphor safe simply by adding 'like' or 'as'? The answer is 'no' to both if we follow Sergey S. Zharikov and Dedre Gentner. To them, similes and metaphors make different statements and express different intentions. Speakers typically use similes if a comparison is meant to emphasise attributes of size or form; metaphors are preferred when the comparison focuses on the relationship between source and target (Zharikov and Gentner 979). For example, 'the sun is like an orange' foregrounds characteristics such as shape and color – what something *is like* – whereas the comparison 'television is a magnet' emphasises what source and target *do* – they attract – and how their actions or effects are similar (977). That is, adding 'like' to a metaphor changes the function of the comparison. A metaphor such as '(The treatment) is the bullet, or missile, that we'll aim at the target' emphasises how the bullet or missile – that is, the treatment – and the target – for example cancerous cells – relate to one another: Both destroy (Casarett et al. 258). If we changed the metaphor into a simile, the comparison still foregrounds the destructive power of bullet and treatment, but it also highlights the attributes of the bullet – it is small, fast, slick. These features are less relevant to the scenario; as a simile, the comparison does not work as well.

With common metaphors such as 'illness is (like) a fight or journey', the distinction between simile and metaphor, characteristic features and actions, may matter less. Still, inserting 'like' into these metaphors does send a different signal because the simile reminds us and makes transparent that we are merely making a comparison, extending a suggestion or invitation to see illness 'like this'. Such a shift from metaphor to simile is easily done if the metaphor is based on nouns – illness is (like) a fight; the task is more onerous though when the metaphor appears in a different grammatical form, such as 'he is fighting against the virus'. In this case, we have to go to great lengths to render the comparison transparent, for example by prefacing the expression with 'we can think of him as someone who is fighting'. In other words, distinguishing between metaphor and simile does matter, albeit in various different ways.

Symbols are of a different cast altogether. In contrast to metaphors and similes, symbols do not suggest similarities between two objects or ideas. A symbol is 'an object, action, or event that represents something, or creates a range of associations, beyond itself'; it is something 'that stands for something else' (Hamilton 93; Mays 848). Flowers brought to a patient, for example, represent a loving family, sympathy and concern; but such flowers share no common features with the people who bring them to the hospital bed (Mays 848).[23] For this reason, 'symbols give rise to an endless exegesis' (Ricœur, 'Metaphor and Symbol' 57). We know intuitively that 'it means more than it says, but it cannot be made out what exactly that might be' (Bode 150). For example, the figurative meanings of a cross depend on the context in which it appears: it means different things in health care than in religion or traffic, of course, and may mean different things within these domains as well.

Conventional symbols have been shaped by habit or cultural tradition, and it is this implicit knowledge that helps us identify something as a symbol and connect it to what it represents. Nonconventional symbols, on the other hand, are invented and appear only in singular contexts, such as the green light in F. Scott Fitzgerald's novel *The Great Gatsby* (1925), which can be interpreted as a symbol of Gatsby's devotion for the woman he loves, Daisy, or as a symbol of money and prosperity, and thus the American Dream. Similarly, if a hospital patient repeatedly mentions a word, expressing a desire for 'honey', say, practitioners may rightly suspect an additional, figurative meaning beyond that of a sweet breakfast topping.[24] Relying on intuition is typical for identifying non-traditional symbols: we have a feeling that another meaning is implied, even though it is not articulated in any explicit way. Repetition can be a clue that alerts us to an extra, non-literal meaning; Hamilton also suggests that words may assume symbolic weight when they are closely connected to the fate of a person or character, or when they are embedded in a detailed description (Hamilton 94). These suggestions serve as a markedly vague starting point for identifying an expression as a symbol. The implication seems to be that 'any word or incident that calls attention to itself, anything unexpected, whatever seems particularly effective, should be looked at for symbolic implication' (Bartel 72). Yet expecting symbolic meaning everywhere can easily lead to overinterpretation and semantic appropriation, encouraging us to 'look through' the literal expression and pay less attention to what is in plain sight. For this reason, Michael Ferber advises: 'What Freud said about cigars is sometimes true of literary symbols: sometimes a nightingale is just a nightingale, or little more than a way of saying that night has come' (4). What is true of metaphor is also true of symbol, then: the interpreter's desire – to pin down meaning or to see her own interpretation acknowledged, for example – might easily override or ignore the literal needs of another person. Instead of overreading figurative language, the method I am suggesting encourages us to activate several meanings at once, both literal and figurative, and to flexibly navigate between them.

FINAL THOUGHTS

The five steps I have laid out above represent a method – a description of an idealised process of engagement with metaphor. I have worked with this method in narrative medicine workshops, and the informal feedback from the participants has been positive. The effectiveness of this method has never been formally tested, however, and while the participants reported that their awareness for metaphors was increased, it is not clear whether this awareness persists over time and if that increased awareness also implies an increased competence in dealing with metaphors.

Importantly, this method, and the concrete strategies and actions it comprises, is only one side of the coin. A critical and mindful use of metaphor is closely interrelated with other skills, abilities and attitudes, such as a heightened attunement to language, a tolerance for ambiguity and uncertainty, a willingness to take on different perspectives and a critical, self-reflexive consciousness. What I am advocating is not some rigid step-by-step schema, although I am aware that the five steps I present here do invoke the promises of manuals: once we have ticked all boxes, we have covered our bases and can tackle any metaphor. There is a great merit in manuals and guidelines, of course, but my aim is not to produce metaphor experts whose mastery disciplines and domesticates unruly language. If this book has made one thing plain, it is how *little* we can actually control a metaphor, its effects and functions, and how inherently unpredictable the uses are to which metaphors can be put. This is not a reason to lose heart, however, but a fact to acknowledge as part of a broader understanding of what it means to explore the varied usability of metaphors.

The method I described is best understood as an interactive, cooperative and reflexive process, in which meanings change dynamically and we enter into multiple relationships. Such an undertaking necessarily involves continuous, self-critical analysis: Which metaphors do *I* live by? How do they structure *my* way of thinking and living? This self-reflexivity also implies that there is no such thing as an ideal agentic, autonomous user in full control of metaphor's intended and effective meanings. After all, we are embedded in dynamic contexts in which we are often externally controlled, in which we react rather than act, and in which we are always entangled with and dependent on others.

There are more limitations to this method. The scenarios I have analysed tend to focus on exclusive, individual conversations between practitioner and patient or among colleagues. These small-scale, intersubjective encounters neglect the role of metaphors on a broader structural level, as for example in social policies, political speeches and institutional regulations.[25] While the method pays attention to cultural context, it does not cover in a comprehensive or satisfactory manner the role of metaphors in this broader, social dimension. It is such a structural aspect that my choice of close reading as the core method cannot address in a satisfactory way and that I hope other scholars, who are more knowledgeable in the analysis of social structures, will take up.

NOTES

1. Models for framing such metaphor competence already exist in fields like developmental psychology and language education. For example, the metaphoric competence of children has been evaluated with the help of concrete tasks and skills,[1] such as 'the capacity to paraphrase a metaphor, to explain the rationale for the metaphor's effectiveness, to produce a metaphor appropriate to a given context, [and] to evaluate the appropriateness of several competing metaphoric expressions (Gardner and Winner 128–9).'[1] Similar frameworks in language learning describe specific, observable actions corresponding to stages of metaphor competence, such as the ability to 'summarize' a metaphor, to 'decouple [it] from a narrative or conversational topic', to extend a metaphor, and to recognise when another speaker is 'extending or elaborating beyond conventional language and why' (Low 221). To my knowledge, these models have not yet been applied yet to health care contexts. However, other competence models have been suggested for health care, such as narrative competence (Charon, *Narrative Medicine*), structural competency (Metzl and Hansen), and cultural competence (e.g. Kumagai and Lypson; Luquis and Pérez).
2. For a critical discussion of the term 'method', see endnote 24 in the introduction.
3. Metaphor safety has been tested in a study by Nathaniel Kendall-Taylor and Abigail Haydon who use quantitative and qualitative methods

(such as a usability test and a persistence trial) to examine how well a metaphor conveys the intended information. The context of this study is policy making and the question how complex information on health-related issues, such as the factors that contribute to and prevent the development of resilience in children, can best be translated to a wider public.
4. An anonymous reviewer suggested that these lists could be read as a form of 'academic metaphor tennis' because Bleakley might be alluding to, for example, Wallace Stevens' poem 'Thirteen Ways of Looking at a Blackbird'.
5. Bob Spall and colleagues also recommend that practitioners engage in regular discussions with their colleagues about the metaphors used by patients or themselves (352).
6. I have written about methods for metaphor analysis in a previous publication, 'Analyzing Metaphors', published in *Research Methods in Health Humanities*, edited by Erin Gentry Lamb and Craig Klugman).
7. I am very grateful to Susanne Michl who shared this metaphor with me. It was used during a meeting of health care professionals, which she attended as an ethics consultant. In the discussion, the expression was used to describe a patient's critical health condition.
8. The exact age is debated and depends on the cognitive abilities used to define metaphor comprehension (e.g. pretence or meaning extension). Some studies suggest that the comprehension of novel metaphors develops progressively until adulthood (see Carriedo 2016).
9. Geary summarises in a chapter dedicated to 'Metaphor and Children' that 'though metaphor making starts early, metaphor comprehension develops in stages, beginning with basic physical comparisons before moving on to more conceptual and psychological domains. As children's knowledge of the world grows, so does their metaphorical range' (161).
10. A quick PubMed search illustrates this prominence: a search for 'vegetative' and 'cognitive' results in over 1,300 articles; 709 of them were published between 2010 and 2020. For a recent and nuanced evaluation of the term 'vegetative' in the context of intensive care, see Wijdicks (2021).
11. Another aspect of mapping to consider is the principle of *unidirectionality*. The process of mapping, as some scholars argue, usually occurs in one direction only – from source to target. The source is typically more concrete and tangible than the target. However, there are other theories that suggest different relations between source and target, such as mutual interaction (e.g. Beardsley and Black) as well as blending or integration (e.g. Fauconnier and Turner). Yet, the principle of unidirectionality is compelling because of its simplicity and because it demonstrates that, while some source and target domains can be reversed, this reversal results in different mappings. For example, to stay with the plant metaphor, one can also think of plants as people (and not only people as plants).

When we personify a willow as weeping or mourning, human qualities are ascribed to a plant. The meanings, then, are different because other constituent elements are transferred or mapped.

12. A number of books on metaphors in medicine provide historical or etymological information on medical metaphors (e.g. Bleakley; Vaisrub; van Rijn-van Tongeren;).
13. Also see: Lindsey Fitzharris. *The Butchering Art: Joseph Lister's Quest to Transform the Grisly World of Victorian Medicine*. Scientific American, 2017.
14. Blending Theory accounts for this incongruence by suggesting a 'cross-domain mapping' or 'conceptual integration' (Kövecses, *Metaphor* 318): The butcher's actions and characteristics emerge in the light of the surgeon's actions and characteristics; they do not exist per se but are contingent on the context (318). 'The blend" or blended space thus introduces a new element that does not need to be constitutive of either source or target domain. In contrast to Conceptual Metaphor Theory, Blending Theory does not see a hierarchy between the input spaces. Moreover, Blending Theory allows for new ways to conceptualise metaphoric creativity because the blend 'contains more than the sum of the parts of the input spaces' (Busse 179).
15. For more information on the historical dimension of the gendered body and its metaphors, see, for example, Emily Martin's *Women in the Body* or Diane Price Herndl's *Invalid Women*.
16. I encountered the example through Elena Semino and Zsófia Demjén's research on online support groups on cancer. My analysis below draws on and is inspired by their discussion (*Metaphor* 233).
17. The old-mare metaphor is taken from an old American folk and children's song. The basic lyrics have been taken up and developed in parodies of the song. For example, in one version, the old mare is said to go 'swimming in the Delaware' with 'her yellow underwear' pretending 'she didn't give a care' (Miller).
18. There is another issue that further complicates the matter. The old-mare comparison is, in fact, uttered as a simile: 'I'm like the old gray mare', the patient is quoted by Berger and colleagues (828). Following my suggestions on similes below, a simile tends to be true because everything can be said to be like everything else. Had the patient said, 'I'm an old mare,' the falseness of the comparison would be easier to surmise. A simile, it seems, complicates how ironic the statement is actually meant, whereas a metaphor seems to heighten the irony.
19. I am grateful to Anna Fenton-Hathaway who brought this example to my attention.
20. In one exercise, Bolton lists questions such as 'If x were an animal, what kind of animal (or food or plant) would it be?' (125). With this exercise, our imagination is activated and the questions can generate surprising comparisons and new insights.

21. For a critical discussion of the dangers of such intimate work with metaphors, see Cohen (1978, 11–12).
22. This subchapter draws on my article 'Symbol or Simile? Sylvia Plath's Poem "Tulips" and the Role of Language in Medicine', published in *Lyrik und Medizin. Jahrbuch Literatur und Medizin*, edited by Florian Steger and Katharina Fürholzer.
23. The definition is, to some extent slippery, because, strictly speaking, all words point beyond themselves and signify something else than the sounds or succession of letters that they are: rock, tree or cloud signify, literally, material objects in the world, but they may also take on a figurative meaning and imply solidity, life or dreams (Mays 848).
24. I take this example from a course on health care communication, in which a medical student relayed an encounter with a so-called difficult patient, who kept complaining about the care she received. The missing honey on her breakfast tray, we surmised, could be a symbol of anything she found lacking and insufficient.
25. See Olivia Banner for a similar critique of narrow focus applied to 'cultural competence'.

Conclusion

Metaphors can be used creatively, imaginatively and generatively in health care as well as in life. Even a famously problematic metaphor such as the battle metaphor for illness can be rethought and continually reimagined. Such reusability may involve several strategies: a metaphor can be traced, challenged, extended and combined with others. Extension can imply new characters (civilians, marathon runners, Amazon warriors), different settings (a courtroom, a baseball field, outer space), new trajectories (defeat, surrender) and a range of attitudes (contentiousness, irony, humour, playfulness). A close reading of a metaphor's context illuminates how the metaphor's meaning is thickened when it is embedded, for example, in (or alongside) questions, exaggerations, second-person narration, negation and other stories that run parallel to it or function as frames. The aims of activating a metaphor's usability are varied, too: while agency and resistance are recurring motivations (including resistance to social hierarchies, racial injustice and the biomedical discourses that uphold them), there are other important aims and outcomes including repair, self-knowledge, intensification and pleasure.

The five central texts here speak with and about metaphor in remarkable ways. Susan Sontag's *Illness as Metaphor* cautions us against metaphors that intensify affective states, such as shame and guilt; at the same time, Sontag looks for ways of writing and interpretation that evoke and grant access to sensory perception. Audre Lorde and Anatole Broyard respond to Sontag's quest by exploring metaphor's sensory and embodied side. For them, metaphor is at the centre of their grappling with a changed body as well as their fears of diminishment and extinction – both politically and existentially. Lorde and Broyard take self-knowledge and self-care to new levels by linking their search for meaning with social protest and personal growth (Lorde) as well as a playful yet serious style of vanity and campy exaggeration (Broyard). The texts here approach metaphor use and reuse in distinct and individual ways, yet they also speak to each other as they cut across important recurring issues: the ethics of feeling more (Sontag, Broyard), the risks of sameness overriding difference (Eve Ensler, Lorde, David Foster Wallace), the challenges of humour and irony (Broyard, Wallace), and the opportunities and limitations of specific genres and narrative forms (Sontag, Wallace). These issues are addressed in the course of rethinking the metaphor 'illness is a battle'. Accordingly, the strategies used to rethink this metaphor are neither universal nor necessarily benign; as we see in Wallace's example, creative engagement with a metaphor can be put to problematic ends. This is not a limitation per se, but it is an important facet to contemplate in a book dedicated to metaphor's varied usability.

I approach the usability of metaphor in two ways. For one, it is the product or result of *a practice of reimagining metaphors*, illustrated so dexterously by the writers I examine. For another, it is an ongoing process and an *ability to analyse* metaphors with the help of metaphor theory and narrative theory. A lingering question concerns the problem of agency: Who exactly is doing the work of reusing metaphors? Who is the agent of the strategies I identify? I briefly address this question in Chapter 2, where I side with George Lakoff and Mark Turner in considering the writer or poet to be the mastermind of metaphor use and reuse, at least grammatically speaking. One may wonder, however, to what extent were the writers actively and consciously employing all the strategies I ascribe to them? Is it not my reading and subsequent labelling of them *as strategies* that makes them into reusable tools? Benjamin Biebuyck and Gunther Martens propose a third option: metaphor does not stem from anyone; 'it is an *event*, happening to rather than within narration' ('Metaphor and Narrative' 118; original emphasis). In other words, metaphor is 'autopoetic' (125) and beyond the control of any identifiable agent. While Biebuyck and Martens have fresh and surprising metaphors in mind, which can indeed develop a powerful vibrancy of their own, their reasoning, to some degree, also applies to the metaphors that are the focus of this book: highly conventionalised, ingrained metaphors, too, can take on a creative life of their own when they inspire someone to think of surprising new ways and meanings as they negotiate a metaphor's problematic or inadequate implications. This third option, however, seems to relegate the writers in this book to a secondary role: they *react to* a metaphor and are enthralled by it, rather than actively and consciously belabouring it.

In this book, I consider the usability of metaphor a collaborative effort. To use and reuse a metaphor requires agents – a writer, a narrator, a character, a reader – to reanimate conventionalised mappings and entailments; but that active engagement is not entirely under the control of any of them. Additional dimensions will always factor in, from the narrative context in which an author embeds a metaphor to the knowledge readers bring to a source domain to the sudden insights and inspirations that come out of nowhere and spark a new association. Treating writers as crucial (but not the sole) agents of metaphor allows me to explore how we are all active and creative *reusers* of metaphor. Published authors of literature may have greater practice with imaginatively reusing metaphors, but we all have the capacity for exploring metaphor's varied usability.

There are limits to the (re)usability of metaphors, however. As I acknowledge throughout the book, metaphor is not an object that can be mastered or ever absolutely controlled. This implies that reuse is not per se a commendable practice, nor that the outcome of creatively engaging with a harmful metaphor is automatically beneficial. Some metaphors are better left at the door and not dragged again into the limelight. In short, the varied usability of metaphors does not prompt a fail-safe undertaking. And yet, metaphor's slippery, evasive nature is in fact the precondition for its magic to unfold, and it is this unpredictability that allows writers like Lorde, Broyard and others to tease out ever new associations and meanings. Metaphor's usability is a fusion of two perspectives: it is a creative practice whose results can be and need to be critically analysed; it is also a set of analytical tools and strategies that can be actively and mindfully applied.

In focusing primarily on *one* metaphor – the battle or fight metaphor for illness – I show how 'reuse' may have more benefits than, for example, inventing new metaphors for illness – a task that is challenging as well as risky.[1] Practices of reuse are not only resource-efficient, they also come naturally to us; each day, we are already engaged in continually shaping and appropriating language with our individual voices, our humour, socio-dialectal inflections and context-specific vocabulary.

Attending to *one* metaphor only has also helped me develop a methodology of metaphor use that is applicable to other prominent metaphors. In fact, there are numerous metaphors like the fight metaphor that seem so natural to us that they have disappeared *as* metaphors.[2] By way of closing, I want to focus on one final example, the notion that 'time is money', which is not only a ubiquitous metaphor in our everyday lives, it also affects health care in complex ways.

The comparison of time to money has been popular since the mid-eighteenth century.[3] The metaphor uses 'money' as the source domain to define a target that is otherwise elusive and abstract. In likening money to time, we claim that 'any period of time has the potential to generate income'; the comparison is also 'frequently used to discourage occupations or engagements that would be injurious to this' ('time'). Not only do 'we *act* as if time is a valuable commodity – a limited resource' like money, Lakoff and Johnson argue, 'we *conceive* of time that way. Thus we understand and experience time as the kind of thing that can be spent, wasted, budgeted, invested wisely or poorly, saved, or squandered' (*Metaphors* 8). The metaphor suggests, among other things, that time is limited, and that this scarcity is a simple fact of life – concealing, of course, the concept's neoliberal, post-Fordist and capitalist underpinnings. Both the explicit and implicit features of this source bear down on health care practitioners who feel constrained by what seems like a chronic shortage of time.

Metaphor analysis can help broaden our ways of thinking about this concept. For example, we can replace the source domain by comparing time not to money but to a gift, making it something that is bestowed upon us (not bought), something that it is valuable but does not have a set price (e.g. Hyde). This replacement forces us to see that 'time is money' is a metaphor and thus necessarily based on a mistake. With that awareness comes the mental room to evaluate both what *is* and what *is not* true about the comparison: while we might be able to save time (or money) through efficient actions, we cannot store time (like money in a bank) because we cannot claim ownership of it, because time is not physical in the way coins or bills are and because it is not a simple fact (like an object) but a theoretical construct or concept.

Another way of broadening the metaphor is to trace how 'time is money' and its entailments are used in health care. This strategy reveals some of the metaphor's ambiguity. In emergency medicine, for example, the feature of scarcity is emphasised when health professionals use phrases such as 'time is brain' and 'time is muscle' (e.g. Saver).[4] These phrases indicate that a shortage of time – as for example in the case of a stroke – positively affects a patient's health. That is, the less time it takes to attend to a patient, the better the outcome of the health care intervention (i.e., patients suffer fewer damages and their chances of survival increase).[5] This positive view of time reduction contrasts with the common view of time famine among health care professionals, who argue that the increasing economisation of health care allots less time for each patient, which results in poorer care and more stress for practitioners.

There are many additional ways to rethink 'time is money' and its prominent entailment of shortage,[6] but one unusual suggestion comes from Albert Camus. I mention this as my last example because Camus's linking of time with an embodied experience reflects in intriguing ways Sontag's 'aesthetic strategy or pedagogy of the senses', that is her inquiry into modes of expression that make space for sensory experiences (Nelson 117). In *The Plague* (1947), Camus's narrator asks rhetorically how we can avoid losing or wasting time. Like Lorde, his answer relies on stretching the metaphor: the narrator recommends the following '*[w]ays in which this can be done*':

> By spending one's days on an uneasy chair in a dentist's waiting room; by remaining on one's balcony all of a Sunday afternoon; by listening to lectures in a language one doesn't know; by traveling by the longest and least-convenient train routes, and of course standing all the way; by lining up at the box-office of theaters and then not buying a seat; and so forth. (26; original emphasis)

Camus's narrator stresses sensory experiences such as physical discomfort as well as specific embodied actions like sitting, standing and queuing. These actions are counter-intuitive because they flout economic paradigms of efficiency. Moreover, the suggestions are invitations to *feel* time's slow passing in and through the body. Camus's example returns us to Sontag's quest: How can we approach artworks – and metaphors – in order 'to *see* more, to *hear* more, to *feel* more' ('Against Interpretation' 14; original emphasis)? Camus's reuse of this highly familiar metaphor encourages, for one, a critical, intellectual stance, a belabouring and 'thinking with' metaphor; for another, it invites a sensory, aesthetic undergoing in which we 'feel with' a metaphor and let it unfold new visions and experiences as they arise.

Using and reusing metaphors is a process that takes time – to acquire, to rehearse, to apply. It is grounded in close reading and careful attention to details, meanings and affordances; and it can be complemented by contextual analyses. Its value, I hope, lies in improving our understanding of the varied potential of figurative language. While it may make communication more efficient in an economic sense, it is more important to me that the uses of metaphor I described in this book render communication more saturated with diversity – of experiences, perspectives and values – and more resonant with what is (or may be) at stake in the language we choose – thematically, emotionally, existentially.

NOTES

1. Imagine a health care practitioner who, like Broyard, decides to speak of illness as a dance. Not only might the patient feel alienated, she might also wonder if someone is trying to flaunt their poetic ingenuity. Moreover, Brit Trogen has questioned whether new metaphors should be left to 'the

whims' of individual physicians (1411). At the same time, of course, we have all surprised ourselves with a new metaphor that has just sprung to mind. (If the moment is right, why not test its usability?)
2. Take, for instance, the work on metaphors of old age by colleagues in age studies who have identified widely internalised – and insidious – metaphors such as old age as decline, as burden, as natural catastrophe (tsunami), as tragedy (e.g. Gullette; Charise).
3. The metaphor was first used in 1719, in a British newspaper called *The Freethinker*. Benjamin Franklin employed the metaphor in his essay 'Advice to a Young Tradesman' in 1749 (*OED*).
4. Another question is, of course, if these phrases are actually metaphors or if they function more like mathematical formulas or equations, where one factor (time) behaves inversely proportional to another (brain).
5. Scarcity can be rethought in other ways, too: a poem uses only a few lines or words even to express dense, saturated ideas; a metaphor is also a condensed expression of complex relations. In other words, scarcity does not necessarily imply poverty but can also be a sign of complexity (see Wohlmann and Michl).
6. Time is not only a limited resource but also unequally distributed and thus dependent on social factors, such as class and gender. For example, the gender pay gap implies that women do not only earn less money, they also have less free time (because they take over more care work).

Bibliography

Abbott, H. Porter. 'Unnarratable Knowledge: The Difficulty of Understanding Evolution by Natural Selection'. *Narrative Theory and the Cognitive Sciences*, edited by David Herman, University of Chicago Press, 2003, 143–62.
Abrams, M. H. *A Glossary of Literary Terms*. 7th edn, Heinle & Heinle, 1999.
Agstner, Irene. *Krebs und seine Metaphern in der Psychotherapie: Ein gestalttheoretischer Ansatz*. Klammer, 2008.
Ahmad, Sara. *What's The Use?* Duke University Press, 2019.
Alexander, Elizabeth. '"Coming out Blackened and Whole": Fragmentation and Reintegration in Audre Lorde's *Zami* and *The Cancer Journals*'. *American Literary History*, vol. 6, no. 4, Winter 1994, pp. 695–715.
Allsopp, Gail. 'Medicine within Health Humanities'. *The Routledge Companion to Health Humanities*, edited by Paul Crawford, Brian Brown and Andrea Charise. Routledge, 2020, pp. 66–71.
Alpern, Stanley. *Amazons of Black Sparta: The Women Warriors of Dahomey*. New York University Press, 2011.
Aristotle. *Poetics*. edited by S. Halliwell. Harvard University Press, 1995.
Atkinson, Sarah, Bethan Evans, Angela Woods and Robin Kearns. '"The Medical" and "Health" in a Critical Medical Humanities'. *The Journal of Medical Humanities*, vol. 36, no. 1, 2014–15, pp. 71–81.
Banner, Olivia. 'Structural Racism and Practices of Reading in the Medical Humanities'. *Literature and Medicine*, vol. 34, no. 1, Spring 2016, pp. 25–52.
Barron, Carrie, David Ring and Matt McGlone. 'Is There a Better Term for "Burnout"?' *Dell Medical School*, 9 May 2017, https://dellmed.utexas.edu/blog/is-there-a-better-term-for-burnout. Accessed 29 August 2021.
Bartel, Roland. *Metaphors and Symbols: Forays into Language*. National Council of Teachers of English, 1983.
Becker, Gay. *Disrupted Lives: How People Create Meaning in a Chaotic World*. University of California Press, 1997.
Becker, Gay. 'Metaphors in Disrupted Lives: Infertility and Cultural Constructions of Continuity'. *Medical Anthropology Quarterly*, vol. 8, no. 4, 1994, pp. 383–410.

Belling, Catherine. 'A Happy Doctor's Escape from Narrative: Reflection in Saturday'. *Medical Humanities*, vol. 38, no. 2, 2012, pp. 2–6.

'be out of the woods'. *Cambridge Dictionary*, 2014, https://dictionary.cambridge.org/de/worterbuch/englisch/be-out-of-the-woods. Accessed 30 August 2021.

Berger, Jeffery T., Jack Coulehan and Catherine Belling. 'Humor in the Physician–Patient Encounter'. *Archives of Internal Medicine*, vol. 164, 2004, pp. 825–30.

Best, Stephen and Sharon Marcus. 'Surface Reading: An Introduction'. *Representations*, vol. 108, Fall 2009, pp. 1–21.

Biebuyck, Benjamin and Gunther Martens. 'Metaphor and Narrative. With References to Nietzsche's *Bildungsanstalten*'. *In Search of (Non)Sense. Literary Semantics and the Related Fields and Disciplines*, edited by E. Kluszewska and G. Spila. Cambridge Scholars Publishing, 2009, pp. 115–27.

Biebuyck, Benjamin. 'Figurativeness figuring as a Condenser between Event and Action: How Tropes Generate Additional Dimensions of Narrativity'. *Amsterdam Electronic Journal of Cultural Narratology*, no. 4, Autumn 2007, https://cf.hum.uva.nl/narratology/a07_biebuyck.htm. Accessed 28 August 2021.

Biebuyck, Benjamin and Gunther Martens. 'Literary Metaphor between Cognition and Narration: *The Sandmann* revisited'. *Beyond Cognitive Metaphor Theory: Perspectives on Literary Metaphor*, edited by Monika Fludernik. Routledge, 2011, pp. 58–76.

Black, Max. 'More about Metaphor'. *Dialectica*, vol. 31, nos 3/4, 1977, pp. 431–57.

Bleakley, Alan. *Thinking with Metaphors in Medicine: The State of the Art*. Routledge, 2017.

Bleakley, Alan and Shane Neilson. *Poetry in the Clinic: Towards a Lyrical Medicine*. Routledge, 2021.

Bode, Christoph. 'Tropes'. *Literature: An Introduction to Theory and Analysis*, edited by Mads Rosendahl Thomsen, Lasse Horne Kjældgaard, Lis Møller, Dan Ringgard, Lilian Munk Rösing and Peter Simonsen. Bloomsbury, 2017, pp. 144–56.

Bolaki, Stella. *Illness as Many Narratives: Arts, Medicine and Culture*. Edinburgh Universtiy Press, 2016.

Bolaki, Stella. *Unsettling the Bildungsroman: Reading Contemporary Ethnic American Women's Fiction*. Rodopi, 2011.

Bolton, Gillie. *Reflective Practice: Writing and Professional Development*. Sage, 2018.

Bono, James J. 'Science, Discourse, and Literature: The Role/Rule of Metaphor in Science'. *Literature and Science: Theory and Practice*, edited by Stuart Peterfreund. Northeastern University Press, 1990, pp. 59–89.

Boyer, Anne. 'What Cancer Takes Away'. *The New Yorker*, 8 April 2019, https://www.newyorker.com/magazine/2019/04/15/what-cancer-takes-away. Accessed 29 August 2021.

Brody, Howard. '"My Story is Broken: Can You Help Me Fix It?" Medical Ethics and the Joint Construction of Narrative'. *Literature and Medicine*, vol. 13, no. 1, Spring 1994, pp. 79–92.

Broyard, Anatole. *Intoxicated by My Illness: And Other Writings on Life and Death*. Fawcett Columbine, 1992.

Broyard, Anatole. 'Portrait of the Inauthentic Negro: How Prejudice Distorts the Victim's Personality'. *Commentary Magazine*, 10 July 1950, https://www.commentarymagazine.com/articles/anatole-broyard/portrait-of-the-inauthentic-negrohow-prejudice-distorts-the-victims-personality/. Accessed 29 August 2021.

Broyard, Bliss. *One Drop: My Father's Hidden Life: A Story of Race and Family Secrets*. Little, Brown and Company, 2007.

Brown, Carolyn S. *The Tall Tale in American Folklore and Literature*. University of Tennessee Press, 1989.

Bruner, Jerome. 'The Narrative Construction of Reality'. *Critical Inquiry*, vol. 18, no. 1, 1991, pp. 1–21.

Busse, Beatrix. 'Writing and Reading as Therapy in Paul Auster's Novels'. *Beyond Cognitive Metaphor Theory: Perspectives on Literary Metaphor*, edited by Monika Fludernik. Routledge, 2011, pp. 176–95.

'butcher'. *The Oxford English Dictionary*. 2020. *OED Online*. https://www-oed-com.proxy1-bib.sdu.dk/view/Entry/25324?rskey=S9ykis&result=1&isAdvanced=false#eid. Accessed 26 August 2021.

Butler, Judith. *Giving an Account of Oneself*. Fordham University Press, 2005.

Cameron, Lynne. 'Patterns of Metaphor Use in Reconciliation Talk'. *Discourse and Society*, vol. 18, 2007, pp. 197–222.

Camus, Albert. *The Plague*, translated by Stuart Gilbert. Vintage International, 1991.

Carel, Havi. *Illness*. Routledge, 2008.

Carel, Havi. *Phenomenology of Illness*. Oxford University Press, 2016.

Carel, Havi. 'A Reply to "Towards an Understanding of Nursing as a Response to Human Vulnerability" by Derek Sellman: Vulnerability and Illness'. *Nursing Philosophy*, vol. 10, 2009, pp. 214–19.

Carel, Havi, Ian James Kidd and Richard Pettigrew. 'Illness as Transformative Experience'. *The Lancet*, vol. 388, no. 10050, 17 September 2016, pp. 1152–3, doi.org/10.1016/S0140-6736(16)31606-3. Accessed 29 August 2021.

Carriedo Nuria, Corral Antonio, Montoro Pedro R, Herrero Laura, Ballestrino Patricia and Sebastián Iraia. 'The Development of Metaphor Comprehension and Its Relationship with Relational Verbal Reasoning and Executive Function'. *PLoS ONE*, vol. 11, no. 3, 2016, doi:10.1371/journal.pone.0150289. Accessed 28 August 2021.

Carter, Sherrie Bourg. 'When Life Loses Its Meaning: The Heavy Price of High Achievement'. *Psychology Today*, 30 September 2011, https://www.psychologytoday.com/intl/blog/high-octane-women/201109/when-life-loses-its-meaning-the-heavy-price-high-achievement. Accessed 29 August 2021.

Casarett, David, Amy Pickard, Jessica M. Fishman, Stewart C. Alexander, Robert M. Arnold, Kathryn I. Pollak and James A. Tulsky. 'Can Metaphors and Analogies Improve Communication with Seriously Ill Patients?' *Journal of Palliative Medicine*, vol. 13, no. 3, 2010, pp. 255–60.

Chambers, Tod. 'Metaphors as Equipment for Living'. *The American Journal of Bioethics*, vol. 16, no. 10, 2016, pp. 12–13.

Charise, Andrea. '"Let the Reader Think of the Burden": Old Age and the Crisis of Capacity'. *Occasion: Interdisciplinary Studies in the Humanities*, vol. 4, 2012, http://occasion.stanford.edu/node/96. Accessed 28 August 2021.

Charon, Rita. 'Close Reading: The Signature Method of Narrative Medicine'. *The Principles and Practice of Narrative Medicine*, co-authored by Rita Charon, Sayantani DasGupta, Nellie Hermann, Craig Irvine, Eric R. Marcus, Edgar Rivera Colón, Danielle Spencer and Maura Spiegel. Oxford University Press, 2017, pp. 157–79.

Charon, Rita. 'Narrative Medicine: Attention, Representation, Affiliation'. *Narrative*, vol. 13, no. 3, October 2005, pp. 261–70.

Charon, Rita. *Narrative Medicine: Honoring the Stories of Illness*. Oxford University Press, 2006.

Charon, Rita. 'The Novelization of the Body, or, How Medicine and Stories Need One Another'. *Narrative*, vol. 19, no. 1, 2011, pp. 33–50.

'cloud'. *The Oxford English Dictionary*. 2020. OED Online. https://www-oed-com.proxy1-bib.sdu.dk/view/Entry/34689?rskey=acc1oV&result=1&isAdvanced=false#eid. Accessed 26 August 2021.

'a cloud on the horizon'. *Cambridge Dictionary*, 2014, https://dictionary.cambridge.org/de/worterbuch/englisch/a-cloud-on-the-horizon?q=cloud+on+the+horizon'. Accessed 30 August 2021.

Clow, Barbara. 'Who's Afraid of Susan Sontag? Or, the Myths and Metaphors of Cancer Reconsidered'. *Social History of Medicine*, vol. 14, no. 2, 2001, pp. 293–312.

Cohen, Ted. 'Metaphor'. *The Oxford Handbook of Aesthetics*, edited by Jerrold Levinson. Oxford University Press, 2009, 366–7.

Cohen, Ted. 'Metaphor and the Cultivation of Intimacy'. *Critical Inquiry*, vol. 5, no. 1, Autumn 1978, pp. 3–12.

Cohen, Ted. *Thinking of Others: On the Talent for Metaphor*. Princeton University Press, 2008.

Colebrook, C. 'Irony'. *The Princeton Encyclopedia of Poetry and Poetics*, 4th edn, edited by Stephen Cushman, Clare Cavanagh, Jahan Ramazani and Paul Rouzer. Princeton University Press, 2012, pp. 731–3.

Conway, Kathleen. *Beyond Words: Illness and the Limits of Expression*. University of New Mexico Press, 2013.

Cooper, Christine M. 'Worrying about Vaginas: Feminism and Eve Ensler's *The Vagina Monologues*'. *Signs: Journal of Women in Culture and Society*, vol. 32, no. 3, Spring 2007, pp. 727–58.

Couser, G. Thomas. 'Disability as Metaphor'. *Prose Studies: History, Theory, Criticism*, vol. 27, nos 1–2, 2005, pp. 141–54.

Couser, G. Thomas. *Recovering Bodies: Illness, Disability, and Life Writing*. University of Wisconsin Press, 1997.

Crawford, Paul, Brian Brown, Victoria Tischler and Charley Baker. 'Health Humanities: The Future of Medical Humanities?' *Mental Health Review Journal*, vol. 15, no. 3, 2010, pp. 4–10.

Culler, Jonathan. 'Narrative Theory and the Lyric'. *Cambridge Companion to Narrative Theory*, edited by Matthew Garrett. Cambridge University Press, 2018, pp. 201–16.

Dash, Mike. 'Dahomey's Women Warriors'. *Smithsonian Magazine*, 23 September 2011, https://www.smithsonianmag.com/history/dahomeys-women-warriors-88286072/. Accessed 29 August 2021.

'David Foster Wallace at Amherst College'. *Amherst College*, https://www.amherst.edu/library/archives/holdings/david-foster-wallace. Accessed 29 August 2021.

Davidson, Donald. 'What Metaphors Mean'. *Critical Inquiry*, vol. 5, 1978, pp. 31–47.

Deerwester, Jayme. '"SNL": RuPaul declares, "The Library is Open" for Snarky Storytime Hour'. *USA TODAY*, 9 February 2020, https://www.usatoday.com/story/entertainment/tv/2020/02/09/saturday-night-live-library-open-drag-queen-storytime/4703493002/. Accessed 29 August 2021.

Desmarais, Jane and David Weir. *Decadence and Literature*. Cambridge University Press, 2019.

Didion, Joan. 'In Bed'. *The White Album*. Simon & Schuster, 1979, pp. 168–72.

Diedrich, Lisa. *Treatments: Language, Politics, and the Culture of Illness*. University of Minnesota Press, 2007.

Donoghue, Denis. 'Disease Should Be Itself'. *The New York Times*, 16 July 1978, https://archive.nytimes.com/www.nytimes.com/books/00/03/12/specials/sontag-illness.html. Accessed 29 August 2021.

Donoghue, Denis. *Metaphor*. Harvard University Press, 2014.

Doty, Mark. *The Art of Description: World into Word*. Graywolf Press, 2010.

Dowling, William C. *Ricœur on Time and Narrative: An Introduction to Temps et Récit*. University of Notre Dame Press, 2011.

Dyer, Richard. *The Culture of Queers*. Routledge, 2002.

Eakin, Paul John. *Living Autobiographically: How We Create Identity in Narrative*. Cornell University Press, 2008.

Ehrenreich, Barbara. *Smile or Die: How Positive Thinking Fooled America and the World*. Granta, 2010.

Ehrenreich, Barbara. 'Welcome to Cancerland: A Mammogram leads to a Cult of Pink Kitsch'. *Harper's Magazine*, November 2001, pp. 43–53.

Empson, William. *Seven Types of Ambiguity*. 3rd edn, Chatto & Windus, 1970.

Engberg-Pedersen, Anders. 'COVID-19 and War as Metaphor'. *b20: an online journal*, 22 April 2020, https://www.boundary2.org/2020/04/anders-engberg-pedersen-covid-19-and-war-as-metaphor/. Accessed 29 August 2021.

Epple, Angelika and Walter Erhart. 'Practices of Comparing: A New Research Agenda between Typological and Historical Approaches'. *Practices of Comparing: Towards a New Understanding of a Fundamental Human Practice*, edited by Angelika Epple, Walter Erhart and Johannes Grave, Transcript, 2020, pp. 11–38.

Erard, Michael. 'See through Words'. *Aeon*, 9 June 2015, https://aeon.co/essays/how-to-build-a-metaphor-to-change-people-s-minds. Accessed 29 August 2021.

Eubanks, Philip. 'The Story of Conceptual Metaphor: What Motivates Metaphoric Mappings?' *Poetics Today*, vol. 20, no. 3, Fall 1999, pp. 419–42.

Felski, Rita. 'Comparison and Translation: A Perspective From Actor-Network Theory'. *Comparative Literature Studies*, vol. 53, no. 4, 2016, pp. 747–65.

Felski, Rita. *The Limits of Critique*. University of Chicago Press, 2015.

Felski, Rita. *Literature after Feminism*. University of Chicago Press, 2003.

Felski, Rita. *The Uses of Literature*. Blackwell, 2008.

Felski, Rita and Susan Stanford Friedman (eds). *Comparison: Theories, Approaches, Uses*. The Johns Hopkins University Press, 2013.

Ferber, Michael. *A Dictionary of Literary Symbols*. Cambridge University Press, 2017.

Fink, Dennis L. *The Battle of Marathon in Scholarship: Research, Theories and Controversies since 1850*. McFarland, 2014.

Fischlin, Daniel T. '"I know not what yet that I feel is much". The Rhetoric of Negation in the English Air." *Rhetoric Society Quarterly*, vol. 19, no. 2, 1989, pp. 153–70.

Fitzpatrick, Kathleen. 'Infinite Summer: Reading, Empathy, and the Social Network'. *The Legacy of David Foster Wallace*, edited by Samuel Cohen and Lee Konstantinou. University of Iowa Press, 2012, pp. 182–207.

Fleischman, Suzanne. 'I am…, I have…, I suffer fro….: A Linguist Reflects on the Language of Illness and Disease'. *Journal of Medical Humanities*, vol. 20, no. 1, 1999, pp. 3–32.

Fludernik, Monika (ed.). *Beyond Cognitive Metaphor Theory: Perspectives on Literary Metaphor*. Routledge, 2011.

Fludernik, Monika. 'The Cage Metaphor: Extending Narratology into Corpus Studies and Opening it to the Analysis of Imagery'. *Narratology in the Age of Cross-Disciplinary Narrative Research*, edited by Sandra Heinen and Roy Sommer. de Gruyter, 2009, pp. 109–28.

Fludernik, Monika. 'Narrative and Metaphor'. *Language and Style. In Honour of Mick Short*, edited by Dan McIntyre and Beatrix Busse, Palgrave, 2010, pp. 347–63.

Fludernik, Monika. 'Second Person Fiction: Narrative *You* as Addressee And/Or Protagonist'. *AAA – Arbeiten aus Anglistik und Amerikanistik*, vol. 18, no. 2, 1993, pp. 217–47.

Fogelin, Robert J. *Figuratively Speaking: Revised Edition*. Oxford University Press, 2011.

'For Those with a Warped Sense of Humour Warning – No Punches Pulled Here'. *Macmillan Cancer Support*, https://community.macmillan.org.uk/cancer_experiences/chat/f/chat-13/40784/for-those-with-a-warped-sense-of-humour-warning--no-punches-pulled-here?pi5520=2&pifragment-13906=38. Accessed 29 August 2021.

Frank, Arthur. 'Metaphors of Pain'. *Literature and Medicine*, vol. 29. no. 1, Spring 2011, pp. 182–96.

Frank, Arthur. *At the Will of the Body: Reflections on Illness*. Mariner Books, 2002.

Frank, Arthur. *The Wounded Storyteller: Body, Illness and Ethics*. University of Chicago Press, 1995.

Friedman, Susan Stanford. 'Lyric Subversion of Narrative in Women's Writing: Virginia Woolf and the Tyranny of Plot'. *Reading Narrative: Form, Ethics, Ideology*, edited by James Phelan, Ohio State University Press, 1989, pp. 162–85.

Friedman, Susan Stanford. 'Why Not Compare?' *PMLA*, vol. 126, no. 3, May 2011, pp. 753–62.

Frommelt, Peter. 'Kurt Goldstein und Adhémar Gelb: Haben sie eine Aktualität für die heutige Neurorehabilitation und Neuropsychologie?' *Neurologie & Rehabilitation*, vol. 21, no. 6, 2015, pp. 353–63.

Gallop, Jane. 'The Historicization of Literary Studies and the Fate of Close Reading'. *Profession*, vol. 1, 2007, pp. 181–6.

Garber, Marjorie. *The Use and Abuse of Literature*. Anchor Books, 2011.

Garden, Rebecca. 'Telling Stories about Illness and Disability: The Limits and Lessons of Narrative'. *Perspectives in Biology and Medicine*, vol. 53, no. 1, 2010, pp. 121–35.

Gardner, Howard and Ellen Winner. 'The Development of Metaphoric Competence: Implications for Humanistic Disciplines'. *Critical Inquiry*, vol. 5, no. 1, Autumn 1978, pp. 123–41.

Gates, Henry Louis. 'White Like Me'. *The New Yorker*, 10 June 1996, https://www.newyorker.com/magazine/1996/06/17/white-like-me. Accessed 29 August 2021.

Geary, James. *I is Another: The Secret Life of Metaphor and How it Shapes the Way We see the World*. Harper Perennial, 2011.

Gillis, Alan. 'Poetry: An Introduction'. *The Edinburgh Introduction to Studying English Literature*, edited by Dermot Cavanagh, Alan Gillis, Michelle Known, James Loxley and Randall Stevenson, 2nd edn. Edinburgh University Press, 2014, pp. 37–46.

Goodman, Nelson. *Languages of Art*. Bobbs-Merrill, 1968.

Gordon, Linda. 'A Meditation on Comparison in Historical Scholarship'. *Comparison: Theories, Approaches, Uses*, edited by Rita Felski and Susan Stanford Friedman. The Johns Hopkins University Press, 2013, pp. 315–35.

Grady, Joseph E., Todd Oakley and Seana Coulson. 'Blending and Metaphor'. *Metaphor in Cognitive Linguistics*, edited by Gerard Steen and Raymond Gibbs. John Benjamins, 1999, pp. 101–24.

Greenhalgh, Trisha and Brian Hurwitz. 'Narrative-based Medicine: Why Study Narrative?' *BMJ*, vol. 318, 1999, pp. 48–50.
Greenhouse, Emily. 'Can We Ever Know Sontag?' *The New Yorker*, 25 April 2012, https://www.newyorker.com/books/page-turner/can-we-ever-know-sontag. Accessed 29 August 2021.
'guerrilla war'. *The Oxford English Dictionary*. 2020. OED Online. https://www-oed-com.proxy1-bib.sdu.dk/view/Entry/82246?redirectedFrom=guerrilla+war#eid2295351. Accessed 26 August 2021.
Gullette, Margaret Morganroth. *Aged by Culture*. University of Chicago Press, 2004.
Gustafsson, Anna W, Charlotte Hommerberg and Sandgren Anna. 'Coping by Metaphors: The Versatile Function of Metaphors in Blogs about Living with Advanced Cancer'. *Medical Humanities*, vol. 46, 2020, pp. 267–77.
Gwyn, Richard. '"Captain of My Own Ship": Metaphor and Discourse of Chronic Illness'. *Researching and Applying Metaphor*, edited by Lynne Cameron and Graham Low. Cambridge University Press, 2012, pp. 203–220.
Gygax, Franziska. 'On Being Ill (in Britain and the US): Illness Narratives of the Self'. *The European Journal of Life Writing*, vol. 2, 2013, pp. 1–17.
Halberstam, Jack J. *The Queer Art of Failure*. Duke University Press, 2011.
Hamilton, Sharon. *Essential Literary Terms: A Brief Norton Guide with Exercises*, 2nd edn, W. W. Norton, 2017.
Hanne, Michael (ed.). *Binocular Vision: Narrative and Metaphor in Medicine*. Special issue of *Genre*, vol. 44, no. 3, 2011.
Hanne, Michael. 'Diagnosis and Metaphor'. *Perspectives in Biology and Medicine*, vol. 58, no. 1, Winter 2015, pp. 35–52.
Hansen, Per Krogh. 'Illness and Heroics: On Counter-narrative and Counter-metaphor in the Discourse on Cancer'. *Frontiers of Narrative Studies*, vol. 4, no. 1, 2018, s213–s228.
Harries, Karsten. 'Many Uses of Metaphors'. *Critical Inquiry*, vol. 5, no. 1, 1978, pp. 167–74.
Harrington, Kristine J. 'The Use of Metaphor in Discourse about Cancer: A Review of the Literature'. *Clinical Journal of Oncology Nursing*, vol. 16, no. 4, August 2012, pp. 408–12.
Haslett, Tobi. 'The Other Susan Sontag'. *The New Yorker*, 4 December 2017, https://www.newyorker.com/magazine/2017/12/11/the-other-susan-sontag. Accessed 29 August 2021.
Hauser, David J. and Norbert Schwarz. 'The War on Prevention: Bellicose Cancer Metaphors Hurt (Some) Prevention Intentions'. *Personality and Social Psychology Bulletin*, vol. 4, no. 1, 2015, pp. 66–77.
Hawkins, Anne Hunsaker. *Reconstructing Illness: Studies in Pathography*, 2nd edn. Purdue University Press, 1993.
Herndl, Diane Price. *Invalid Women: Figuring Feminine Illness in American Fiction and Culture, 1840–1940*. University of North Carolina Press, 1993.

Holmes, Martha Stoddard. 'After Sontag: Reclaiming Metaphor'. *Binocular Vision: Narrative and Metaphor in Medicine*, edited by Michael Hanne, special issue of *Genre*, vol. 44, no. 3, 2011, pp. 239–261.

Hommerberg, Charlotte, Anna W. Gustafsson and Anna Sandgren. 'Battle, Journey, Imprisonment, and Burden: Patterns of Metaphor Use in Blogs about Living with Advanced Cancer'. *BMC Palliative Care*, vol. 19, no. 59, 2020, https://doi.org/10.1186/s12904-020-00557-6. Accessed 28 August 2021.

Horn, Laurence R. and Heinrich Wansing. 'Negation'. *The Stanford Encyclopedia of Philosophy*, edited by Edward N. Zalta, 20 February 2020 https://plato.stanford.edu/archives/spr2020/entries/negation/. Accessed 28 August 2021.

Hunter, Kathryn Montgomery. *Doctors' Stories: The Narrative Structure of Medical Knowledge*. Princeton University Press, 1991.

Hustvedt, Siri. *Living, Thinking, Looking*. Sceptre, 2012.

Hustvedt, Siri. *The Shaking Woman: A History of My Nerves*. Hodder & Stoughton, 2011.

Hutcheon, Linda. *Irony's Edge: The Theory and Politics of Irony*. Routledge, 1995.

Hutchings, Deanna. 'Communicating with Metaphor: A Dance with Many Veils'. *American Journal of Hospice and Palliative Care*, September/October 1998, pp. 282–4.

Huyssen, Andreas. *After the Great Divide: Modernism, Mass Culture, Postmodernism*. Indiana University Press, 1986.

Hyde, Lewis. *The Gift: Creativity and the Artist in the Modern World*. Vintage, 2007.

Jakobson, Roman. 'Two Aspects of Language and Two Types of Aphasic Disturbances'. *The Norton Anthology of Theory and Criticism*, edited by Vincent B. Leitch, 3rd edn. W.W. Norton, 1074–8.

Jamison, Leslie. *The Empathy Exams: Essays*. Granta, 2014.

Jamison, Leslie. *The Recovering: Intoxication and Its Aftermath*. Granta, 2018.

Johnson, Mark. 'Introduction: Metaphor in the Philosophical Tradition'. *Philosophical Perspectives on Metaphor*, edited by Mark Johnson. University of Minnesota Press, 1981, pp. 3–47.

Jurecic, Ann. 'The Illness Essay'. *Life Writing*, vol. 13, no. 1, 2016, pp. 13–26.

Jurecic, Ann. *Illness as Narrative*. University of Pittsburgh Press, 2012.

Karabanowicz, Ewa, Ernest Tyburski, Karol Karasiewicz, Andrzej Sokołowski, Monika Mak, Monika Folkierska-Żukowska and Wioletta Radziwiłłowicz. 'Metaphor Processing Dysfunctions in Schizophrenia Patients with and without Substance Use Disorders'. *Frontiers in Psychiatry*, vol. 11, 24 April 2020, doi.org/10.3389/fpsyt.2020.00331. Accessed 29 August 2021.

Kay, Lily E. *Who Wrote the Book of Life: A History of the Genetic Code*. Stanford University Press, 2000.

Kendall-Taylor Nathaniel and Abigail Haydon. 'Using Metaphor to Translate the Science of Resilience and Developmental Outcomes'. *Public Understanding of Science*, vol. 25, 2016, pp. 576–87.

Khalid, Robina Josephine. 'Demilitarizing Disease: Ambivalent Warfare and Audre Lorde's *The Cancer Journals*'. *African American Review*, vol. 42, nos 3–4, Fall/Winter 2008, pp. 697–714.

Kirmayer, Laurence J. 'The Body's Insistence on Meaning: Metaphor as Presentation and Representation in Illness Experience'. *Medical Anthropology Quarterly*, vol. 6, no. 4, December 1992, pp. 323–46.

Kistner, Ulrike. 'Illness as Metaphor? The Role of Linguistic Categories in the History of Medicine'. *Studies in 20th Century Literature*, vol. 22, no. 1, 1998, pp. 11–30.

Kleinman, Arthur. *The Illness Narratives: Suffering, Healing, and the Human Condition*. Basic Books, 1988.

Konstantinou, Lee. 'No Bull: David Foster Wallace and Postironic Belief'. *The Legacy of David Foster Wallace*, edited by Samuel Cohen and Lee Konstantinou. University of Iowa Press, 2012, pp. 83–112.

Kövecses, Zoltán. *Metaphor: A Practical Introduction*. Oxford University Press, 2010.

Kövecses, Zoltán. 'Metaphor and Culture'. *Acta Universitatis Sapientiae, Philologica*, vol. 2, no. 2, 2010, pp. 197–220.

Kövecses, Zoltán. *Metaphor in Culture: Universality and Variation*. Cambridge University Press, 2005.

Kumagai, Arno K. and Monica L. Lypson. 'Beyond Cultural Competence: Critical Consciousness, Social Justice, and Multicultural Education'. *Academic Medicine*, vol. 84, no. 6, June 2009, pp. 782–7.

Kurz, Gerhard. *Metapher, Allegorie, Symbol*. Vandenhoeck & Ruprecht, 1988.

Lahn, Silke and Jan Christoph Meister. *Einführung in die Erzähltextanalyse*. 3rd edn, Metzler, 2016.

Lakoff, George and Mark Johnson. *Metaphors We Live By*. University of Chicago Press, 1980; republished with a new afterword in 2003.

Lakoff, George and Mark Johnson. *Philosophy in the Flesh: The Embodied Mind and Its Challenge to Western Thought*. Basic Books, 1999.

Lakoff, George and Mark Turner. *More Than Cool Reason: A Field Guide to Poetic Metaphor*. University of Chicago Press, 1989.

Lepore, Jill. 'Burnout: Modern Affliction or Human Condition?' *The New Yorker*, 24 May 2021, https://www.newyorker.com/magazine/2021/05/24/burnout-modern-affliction-or-human-condition. Accessed 29 August 2021.

Linfield, Susie. 'Stories of Father Obsession and Betrayal'. *Los Angeles Times*, 26 August 1999, https://www.latimes.com/archives/la-xpm-1999-aug-26-cl-3670-story.html. Accessed 29 August 2021.

Lorde, Audre. 'A Burst of Light'. *A Burst of Light: Essays*. Sheba Feminist Publishers, 1988, pp. 49–134.

Lorde, Audre. *The Cancer Journals*. Aunt Lute Books, 1997.

Lorde, Audre. 'The Master's Tools Will Never Dismantle the Master's House'. *Sister Outsider: Essays and Speeches*. Crossing Press, 1984, pp. 110–13.

Love, Heather. 'Truth and Consequences: On Paranoid Reading and Reparative Reading'. *Criticism*, vol. 52, no. 2, 2010, pp. 235–41.

Low, Graham. 'Metaphor and Education'. *The Cambridge Handbook of Metaphor and Thought*, edited by Raymond W. Gibbs, Jr, Cambridge University Press, 2008, pp. 212–31.

Luquis, Raffy R. and Miguel A. Pérez. 'Achieving Cultural Competence: The Challenges for Health Educators'. *American Journal of Health Education*, vol. 34, no. 3, May/June 2003, pp. 131–8.

McAdam, Dan P. *The Redemptive Self: Stories Americans Live By*. Oxford University Press, 2005.

McAdams, Dan P. and Keith S. Cox. 'Self and Identity across the Life Span'. *The Handbook of Life-Span Development*, vol. 2, edited by Richard M. Lerner, Michael E. Lamb and Alexandra M. Freund. John Wiley & Sons, 2010, pp. 158–207.

McCaffery, Larry. 'A Conversation with David Foster Wallace by Larry McCaffery'. *The Review of Contemporary Fiction*, vol. 13, no. 2 (Summer 1993), https://www.dalkeyarchive.com/a-conversation-with-david-foster-wallace-by-larry-mccaffery/. Accessed 29 August 2021.

McGee, Micki. *Self-Help, Inc.: Makeover Culture in American Life*. Oxford University Press, 2005.

McHale, Brian. 'Beginning to Think about Narrative in Poetry'. *Narrative*, vol. 17, no. 1, 2009, pp. 11–30.

Major, William. 'Aesthetics and Social Critique in Anatole Broyard's *Intoxicated by My Illness*'. *Journal of Narrative Theory*, vol. 32, no. 1, Winter 2002, pp. 97–121.

Manguso, Sarah. *The Two Kinds of Decay* [2008], Granta, 2012.

Marks, Christine. 'Metaphor, Myth, and Universality in Eve Ensler's *In the Body of the World*'. *Symbolism: An International Annual of Critical Aesthetics*, edited by Katja Sarkowsky. deGruyter, 2018, pp. 13–28, doi.org/10.1515/9783110580822-002. Accessed 28 August 2021.

Marks, Christine. 'Metaphors We Heal By: Communicating Pain through Illness Narratives'. *Communicating Disease: Cultural Representations of American Medicine*, edited by Carmen Birkle and Johanna Heil. Winter Verlag, 2013, pp. 291–307.

Martin, Emily. 'The Egg and the Sperm: How Science Has Constructed a Romance Based on Stereotypical Male-Female Roles'. *Signs: Journal of Women in Culture and Society*, vol. 16, no. 3, 1991, pp. 485–501.

Martin, Emily. *The Woman in the Body: A Cultural Analysis of Reproduction*. 1992, Beacon, 2001.

Martínez, Matías and Michael Scheffel. *Einführung in die Erzähltheorie*, 9th edn. Beck, 2012.

Mathiasen, Helle and Joseph S. Alpert. 'On Illness. Review of *Intoxicated by My Illness: And Other Writings on Life and Death*, by Anatole Broyard'. *JAMA*, vol. 268, no. 19, 1992, pp. 2711.

Mattingly, Cheryl. 'The Machine-Body as Contested Metaphor in Clinical Care'. *Binocular Vision: Narrative and Metaphor in Medicine*, edited by Michael Hanne, special issue of *Genre*, vol. 44, no. 3, 2011, pp. 363–80.

Mattingly, Cheryl. *The Paradox of Hope: Journeys through a Clinical Borderland*. University of California Press, 2010.
Mays, Kelly J. *The Norton Introduction to Literature*. W. W. Norton, 2016.
Max, D. T. *Every Love Story is a Ghost Story: A Life of David Foster Wallace*. Penguin, 2013.
Max, D. T. 'The Unfinished'. *The New Yorker*, 9 March 2009, pp. 48–61.
Melzack, Ronald. 'The McGill Pain Questionnaire: Major Properties and Scoring Methods'. *Pain*, vol. 1, no. 3, 1975, pp. 277–99.
Meretoja, Hanna. 'Stop Narrating the Pandemic as a Story of War'. *Instrumental Narratives*, 25 May 2020, https://instrumentalnarratives.wordpress.com/2020/05/25/hanna-meretoja-pandemic-story-of-war/. Accessed 6 November 2021.
Mignolo, Walter D. 'On Comparison: Who Is Comparing What and Why?' *Comparison: Theories, Approaches, Uses*, edited by Rita Felski and Susan Stanford Friedman. Baltimore: The Johns Hopkins University Press, 2013. 99–119.
Miller, Adam. 'Lyr Add: Parodies of "The Old Gray Mare"'. *The Mudcat Café*, 21 July 2009. https://mudcat.org/thread.cfm?threadid=122425. Accessed 29 August 2021.
Mink, Louis O. 'Narrative Form as a Cognitive Instrument'. [1978] *The History and Narrative Reader*, edited by Geoffrey Roberts. Routledge, 2001.
Moi, Toril. *Revolution of the Ordinary: Literary Studies after Wittgenstein, Austin, and Cavell*. The University of Chicago Press, 2017.
Musolff, Andreas. *Metaphor and Political Discourse: Analogical Reasoning in Debates about Europe*. Palgrave, 2004.
Nelson, Deborah. *Tough Enough: Arbus, Arendt, Didion, McCarthy, Sontag, Weil*. University of Chicago Press, 2017.
North, Joseph. *Literary Criticism: A Concise Political History*. Harvard University Press, 2017.
Nünning, Ansgar. 'On the Discursive Construction of an Empire of the Mind: Metaphorical Re-Membering as a Means of Narrativizing and Naturalizing Cultural Transformations'. *Metamorphosis: Structures of Cultural Transformations*, edited by Jürgen Schlaeger, special issue of *REAL: Yearbook of Research in English and American Literature*, vol. 20, 2005, pp. 59–97.
Nünning, Ansgar. 'Steps towards a Metaphorology (and Narratology) of Crises: On the Functions of Metaphors as Figurative Knowledge and Mininarrations'. *Metaphors Shaping Culture and Theory*, edited by Herbert Grabes, Ansgar Nünning and Sibylle Baumbach, special issue of *REAL: Yearbook of Research in English and American Literature*, vol. 25, 2009, pp. 229–61.
Nünning, Vera and Ansgar Nünning. *An Introduction to the Study of English and American Literature*. Klett, 2014.
Oransky, Ivan. 'Susan Sontag: Obituary'. *The Lancet*, vol. 365, 2005, p. 468.

Otis, Laura. *Membranes: Metaphors of Invasion in Nineteenth-Century Literature, Science, and Politics.* Johns Hopkins University Press, 1999.

Pamboukian, Sylvia A. 'Denotation and Connotation'. *Research Methods in Health Humanities*, edited by Craig Klugman and Erin Gentry Lamb. Oxford University Press, 2019, pp. 15–24.

Penson, Richard T., Lidia Schapira, Kristy J. Daniels, Bruce A. Chabner and Thomas J. Lynch. 'Cancer as Metaphor'. *The Oncologist*, vol. 9, 2004, pp. 708–16.

Percy, Walker. 'Metaphor as Mistake'. *The Sewanee Review*, vol. 66, no. 1, 1958, pp. 79–99.

Perreault, Jeanne. *Writing Selves: Contemporary Feminist Autography.* University of Minnesota Press, 1995.

Phelan, James. 'Estranging Unreliability, Bonding Unreliability, and the Ethics of *Lolita*'. *Narrative*, vol. 15, 2007, pp. 222–38.

Phelan, James. *Experiencing Fiction: Judgments, Progressions, and the Rhetorical Theory of Narrative.* The Ohio State University Press, 2007.

Phelan, James. *Narrative as Rhetoric: Technique, Audiences, Ethics, Ideology.* Ohio State University Press, 1996.

Plath, Sylvia. 'Tulips'. *The Collected Poems: Sylvia Plath*, edited by Ted Hughes. Harper & Row, 1981, pp. 160–2.

Pragglejaz Group. 'MIP: A Method for Identifying Metaphorically Used Words in Discourse'. *Metaphor and Symbol*, vol. 22, no. 1, 2007, pp. 1–39.

Prince, Gerald. 'The Disnarrated'. *Style*, vol. 22, no. 1, 1988, pp. 1–8.

Prosser, Jay. 'Metaphors Kill: "Against Interpretation" and the Illness Books'. *The Scandal of Susan Sontag*, edited by Barbara Ching and Jennifer A. Wagner-Lawlor. Columbia University Press, 2009, pp. 188–204.

Radhakrishnan, Rajagopalan. 'Why Compare?' *New Literary History*, vol. 40, 2009, pp. 453–71.

Ratzan, Richard M. 'Intoxicated by My Illness and Other Writings on Life and Death'. *LitMed: Literature, Arts, Medicine Database.* New York University, 29 August 2006, http://medhum.med.nyu.edu/view/226. Accessed 30 August 2021.

Redgate, Jamie. 'David Foster Wallace's Treatment of Therapy after Postmodernism'. *Critique: Studies in Contemporary Fiction*, vol. 59, no. 3, 2018, pp. 284–94, doi.org/10.1080/00111619.2017.1398712. Accessed 29 August 2021.

Rees, Geoffrey. 'The Clinic and the Tearoom'. *Journal of Medical Humanities*, vol. 34, 2013, pp. 109–21.

Regarding Susan Sontag. Directed by Nancy Kate, Women Make Movies, HBO, 2014.

Reiffenrath, Tanja. *Memoirs of Well-Being: Rewriting Discourses of Illness and Disability.* Transcript, 2016, pp. 97–103.

Reisfield, Gary M. and George R. Wilson. 'Use of Metaphor in the Discourse on Cancer'. *Journal of Clinical Oncology*, vol. 22, no. 19, 2004, pp. 4024–7.

Richards, I. A. *The Philosophy of Rhetoric*. Oxford University Press, 1936.
Richards, I. A. *Practical Criticism: A Study of Literary Judgment*. Kegan Paul, Trench, Turner, 1930.
Ricœur, Paul. 'Metaphor and Symbol'. *Interpretation Theory: Discourse and the Surplus of Meaning*. The Texas Christian University Press, 1976, pp. 45–69.
Ricœur, Paul. *The Rule of Metaphor: The Creation of Meaning in Language* [1975, 1977]. Taylor & Francis, 2004.
Ricœur, Paul. *Time and Narrative*, vol. 1, translated by Kathleen McLaughlin and David Pellauer. University of Chicago Press, 1984.
Rieff, David. 'Illness as More Than a Metaphor'. *The New York Time Magazine*. 4 December 2005.
Rieff, David. *Swimming in a Sea of Death: A Son's Memoir*. Granta, 2009.
Ritchie, L. David. 'Gateshead Revisited: Perceptual Simulators and Fields of Meaning in the Analysis of Metaphors'. *Metaphor and Symbol*, vol. 23, 2008, pp. 24–49.
Ritchie, L. David, and Char Schell. '"The Ivory Tower" and an "unstable foundation": Playful Language, Humor, and Metaphor in the Negotiation of Scientists' Identities'. *Metaphor and Symbol*, vol. 24, 2009, pp. 90–104.
Rohe, Miriam, Joachim Funke, Maja Storch and Julia Weber. 'Can Motto-goals Outperform Learning and Performance Goals? Influence of Goal Setting on Performance and Affect in a Complex Problem Solving Task'. *Journal of Dynamic Decision Making*, vol. 2, no. 3, 2016, pp. 1–15.
Roiphe, Katie. 'Without Metaphor. Review of Swimming in a Sea of Death: A Son's. Memoir, by David Rieff'. *New York Times Book Review*, 3 February 2008.
Sacks, Oliver. *Awakenings*. Vintage, 1999.
Sana, Loue. *The Transformative Power of Metaphors in Therapy*. Springer, 2008.
Saver, Jeffrey L. 'Time is Brain – Quantified'. *Stroke*, vol. 37, no. 1, 2006, pp. 263–66.
Scarry, Elaine. *The Body in Pain: The Making and Unmaking of the World*. Oxford University Press, 1985.
Schleifer, Ronald and Jerry B. Vannatta. *The Chief Concern of Medicine: The Integration of the Medical Humanities and Narrative Knowledge into Medical Practices*. University of Michigan Press, 2013.
Schmidt, Nina. *The Wounded Self: Writing Illness in Twenty-First-Century German Literature*. Camden House, 2018.
Schwibbe, Gudrun. *Erzählungen vom Anderssein: Linksterrorismus und Alterität*. Waxmann, 2013.
Scott, Maria C. *Empathy and the Strangeness of Fiction: Readings in French Realism*. Edinburgh University Press, 2020.
Sedgwick, Eve Kosofsky. *Touching Feeling: Affect, Pedagogy, Performativity*. Duke University Press, 2003.

Semino, Elena. *A 'Metaphor Menu' for People Living With Cancer*. Lancaster University, 2019. http://wp.lancs.ac.uk/melc/the-metaphor-menu/. Accessed 29 August 2021.

Semino, Elena and Gerard Steen. 'Metaphor in Literature'. *The Cambridge Handbook of Metaphor and Thought*, edited by Raymond W. Gibbs, Jr. Cambridge University Press, 2008, pp. 232–46.

Semino, Elena, Zsófia Demjén, Jane Demmen, Veronika Koller, Sheila Payne, Andrew Hardie, Paul Rayson. 'The Online Use of Violence and Journey Metaphors by Patients with Cancer, as Compared with Health Professionals: A Mixed Methods Study'. *BMJ Supportive and Palliative Care*, vol. 7, 2017, pp. 60–6, doi.org/10.1136/bmjspcare-2014-000785. Accessed 29 August 2021.

Semino, Elena, Zsófia Demjén, Andrew Hardie, Sheila Payne and Paul Rayson. *Metaphor, Cancer and the End of Life: A Corpus-Based Study*. Routledge, 2018.

Servitje, Lorenzo. *Medicine is War: The Martial Medical Metaphor in Victorian Literature and Culture*. New York University Press, 2021.

Shen, Dan. 'Unreliability'. *The Living Handbook of Narratology*, edited by Peter Hühn, John Pier, Wolf Schmid and Jörg Schönert. Hamburg University, 31 December 2013, http://www.lhn.uni-hamburg.de/article/unreliability. Accessed 5 August 2020.

Shklovsky, Victor. 'Art as Technique'. 1917, *Russian Formalist Criticism: Four Essays*, translated and edited by Lee T. Lemon and Marion J. Reis. University of Nebraska Press, 1965, pp. 3–24.

Smith, Barbara Herrnstein. 'What Was "Close Reading"? A Century of Method in Literary Studies'. *Minnesota Review*, vol. 87, 2016, pp. 57–75.

Smith, Sidonie and Julia Watson. *Reading Autobiography: A Guide for Interpreting Life Narratives*, 2nd edn. University of Minnesota Press, 2010.

Sontag, Susan. 'Against Interpretation'. 1961. *Against Interpretation and Other Essays*. Penguin Classics, 2009, pp. 3–14.

Sontag, Susan. *As Consciousness Is Harnessed to Flesh: Journals and Notebooks, 1964–1980*, edited by David Rieff. Farrar, Straus, Giroux, 2012.

Sontag, Susan. *Illness as Metaphor and AIDS and Its Metaphors*. 1978. Penguin Classics, 2002.

Sontag, Susan. 'Notes on "Camp"'. 1964. *Against Interpretation and Other Essays*. Penguin Classics, 2009, pp. 275–92.

Spall, Bob, Sue Read and David Chantry. 'Metaphor: Exploring Its Origins and Therapeutic Use in Death, Dying and Bereavement'. *International Journal of Palliative Nursing*, vol. 7, no. 7, 2001, pp. 345–53.

Spencer, Danielle. 'Narrative Medicine'. *Routledge Companion to Philosophy of Medicine*, edited by Miriam Solomon, Jeremy R. Simon and Harold Kincaid, Routledge, 2017, pp. 372–82.

Stafford, Barbara Maria. *Visual Analogy: Consciousness as the Art of Connecting*. The MIT Press, 2001.

Steen, Gerard. 'Metaphor'. *Routledge Encyclopedia of Narrative Theory*, edited by David Herman, Manfred Jahn and Marie-Laure Ryan. Routledge, 2005, pp. 305–7.

Steen, Gerard. 'Parable'. *Routledge Encyclopedia of Narrative Theory*, edited by David Herman, Manfred Jahn and Marie-Laure Ryan. Routledge, 2005, pp. 418–19.

Strawson, Galen. 'Against Narrativity'. *Ratio*, vol. 17, no. 4, 2004, pp. 428–52.

Sword, Helen. *Air & Light & Time & Space: How Successful Academics Write*. Harvard University Press, 2017.

Sword, Helen. 'Snowflakes, Splinters, and Cobblestones: Metaphors for Writing'. *Innovations in Narrative and Metaphor: Methodologies and Practices*, edited by Sandy Farquhar and Esther Fitzpatrick. Springer Nature, 2019, pp. 39–55. doi.org/10.1007/978-981-13-6114-2_4. Accessed 29 August 2021.

Tammi, Pekka. 'Against Narrative ("A Boring Story")'. *Partial Answers: Journal of Literature and the History of Ideas*, vol. 4, no. 2, 2006, pp. 19–40.

Tay, Dennis. *Metaphor in Psychotherapy: A Descriptive and Prescriptive Analysis*. Benjamins, 2013.

'time'. *The Oxford English Dictionary*. 2020. *OED Online*. https://www-oed-com.proxy1-bib.sdu.dk/view/Entry/202100?rskey=5kJ9J8&result=1&isAdvanced=false#eid. Accessed 26 August 2021.

Treichler, Paula. *How to Have Theory in an Epidemic: Cultural Chronicles of AIDS*. 1999. Duke University Press, 2006.

'trip'. *The Oxford English Dictionary*. 2020. *OED Online*. https://www-oed-com.proxy1-bib.sdu.dk/view/Entry/206230?rskey=YVtanL&result=1&isAdvanced=false#eid. Accessed 26 August 2021.

Trogen, Brit. 'The Evidence-based Metaphor'. *JAMA*, vol. 317, 2017, pp. 1411–12.

Vaisrub, Samuel. *Medicine's Metaphors: Messages and Menaces*. Medical Economics Company, 1977.

van Rijn-van Tongeren, Geraldine W. *Metaphors in Medical Texts*. Rodopi, 1997.

'vanity'. *The Oxford English Dictionary*. 2020. *OED Online*. https://www-oed-com.proxy1-bib.sdu.dk/view/Entry/221396?redirectedFrom=vanity#eid. Accessed 26 August 2021.

'Vegetative'. *Merriam-Webster.com Dictionary*, Merriam-Webster, https://www.merriam-webster.com/dictionary/vegetative. Accessed 30 August 2021.

Verghese, Abraham. 'A Linguistic Prescription for Ailing Communication'. *YouTube*, uploaded by TEDMED. 14 April 2015. https://www.youtube.com/watch?v=Eg_GwMr4IpY. Accessed 29 August 2021.

Verghese, Abraham. 'Hope and Clarity'. *New York Times Magazine*, 22 February 2004, http://www.nytimes.com/2004/02/22/magazine/the-way-we-live-now-2-22-04-hope-and-clarity.html?mcubz=1. Accessed 29 August 2021.

Vidali, Amy. 'Seeing What We Know: Disability and Theories of Metaphor'. *Journal of Literary and Cultural Disability Studies*, vol. 4, no. 1, 2010, pp. 33–54.

Viney, William, Felicity Callard and Angela Woods. 'Critical Medical Humanities: Embracing Entanglement, Taking Risks'. *Medical Humanities*, vol. 41, 2015, pp. 2–7.

Wallace, David. 'The Planet Trillaphon as It Stands in Relation to the Bad Thing'. *The Amherst Review*, vol. 12, 1984, pp. 26–33.

Wallace, David Foster. 'E Unibus Pluram: Television and U.S. Fiction'. *Review of Contemporary Fiction*, vol. 13, no. 2, Summer 1993, pp. 151–94.

Wallace, David Foster. *Infinite Jest*. Abacus, 2007.

Warhol, Robyn R. 'Neonarrative; or, How to Render the Unnarratable in Realist Fiction and Contemporary Film'. *A Companion to Narrative Theory*, edited by James Phelan and Peter J. Rabinowitz, Blackwell, 2008, pp. 220–31.

Wasson, Sara. 'Before Narrative: Episodic Reading and Representations of Chronic Pain'. *Medical Humanities*, vol. 44, no. 2, 2018, pp. 106–12.

Werth, Paul. 'Extended Metaphor: A Text-World Account'. *Language and Literature*, vol. 3, no. 2, 1994, pp. 79–103.

White, Michael. 'Narrative Practice and the Unpacking of Identity Conclusions'. *Gecko: A Journal of Deconstruction and Narrative Ideas in Therapeutic Practice*, vol. 1, 2001, pp. 28–55.

Wiebel-Fanderl, Oliva. *Herztransplantation als erzählte Erfahrung: Der Mensch zwischen kulturellen Traditionen und medizinisch-technischem Fortschritt*. LIT Verlag, 2003.

Wiest-Kellner, Ursula. *Messages from the Threshold: Die* You-*Erzählform als Ausdruck liminaler Wesen und Welten*. Aisthesis, 1999.

Wijdicks, Eelco. '"We believe your father is in a vegetative state". "You mean he is a vegetable? He never wanted that"'. *Intensive Care Medicine*, vol 47, 2021, pp. 363–4, doi.org/10.1007/s00134-020-06332-8. Accessed 7 November 2021.

Wohlmann, Anita. 'Analyzing Metaphors'. *Research Methods in Health Humanities*, edited by Craig Klugman and Erin Gentry Lamb. Oxford University Press, 2019, pp. 25–38.

Wohlmann, Anita. 'Empathie und ihre Grenzen: Die depressive Person von David Foster Wallace'. *Narrative Medizin: Praxisbeispiele aus dem deutschsprachigen Raum*, edited by Anita Wohlmann, Pascal O. Berberat and Daniel Teufel. Böhlau, 2021, pp. 59–78.

Wohlmann, Anita. 'The Illness Is You: Figurative Language in David Foster Wallace's Short Story "The Planet Trillaphon"'. *Embodied Narration: Illness, Death and Dying in Modern Culture*, edited by Heike Hartung. Transcript, 2018, pp. 203–25.

Wohlmann, Anita. 'Illness Narrative and Self-Help Culture – Self-Help Writing on Age-Related Infertility'. *The European Journal of Life Writing*, vol. 3, 2014, pp. 19–41.

Wohlmann, Anita. 'Metaphor as Art – A Thought Experiment on Metaphors in Health Care'. *Handbook for the Medical Humanities*, edited by Alan Bleakley. Routledge, 2019, pp. 136–43.
Wohlmann, Anita. 'Of Termites and Ovaries on Strike: Rethinking Medical Metaphors of the Female Body'. *Signs: Journal of Women in Culture and Society*, vol. 43, no. 1, 2017, pp. 127–50.
Wohlmann, Anita. 'Symbol or Simile? Sylvia Plath's Poem "Tulips" and the Role of Language in Medicine'. *Lyrik und Medizin. Jahrbuch Literatur und Medizin*, edited by Florian Steger and Katharina Fürholzer. Winter Verlag, 2019, pp. 179–97.
Wohlmann, Anita and Susanne Michl. 'The Gains of Reduction in Translational Processes: Illness Blogs and Clinical-Ethics Cases'. *Palgrave Communications*, vol. 6, 2020, doi.org/10.1057/s41599-020-0477-5. Accessed 29 August 2021.
Wohlmann, Anita and Anders Juhl Rasmussen. 'Brugen af litteratur i narrativ medicin'. *Brug af litteratur*, edited by Anne-Marie Mai. Forlaget Spring, 2019, pp. 258–82.
Wonham, Henry B. *Mark Twain and the Art of the Tall Tale*. Oxford University Press, 1993.
Wood, James. *How Fiction Works*. Farrar, Straus and Giroux, 2008.
Wood, James. 'Serious Noticing'. *Michigan Quarterly Review*, vol. 49, no. 4, 2010, http://hdl.handle.net/2027/spo.act2080.0049.410. Accessed 29 August 2021.
Woods, Angela. 'Beyond the Wounded Storyteller: Rethinking Narrativity, Illness and Embodied Self-Experience'. *Health, Illness and Disease: Philosophical Essays*, edited by Havi Carel and Rachel Cooper. Acumen, 2013, pp. 113–28.
Woods, Angela. 'The Limits of Narrative: Provocations for the Medical Humanities'. *Medical Humanities*, vol. 37, 2011, pp. 73–8.
Woolf, Virginia. 'On Being Ill'. *On Being Ill by Virginia Woolf*. Paris Press, 2012, pp. 3–28.
'wrestle, n'. *The Oxford English Dictionary*. 2020. OED Online. https://www-oed-com.proxy1-bib.sdu.dk/view/Entry/230647?rskey=4vVwgZ&result=1&isAdvanced=false#eid. Accessed 26 August 2021.
'wrestle, v'. *The Oxford English Dictionary*. 2020. OED Online. https://www-oed-com.proxy1-bib.sdu.dk/view/Entry/230648?rskey=4vVwgZ&result=2&isAdvanced=false#eid. Accessed 26 August 2021.
Wu, Cynthia. 'Marked Bodies, Marking Time: Reclaiming the Warrior in Audre Lorde's *The Cancer Journals*'. *a/b: Auto/Biography Studies*, vol. 17, no. 2, 2002, pp. 245–61, doi.org/10.1080/08989575.2002.10815294. Accessed 29 August 2021.
Yacobi, Tamar. 'Metaphors in Context: The Communicative Structure of Figurative Language'. *Beyond Cognitive Metaphor Theory: Perspectives on Literary Metaphor*, edited by Monika Fludernik. Routledge, 2011, pp. 113–34.

Zharikov, Sergev S. and Dedre Gentner. 'Why Do Metaphors Seem Deeper than Similes?' *Proceedings of the Twenty-Fourth Annual Conference of the Cognitive Science Society*, edited by W. D. Gray and C. D. Schunn. George Mason University, 2002, pp. 976–91.

Zito, Tom. 'The Big Question Mark'. *The Washington Post*, 28 February 1978, https://www.washingtonpost.com/archive/lifestyle/1978/02/28/the-big-question-mark/50a3d241-266e-41ff-ae7c-ef3bb6202e06/. Accessed 29 August 2021.

Index

allegory, 38–40, 133
Aristotle, 8, 13, 24n

battle
  battlefield, 35, 37, 64, 81, 84, 89, 106–7, 176
  capitulation and surrender, 2, 34, 41, 86, 110, 136–7, 188
  courtroom battle, 20, 106–7, 109, 188
  defeat and failure, 2, 21, 34, 41–2, 83, 85, 132–3, 135–9, 188
  enemy, 1, 34–7, 39, 47, 64, 70, 81, 85–6, 135, 137, 163
  heroism, 34, 42, 59, 81, 90, 106–7, 109, 129n, 135, 166
  sports game, 20, 37, 42, 107
  survival, 31, 36, 39, 85–7, 94, 96, 104n, 106, 113, 135, 191
  triumph, 3, 59, 61, 68, 70, 92, 96, 107–10, 114, 123
  victory, 2, 34, 39, 41–2, 59, 67, 83, 85–6, 107, 122, 135
Biebuyck, Benjamin and Gunther Martens, 43–4, 46–7, 189
Bleakley, Alan, 6, 15, 18, 26–7, 85, 158, 159, 170
Broyard, Anatole, 1–2, 20–1, 51, 77, 79, 103, 105–29, 159, 179, 188–90
burnout, 175–6

cancer, 2, 18, 28, 30–1, 33, 35–6, 48, 58–61, 63–8, 71, 75, 80–91, 95–9, 101–7, 111, 113, 116–17, 124, 128, 144, 159–60, 164, 169, 173–4, 181

Charon, Rita, 8, 16–18, 23n, 160
close reading, 2, 14–18, 22, 109, 142, 144, 152, 158, 160, 162, 170, 184, 188, 192
Cohen, Ted, 9, 28–9, 40, 50, 93, 100–1, 174
comparison, 13–14, 65–7, 81, 95–8, 162–3, 180–1
  appropriation and colonisation, 14, 67–8, 91–3, 95, 146, 180
  difference, 13, 20, 66, 81–2, 85, 91–4, 97–8, 126, 189
  gains, 14, 25n, 29, 81, 88, 96–7, 103, 117, 122, 166, 168–9, 174
  juxtaposition and collage, 14, 88, 96–8, 113, 118, 126–8, 152, 170, 172
  light or small comparisons, 21, 113, 118, 125–6
  resemblance, 9–10, 13–14, 92, 180
  relationality, 14, 20–1, 95–6, 133, 140, 142, 151
  risks, 27–8, 31–2, 84–5, 88, 90, 92–3, 141, 146–7, 167–8, 172
  sameness, 13, 20–1, 92, 94, 143–7, 189
  similarity, 9, 13, 20, 49, 82, 91, 97, 126, 140, 143, 168, 182
competence
  cultural and structural, 25n
  metaphor, 158, 161, 183, 184n
  narrative, 17–18, 160

depression, 18–19, 21, 76, 132–5, 138–44, 149, 151–3

Didion, Joan, 1, 19, 21, 73, 108, 132, 136–8

embodiment, 5, 11, 74, 76–7, 91, 97, 172, 188, 191, 192
Ensler, Eve, 1, 19–20, 90–5, 97, 189
ethics, 92–3, 103, 110, 189

Felski, Rita, 14, 29, 50, 93, 95–6, 103, 115, 121–2, 127
fight
  as struggle, 26, 39, 42–3, 48–9, 81, 89
  as wrestling, 38–9, 47–8, 51
  see also battle; war
figurativeness, 6, 8–9, 13, 16, 22, 39–40, 74, 83, 92, 106, 110, 139, 150, 160–2, 164, 174, 179, 180, 182–3, 192
Fludernik, Monika, 41, 43–5, 47, 49–50, 141
Frank, Arthur, 1–3, 8, 19, 26, 33, 35–44, 46–8, 50–1, 61–2, 107–10, 116, 124, 164

generativity, 1–2, 7, 22, 27, 59, 66, 68, 101–102, 108, 159, 162, 166, 176, 178, 188
genre
  essay, 5–6, 21, 40, 58–60, 67, 71–3, 98, 125, 129, 133
  illness narrative, 3, 8
  short story, 21, 132
  tall tale, 119–20, 130n

Hanne, Michael, 7, 44
Holmes, Martha Stoddard, 61–3, 74–5, 124, 127, 140, 173, 180
Hustvedt, Siri, 1, 19, 111, 136, 144
Hutcheon, Linda, 147, 149–53, 175
hyperbole, 21, 46, 106, 113, 118–19

illness as journey, 3, 7–8, 10, 31, 99, 132, 134, 150–2, 177–8, 180–1
intentionality, 29, 33, 38, 46, 62, 175, 177
irony, 13, 21, 45–6, 70, 117–18, 132–4, 147–53, 157n, 161, 173, 175, 188–9

Kirmayer, Laurence J., 30–1, 53n, 93

Lakoff, George and Mark Johnson
  Metaphors We Live By, 8, 10–11, 31, 64, 69–70, 76–7, 106, 172, 191
Lakoff, George and Mark Turner
  More than Cool Reason, 19, 36–8, 51, 85, 189
literal meanings, 6–9, 27, 39–40, 44–5, 61–2, 75, 84, 92, 108, 136, 143, 147, 150–1, 162–4, 174–6, 181–3
Lorde, Audre, 1–3, 20, 51, 80–91, 92–105, 109, 111, 116–17, 124, 146, 170, 188–9, 190, 192
lyric and sensory side of metaphor, 19, 49–50, 73, 98, 125

Manguso, Sarah, 19, 62
Mattingly, Cheryl, 31–3, 40, 163, 165
metaphor method, 162–179
  metaphor analysis, 8, 19, 26, 32–9, 41–3, 48, 51, 133, 152, 191
  narrative analysis, 15, 26, 38–48, 51, 107, 133, 137–9, 141–2, 145–6, 152–3, 173–6
metaphor theories
  blending theory, 10, 41–2, 50, 54n, 185n, 186n
  comparison, 10, 13, *see also* comparison
  interaction, 10, 13, 24n, 185n
  metaphor as mistake, 12, 123
  resemblance, 9–10, 13–14, 24n, 180
  substitution, 10, 13
  tension, 10–14, 18, 50, 61, 74, 94, 143, 146, 150
  see also strategies
migraine, 18, 21, 132, 136–7, 144, 155n
misuse, 2, 15, 30–3, 38, 66, 77, 93, 152–3

narrative
  analysis *see* metaphor method
  limits, 3–7, 49–50, 125
  metaphor scenarios, 7, 19, 43, 46, 51, 105, 109, 133, 135, 140, 163, 166, 173, 177, 181

Index

mini-narrative or micronarrative, 19, 43–4, 51
side of metaphor, 41–4, 72–3
narrative medicine, 3, 16–17, 21, 105, 132, 183
Nelson, Deborah, 20, 59, 61, 68–9, 72–5

reparative reading, 21, 103, 106, 113–15, 117, 122, 128, 130n
reuse, gains of
  empowerment, 2, 58, 60, 70, 80, 82–3, 94, 99
  enchantment, 50, 121–2, 129
  pleasure, 1–3, 12, 20, 70, 81, 98–103, 106, 112, 115, 117, 120, 124, 188
  repair, 2, 21, 81, 102–3, 106, 110, 113–17, 119, 123–4, 127–30, 188
  resistance and defiance, 2, 20, 31–2, 40–1, 46–7, 67–9, 82, 88, 90, 102–3, 111, 170, 173, 188
  self-affirmation 68–9
  self-care, 87–8, 106, 116–17, 188
  self-knowledge, 2, 20, 81, 97, 99, 188
  sensory side, 6, 20, 59, 73, 77, 101, 188, 192; *see also* embodiment
  thickening and saturating, 18–19, 27, 39, 43, 48–9, 51, 56n, 70, 192
  tinkering and playfulness, 2, 46, 48, 82, 103, 105, 119–20, 126, 174, 188
  see also strategies of reusing metaphors
reuse, risks of
  homogenisation, 14, 20, 91–3, 95; *see also* comparison: appropriation and colonisation
  overextension, 88, 102
  overidentification, 145–7, 149
  see also ethics

parable, 38–40, 43, 48

Ricœur, Paul, 7, 9–14, 94, 143, 198
Rieff, David, 20, 59–60, 67–9, 75

Sedgwick, Eve Kosofsky, 14, 114–15, 117, 122, 127
Semino, Elena, 28–9, 173–4
  metaphor menu, 128, 159, 179
sensory experience *see* embodiment
simile, 9, 13, 22, 45, 62, 131n, 139–43, 153, 158, 179–82
Sontag, Susan, 1–2, 6, 19–20, 47, 51, 58–79, 83, 105–6, 108–9, 116–17, 124–5, 150, 170, 188–9, 192
strategies of reusing metaphors
  5 steps, 162–179
  combining, 2, 20, 36–7, 51–2, 80–1, 87–8, 114, 178
  comparing, 64–6, 77
  elaborating, 2, 21, 30, 36–7, 43, 51, 85, 108–9, 132, 137, 140–2, 144, 166, 174, 178
  embracing mistake and failure, 21, 112–13, 121–3, 139
  exaggerating and intensifying, 20–1, 62, 106–7, 109, 113, 118–20, 122–3, 141–3, 150, 153, 173, 188
  literalising, 62, 84, 108, 151, 163–4
  negation, 13, 46–8, 51, 188
  oscillating, 60, 111–13, 122, 127, 150, 152
  personification, 31, 35, 37, 174
  quantity over quality, 21, 125–8, 133
  questioning or challenging, 21, 26, 36, 77, 81, 95, 132, 142; *see also* reuse, gains of: resistance and defiance
  stretching or extending, 1–2, 20, 30, 36–7, 41, 43, 51, 76, 80–1, 83, 85–9, 94, 102, 114, 132, 136–7, 143, 178, 188, 192
  switching source and target, 20, 64, 66, 101
  tracing, 19, 47, 64–5, 77, 129, 170–1, 188, 191
style, 20–1, 46, 51, 58–9, 69–72, 77, 87, 98, 103, 105–7, 109–11, 113–18, 122, 124–9, 188
  camp, 21, 60, 106, 113, 115, 117, 122, 130n, 188
  vanity, 21, 105, 114, 116–17, 188

surrender *see* battle: capitulation
symbol, 9, 16, 22, 48, 116, 158, 161, 169, 179–80, 182–3

time is money, 172, 190–2

use and usability of metaphors
    effects and functions, 10, 14, 18–19, 26–9, 40, 49, 51, 91–3, 121, 152–3, 159, 167–70, 174–5, 183
    recommendations in health contexts, 159–61
    see also reuse *and* strategies

Wallace, David Foster, 1–2, 18–19, 21, 51, 132–153, 189
war
    Amazon warrior, 20, 81–2, 188
    argument is war, 69–70, 106
    guerrilla war, 135–7, 155n
    imagery during COVID-19, 34, 166
    on cancer, 60, 111
    on terror, 34, 111, 167
    Vietnam war, 67–8, 176
Werth, Paul, extended metaphor, 40

Yacobi, Tamar, 45–7

EU representative:
Easy Access System Europe
Mustamäe tee 50, 10621 Tallinn, Estonia
Gpsr.requests@easproject.com

www.ingramcontent.com/pod-product-compliance
Lightning Source LLC
Chambersburg PA
CBHW070353240426
43671CB00013BA/2482